**"My baby won't stop crying . . .
and I don't know what's *wrong*!"**

Coping with the unrelenting demands of a newborn can be one of the most exhausting and difficult aspects of a mother's life. It can cause tension and family quarrels and evoke feelings of guilt and self-doubt; it can even make a mother angry at her own baby.

Now, in Sandy Jones's carefully researched book, parents who are often in the grip of helpless anger can find honest answers to their most difficult, often-asked questions:

- What does my baby's cry mean?
- Is my infant more or less fussy than most?
- Should I pick the baby up regardless of the hour, day or night?
- When should I *not* respond?
- What about allergies?
- Can I work *and* continue to breastfeed?
- Should my baby sleep in bed with me?
- Is there a "perfect mother"?
- Do smoking and drinking coffee or alcohol make a difference?
- What can I *do* to make life bearable with . . .

CRYING BABY, SLEEPLESS NIGHTS

ALSO BY SANDY JONES

Good Things for Babies
Learning for Little Kids
To Love a Baby

Crying Baby, Sleepless Nights

SANDY JONES

 WARNER BOOKS

A Warner Communications Company

Copyright © 1983 by Sandy Jones
All rights reserved.
Warner Books, 666 Fifth Avenue, New York, NY 10103

⬤ A Warner Communications Company

Printed in the United States of America
First printing: October 1983
10 9 8 7 6 5 4 3 2 1

Book design: H. Roberts Design

Library of Congress Cataloging in Publication Data

Jones, Sandy.
    Crying baby, sleepless nights.

    Includes index.
    1. Infants (Newborn)—Care and hygiene.
2. Crying. I. Title.
RJ253.J66   1983   649'.122   83-5090
ISBN 0-446-37516-0 (USA)
ISBN 0-446-37918-2 (Canada)

ATTENTION: SCHOOLS AND CORPORATIONS

Warner books are available at quantity discounts with bulk purchase for educational, business, or sales promotional use. For information, please write to: **Special Sales Department, Warner Books, 666 Fifth Avenue, New York, NY 10103.**

ARE THERE WARNER BOOKS YOU WANT
BUT CANNOT FIND IN YOUR LOCAL STORES?

You can get any **Warner Books** title in print. Simply send title and retail price, plus 75¢ per order and 50¢ per copy to cover mailing and handling costs for each book desired. New York State and California residents, add applicable sales tax. Enclose check or money order—no cash, please—to: **Warner Books, PO Box 690, New York, NY 10019.** Or send for our complete catalog of Warner Books.

Dedicated to all the mothers who are reading
this book at 4:00 A.M., and to all
the babies who long not to have to cry anymore

Contents

PART III
Crying and Sleep: The Shifting Balance

PART IV
Strategies for Survival

A Closing Parable

APPENDIX

Introduction

"Please, God . . . just four hours of sleep in a row!"

The light shines out of an apartment window down onto the deserted street below. It is four o'clock in the morning, and Sally Burson is awake with her baby, Nathan, who hasn't slept more than three hours at once since he was born three months ago.

The dark stillness of the night is pierced by Nathan's shrill screams. He seems to be in pain, yet neither Sally nor her pediatrician can find an obvious reason for his discomfort.

Once he's asleep, Sally lowers Nathan gently into the crib, hoping that she doesn't wake him up again. She turns out the light and sleepily stumbles back into her bed. It's the third time she's been up since midnight. Wiping a tear from her eye, she pleads silently, *Please, God, just let me have four hours of sleep in a row!*

The story of Sally and her baby, Nathan, is being repeated nightly in homes everywhere, in what has been called by one researcher "a crying baby epidemic." One out of every five babies is currently being labeled as excessively irritable or prone to crying. Of seventy-eight consecutively born babies recently observed, sixty-eight had fussy periods daily, lasting anywhere from half an hour to five hours in duration.

The answers to why a baby cries and doesn't sleep are not simple but myriad and as complicated as the baby himself is. In the past few years an explosion has taken place in infant research in several important areas—psychology, psychiatry, physiology, and gastroenterology. Researchers in each field are now examining infancy from a specific perspective. The result is a new understanding of babies and how they function, develop, and mature.

Up until now, no one has really tried to translate the critical information that is being uncovered and to apply it to the problematic baby, the less than easy one. What all the research seems to be pointing to is that babies are not simply miniature adults but are highly sophisticated beings in their own right whose crying and sleeplessness *mean* something. Never have we come closer to pinpointing the causes of baby misery than now.

Hopefully this book will provide you with *real, useable* answers—and at least some relief from relatives who think your baby is spoiled or doctors who think that you are too nervous. In the past the result of these unfair and inaccurate opinions has been the alienation of parents from each other and their fighting out of tensions and frustrations between themselves, or, more seriously, taking their feelings out on the baby. Now you can rest assured: your baby's screaming is *not* your fault.

The motivation to discover what really causes crying and sleeping problems in babies arose out of two experiences in my life. My daughter, Marcie, was what many parents call "a ten-minute sleeper." I still remember clearly what it feels like to seem totally alone in my exhaustion and grief over the unrelenting demands of my small baby.

My second experience had to do with poring over some forty letters that had been sent to Nancy Kleckner, Editor of *Growing Child*, from mothers of colicky babies, in response to a brief, desperate letter she published from the mother of a fussy baby. These mothers boldly shared their alienation, their guilts, their uncertainties, and their victories in the face of what was probably the most unrelentingly stressful event in their lives. Since that time, and after interviews with over a hundred more mothers of fussy babies, I am continually touched by how the pain of those months of life with a crying baby can bring tears to a mother's eyes sometimes even twenty years later!

This book has been designed, you'll notice, for the reader who has only five minutes a day to devote to anything other than a baby. I hope that I can help you to find answers *quickly*, and that I will have enabled you to continue to be long-suffering and compassionate about responding to your baby's need for your closeness when he's in pain. As one clear-sighted mother said: "If my baby's going to suffer, I don't want him to have to suffer alone."

I hope you won't have to suffer alone, either. I hope you find comfort in knowing that many, many other parents have been through what you've been through and have lived to tell about it. If you find your baby described in this book, please pick up the phone and reach out to someone you know or to a support group. Things will be so much more energized and bearable when you talk about them with other people.

You will notice that I have used "he" throughout the book. I am not a sexist person, and in my last three books I alternated between he and she designations throughout, wanting deeply to give recognition to the reality of having female children as well as male. What happened in many cases is that readers stumbled over the unexpected "she's." Their eyes, instead of flowing across the pages smoothly, got caught on the "she's," even if momentarily. It became a distraction. It was like unconsciously finding a typographical error because of a tiny deviation from the expected. I want you to be able to read this book quickly and easily to get to the information you need without having to get caught up in semantic distractions. So read on . . . and understand that my heart's in the right place but, for the sake of making reading faster for you this time, I'm reverting to the familiar "he."

I would like to thank the many mothers who have shared their crying experiences with me. Thank you, too, to Reid Boates, my editor at Warner, whose son's crying led him to conceive of a book project like this one. Thank you to Kathy Conklin, my typist, who will have had a baby when this reaches print, and to my agent, Charlotte Sheedy, who aggressively sewed up the details of this project on my behalf. As always, my gratitude to my dear, dear Marcie, who now sleeps through most nights, and my husband, Paul, for his consummate patience.

Godspeed to you, my friend. May you have "four hours in a row" tonight, or, if not, the wisdom and flexibility to keep on giving with the trust that "this, too, will pass" in time.

Crying Baby, Sleepless Nights

PART I

Pain: The Physical Causes of Baby's Crying

1
Help Your Doctor to Find the Answer to Your Baby's Pain

Meet Andrew Bendson, a robust, blond-haired, fair-skinned three-month-old baby. If you were to see him out for a walk in his stroller, or in the grocery store, you'd probably remark casually on what a sweet baby he is. Back home, however, Andrew is not a cherub by a long shot.

When his mother settles down to feed him, he refuses to look her in the eyes. After only a few gulps, he starts fussing. Within minutes, he is actively screaming. His crying is so compelling, so shrill, his mother can barely endure it. He seems to want to squirm out of her arms, yet when she tries to put him down, he cries even more inconsolably. His cycles of discomfort and screaming go on day and night, punctuated only by brief rests.

Both of Andrew's parents have decided that he can't handle even mild stimulation, like the turning on of the bedroom light, or too loud a laugh from his mother, or unexpected jiggling by his father. Even diaper changing sends Andrew off the wall with loud screams of protest.

Andrew's mother never knows when he will finally

fall asleep exhausted, or whether he can be expected to sleep for twenty minutes or two hours. She is sure of one thing—her baby will be waking her up three to four times a night, and that prospect fills her with a bleak sense of dread as nighttime nears and her own body begins to cry out for much-needed rest.

> *"My husband and I would like to have another child, but we both still shudder at the idea of having to go through another experience of colic like our baby's. It was truly a nightmare, and only a mother who goes through colic like I and other mothers have can really understand."*

Even trained nurses don't know how to deal with babies like Andrew. In the hospital nursery these babies' bassinets are almost always put off in a far corner so that their cries can be tolerated. Here's how one nurse described the behavior of a baby like Andrew in her daily progress notes:

From early evening onward at age three days this baby has been quite fussy. He cried very vigorously before feeding, took feeding frequently. He is fussier than any baby I have ever seen. *A Day Later.* Again this evening the baby has been very fussy during feeding. He trembles slightly at the beginning of feedings as if ravenous and excited. Placed in his crib after feeding and burping, he immediately cried out lustily. Offered more formula, he took it well. After burping he seemed satisfied, but when I put him back to bed he cried again. He seemed unable to make up his mind. When picked up he's quiet, content. He dozed. *Six Days of Age.* The baby is increasingly unmanageable and more puzzling. *Babies never annoy me but this one does.* I've never seen a baby act like this before. It seems that nothing satisfies him but holding him. It was suggested that I'd just have to hold him in one arm and work with the other until he falls asleep. The baby seemed miserable and uncomfortable. He sputtered and whimpered. In 20 minutes he burst forth again full force. Picked up and patted, almost lulled to sleep, he was replaced in the crib. He went to sleep, was quiet, but woke up shortly and suddenly started crying again. Dropped off to sleep and again awoke crying, off and on until midnight. Finally he went to sleep and slept for three and a half hours.

Wessel, et al.,
"Paroxysmal Fussing in Infancy,"
Pediatrics, 14, November 1954, p. 421.

Not all babies are as difficult to manage as these two babies, but many, many babies have sieges of unexplained crying that definitely appear to come from pain, although the exact source of the pain is usually quite difficult to pinpoint. Some babies cry around the clock. Some cry only in the evenings. Others are totally irregular in their crying.

"If you're wondering if your infant has colic—he doesn't. With a colicky baby, there's no doubt!"

The catch-all word for the "screaming baby syndrome" that these babies epitomize is *colic.* Colic in some form, it appears, has been a part of the human race as far back as recorded time. Descriptions of babies who cry endlessly appear as early as A.D. 400.

Seventy years ago Dr. Emelyn Coolidge described a

typical colic attack in her book, *Home Care of Sick Children,* in the same way that all major pediatric textbooks do today:

> The baby with colic screams lustily and in paroxysms. His face is first red, but it may become pale or even blue around the mouth if the attacks last long or are severe. The hands and feet are cold, the legs are drawn up, the abdomen, as a rule, is very hard and distended, and the baby works his hands in agony.

What has been found in the past decade is that there probably is no single disease entity that can easily be labeled colic. Just as *headache* is simply a word for a certain kind of pain, so *colic* is a word for baby pain that results in crying. The word really doesn't communicate anything about what causes the pain or what can be done for it.

Unfortunately, baby crying is seldom taken seriously by anyone but parents. Those researchers and physicians in the position to carry out critical research into baby pain and crying often select to focus on the rarer, more life-threatening baby illnesses. Because the screaming baby syndrome is seen as self-limiting—that it will go away in time—they are hesitant to institute costly, uncomfortable medical tests on babies who will most likely grow out of their pain.

The Nervous Mother Myth

"Why are you so *tense,* dear?" her baby's doctor asked Andrew's mother, Connie Bendson, giving her a patronizing pat on the shoulder. In tears, she had just spilled out her fear that something was seriously wrong with her irritable, screaming baby. After a quick physical exam, the doctor reported, "There's nothing physically wrong with your baby that I can tell. He's gaining weight well and thriving."

The doctor smiled, a bemused look on his face. "Just *relax* and your baby will settle right down. If things don't get better in a week or two, call me and I'll prescribe a mild sedative for him so he'll sleep and you can get some rest." With that, he whisked off to another small patient.

Connie was tired. Her self-esteem had plummeted to zero, and now the doctor seemed to be putting the blame for her baby's misery squarely on her shoulders. That afternoon she went home and cried *with* Andrew. She wasn't sure she had the stamina to face another night.

It is too bad that Andrew's doctor didn't know that fussy babies aren't caused by nervous mothers. That notion was popular in the fifties, when physicians were unable to find any organic reasons for the so-called colicky baby. Indeed, the mothers of colicky babies did seem markedly more uptight than mothers of relaxed, easy-going babies who had regular sleeping patterns. Psychologists even conducted studies in that decade that appeared to show a relationship between baby fussiness and mother nervousness.

> *"One night at three A.M. when the baby had been crying steadily for four hours and would not stop, when we were worried that she might be really ill, when we were afraid our whole apartment building could hear and would be down the next morning demanding that we move out immediately, we sat down on our living room sofa and cried together. All three of us."*

What psychological tests failed to explain was how baby number one and baby number two could be perfectly even-tempered while baby number three was a fusser. Did the mother suddenly alter her personality? Testing of personality characteristics failed to predict which mothers would be more likely to have a colicky baby.

The most glaring flaw in these research studies was that they failed to take into account the profound stress effects that a nonsleeping, continually demanding baby has on the family, especially the mother, if she is the primary caregiver.

The effect of loss of sleep on the emotional stability of an adult has been well documented. Add to sleeplessness the heightened sense of frustration and helplessness aroused by such a nonstop situation, and the result is depression and anxiety in the most normal and emotionally healthy of mothers.

Researchers are confident now that the colicky baby/nervous mother link is a "chicken and egg" situation in which it is scientifically invalid to claim either as the true cause of the other. Dr. Ronald Illingworth, a British pediatrician who carried on an extensive study of colic in infants, has this to say about the matter in *The Normal Child: Some Problems of the Early Years and Their Treatment:*

> In my opinion most of the so-called tension in parents of babies with colic is the result of the babies' colic and not the cause of it. It is inevitable that severe colic in a baby will cause some degree of tension in a good mother. After careful observation of parents of these babies, I do not believe that they are any different from parents of babies who have no colic.... I do not see how family tension could produce these strictly rhythmical attacks of violent screaming ... which should surely be due to pain from the nature of the scream and the fact that they continue unabated in the mother's arms. If the colic was due entirely to psychological tension, one would expect it to occur more often in the first-born than in subsequent children, but it does not. Furthermore, colic commonly occurs in only one of three or four babies in the family.

Finding a Doctor You Can Trust

Over and over again mothers have communicated to me how important the support and sympathy of their physicians has been to their coping successfully with a crying, sleepless baby.

Unhelpful doctors are patronizing, take colic lightly, or quickly dispense drugs without sensing the seriousness of the baby's problems. In these cases parents are more likely to feel alienated from each other and their babies and to feel isolated, angry, guilty—and a whole host of other negative, stressful emotions. It is exactly these feelings that move parents toward baby abuse.

> *"Do not stay with a doctor who will not help you and the baby. There is a reason for a baby's cries, and any doctor who doesn't take colic seriously should be hung up by his Hippocratic oath."*

Here are some qualities that you should seek in the physician that you choose to help you and your baby:

- He should make you feel that he has plenty of time to listen to you, that you are important, and that your opinions and perceptions about the baby are valuable in finding solutions.
- You shouldn't feel rushed in his office, as though you've been cheated out of valuable sit-and-talk time by his scheduling, and you shouldn't have to wait long with your baby to see him when you have an appointment.
- He should be easily available to give you support over the telephone. (Colic is *important;* your feelings *do matter.*)
- You should feel that he's leaving no stone unturned to discover what's causing your baby's pain.

- He should seem reluctant to give you pat answers that don't help you or your situation, or to prescribe drugs that simply mask the baby's discomfort.
- He should encourage you to seek a second opinion, especially if more extensive tests are going to be done on the baby, or if you feel your baby's problem is more serious than your physician does.
- Most importantly, you should feel that you can *trust* him—that he has excellent training, experience, and up-to-date knowledge on baby problems.

You are paying your physician to render a service to you. If you are unhappy with how you are being treated, you have two options: You can discuss your feelings with your doctor to see if he is willing to change his approaches to you, or you can seek a new physician who is more sensitive to your needs. The latter is one of the joys and privileges of the American medical system, and you should use that freedom if you need to.

Your Doctor's Dilemma

Unfortunately, a baby can't talk. If he could, he would be able to tell your doctor how severe the pain is and where it comes from and how it really feels. The only language that a baby has is his crying, and that doesn't tell anything other than that there is *something* wrong.

Unfortunately, too, most pain attacks don't happen while the baby is in the doctor's office, so it is easy for a physician to pass off your baby's unseen, unheard pain cries as simply being "normal," or as being overblown by your uncertainty and obvious anxiety about the situation.

Your physician has to walk a fine line between giving you the assurance you need that the baby is all right and making medical decisions himself about whether or not to subject the baby to further tests that may only upset you and the baby more, cause separations, and cost you additional money.

"What if," he must ask himself, "I order sophisticated tests in the hospital that show no real problems in the baby? What if the baby really just has something that will be outgrown in just a matter of weeks?" Understandably, many doctors choose to wait out a baby's crying in hopes that it will cure itself, whatever the organic problem causing the discomfort. That does *not* excuse him from the responsibility of taking your baby's crying seriously.

How to Describe Your Baby's Symptoms to Your Doctor

You can help your doctor in diagnosing your baby's source of pain by providing the information that he needs to make a decision.

Baby's Symptoms	How to Describe Them
Pain	
The baby seems whiney and cries frequently. No change in position seems to help.	"He seems to have *chronic* pain" (pain that endures both day and night).
The baby's pain attacks are abrupt and sudden. For example, he's drinking from the bottle and suddenly gasps and lets out a loud, piercing scream.	"He has *acute* pain attacks" (very sharp pain that comes on quickly).

Tip: Make a tape recording of a typical attack and carry the tape and recorder to your doctor's office so that he can hear the way your baby cries.

Baby's Symptoms	How to Describe Them
Location of Pain	
Try pressing gently around the baby's belly to see if touching a particular spot provokes him to scream more. (Note: Most babies feel *all* pain around the belly button area.)	"The pain seems to be centered around his belly button." "It seems to be near his rib cage on the left (or right) side." "It seems to be coming from just above his pubic bone" (the area directly above the genitals).
Try rotating the ear by pressing it with your fingertips in a rhythmical, circular motion.	"It seems to be coming from his left (or right) ear."
Redness	
Look for unusual redness or heat coming from some spot on the baby's body during a crying attack.	"His ear seems hot." "His abdomen feels hot." "His left (or right) testicle feels hot."
Swelling	
Look for swelling or places that seem puffed out.	"His temples seem swollen." "His abdomen (belly) gets (or stays) *distended* (the medical word for swelling outward). "His testicle gets red and swollen when he cries."
Timing	
Keep a record for a few days about your baby's crying so you can describe it better.	"He cries in cycles for about half an hour every two hours." "He cries every evening as though he is in severe pain, beginning usually about 5:00

Baby's Symptoms	How to Describe Them

Baby's Symptoms

How to Describe Them

and ending at about midnight." "He wakes up abruptly during the night with screams of pain unrelated to hunger."

Fever and Cold Symptoms

Fever will indicate a possible infection. The baby's forehead will seem hotter than usual to your lips. His face may be flushed and red, or the opposite, unusually pale. (Note: Fevers in babies tend to run higher than in adults— 103°–104°F may be a sign of an oncoming cold.) Immunizations may cause fevers in babies.

"His temperature rectally at 10:00 P.M. was 102°F. At midnight it was 103°." "He has a fever and a runny nose." "His nose is stopped up." "He has been sneezing a lot." "He has a rattly cough." "He seems cranky." "He seems unusually irritable." "He's lost his appetite."

Stools

Count the number of bowel movements the baby has in a day. Is it more (or less) than usual? Severe diarrhea can cause serious dehydration (loss of body fluids) in less than a day. Call your doctor even on the weekend. (Also see the section on diarrhea in breastfed babies, p. 67.)

For constipation: "His stools are hard, like small pebbles, and leave no trace on the diaper."
For diarrhea: "His stools are loose and runny."
"He's had four more bowel movements than usual."
"His stools have flecks of mucus, blood, and undigested food in them."
"He seems to have persistent, mild diarrhea."

Tip: Carry a dirty diaper with you to the doctor so that he can see your baby's bowel movement.

Baby's Symptoms	How to Describe Them

Spitting Up and Vomiting

All babies spit up one or two mouthfuls of milk occasionally, especially after a burp or a feeding. It's normal, too, for babies to throw up once in a while. Frequent, forceful vomiting may be cause for concern.

"He spits up one to two mouthfuls of milky fluid without much effort."
"He has *projectile* vomiting after every feeding"—vomiting forcefully forward—"it seems to shoot across the room."

Examine the vomit for color, contents, or any bits of leaves or pills that could have been swallowed accidentally by your baby.

"His vomit is white (yellow, brown, green)." "His vomit has flecks of blood in it." "He seems to feel better after he has vomited."
"He doesn't seem to feel any better after he has vomited." "The baby coughs or chokes over and over again after he spits up."

Tip: Take a sample of your baby's vomit on a diaper when you go to the doctor's for his examination.

Breathing

When babies are in active sleep, they often mouth like they are nursing and groan, sigh, and make other strange noises.

"He is *wheezing*" (sounds like the purr of a cat coming from the baby's throat or chest).
"He is breathing very fast," or "He is taking very rapid, shallow breaths."
"He's having trouble getting air in and out." "His nostrils are flared when he breathes and the center of his chest sinks in with each breath" (possibly pneumonia).
"Sometimes he seems to stop breathing."

How to Take Your Baby's Temperature

Fever in a baby is a sign of infection. It is important for your doctor to know if your baby has a temperature when he is excessively fussy in order to tell if what is happening in his body is caused by infection or if his pain is from other sources. The temperature should best be taken when the baby is not upset, or hasn't been lying on a hot water bottle.

There are two kinds of glass thermometers: those with long, slender silver-looking tips that are meant for using in the mouth and those with short, stubby tips that are for putting in the baby's rectum. Mouth temperatures are not taken in babies because the thermometer might break if the baby's jaws clamp shut on it, and also because it's too difficult to be sure that the thermometer is under the baby's tongue, where readings should be taken.

The temperature of the baby is read by where the mercury line ends inside the glass tube. The line goes up with heat, but *it does not go back down on its own.* You have to shake the mercury line down before taking a temperature. Here's how:

- See what the thermometer reads. It should read 95°F. (It's a right-handed instrument, and can only be deciphered well when it faces to your left.)
- Stand away from furniture so you won't hit the thermometer against anything and break it.
- Hold the thermometer by the end *opposite* the rounded silver bulb.
- Shake the thermometer like you are trying to shake water off your hands, "flip, flip, flip," until it reads 95°F or below.

Don't get uptight, now, it won't hurt the baby.

- Lubricate the tip with Vaseline or diaper cream.

15

- Lie the baby on his back, as if you were going to change his diaper, with his feet toward you.
- Hold on to his ankles with one hand, finger in between, and bend his knees so that his anus is visible.
- Gently insert bulb about one inch into his anus and hold it in place near where it enters the baby. (Maybe someone can help with this). Keep it in for at least three minutes.
- Take out the thermometer and write down the time and the reading. The line seems to disappear if you turn the thermometer too far one way or the other. The graduations between the numbers are usually in tenths. The normal reading is 99°–99.6°F (i.e. 99 and 6 tenths—one degree higher than by mouth).
- Clean the thermometer with cool water and soap, rinsing well, and wipe it off for storage.

2
Hidden Causes That You Can Influence

Within the past ten years tremendous advances in the diagnosis of disease and behavior problems in babies have enabled scientists to discover more of what causes babies to behave miserably. At last doctors and researchers are moving beyond the "nervous-mother-causes-colicky-baby" myth to pinpoint real reasons for the mysterious ailment that was labeled colic for over a century.

Before Baby Even Arrives

Recently an association between excessive irritability in young babies and a range of factors that may be related to prenatal oxygen deprivation has been uncovered.

Birth Complications

Research has demonstrated that babies who are premature or are much smaller than expected at birth are more likely to be excessively irritable, fussy, and to sleep less in the months after birth. Similarly, babies who undergo prolonged labors or who suffer from anoxia, an inadequate supply of oxygen during birth and immediately afterward, are more apt to have these same negative behaviors.

High Blood Pressure

Dr. Anneleise Korner and her associates at the Stanford University School of Medicine have found a possible link between high blood pressure in the mother in the later months of pregnancy and extreme irritability in babies. Mothers with blood pressures in the high-normal range were more likely to give birth to superexcitable, crying babies than those mothers with lower readings.

Drugs

Similarly a connection has been found between a mother's use of drugs during pregnancy and labor and baby crying and sleeplessness. Babies born to heroin-addicted mothers have nervous system instabilities, which include sleep disruptions and extreme fussiness. Mothers who have taken barbiturates such as Phenobarbital during pregnancy are more apt to give birth to hyperexcitable, trembling babies who are restless and ravenous. The baby's symptoms may not appear until a week after birth. They peak at between two and six weeks of age and may last until the baby is six months of age. The baby may be undergoing drug withdrawal symptoms—going "cold turkey."

Drugs are now a potent part of the body environment of most unborn babies. A survey of fifty thousand pregnant women in the U.S. found that only six percent of the mothers *took no drugs* during pregnancy. Most mothers averaged four drugs during that critical time.

The old concept that somehow the mother's placenta operates as a master filtering device, barring drugs and unwanted substances from the unborn baby's body, is now known to be wrong. *It is currently thought that any substance found in the mother's blood that isn't altered or destroyed during passage will be directly transferred to the baby.*

Even in the hours and minutes before birth, when drugs are administered to the mother for pain, the baby receives his complement of these chemicals. Once the umbilical cord is cut the baby's immature and extremely inefficient system is on its own to break down the drugs and get rid of them. In most cases this takes days or weeks.

Dr. Inger Asmussen of the University of Copenhagen discovered that infants of mothers who smoked heavily during pregnancy had tissue damage and clogging in their blood vessels even at birth. The babies born to smoking mothers, she found, were approximately 10 percent smaller than normal. The mother's placentas, which supply oxygen and sustenance to the babies in the womb, were 20 percent smaller than those of nonsmoking mothers. Smoking studies in the U.S. have shown it to be related to the premature separation of the placenta from the uterine wall, which radically affects the baby's oxygen supply.

Rhesus monkeys have been used to look at the effects of nicotine on the baby after birth. Nicotine, the drug contained in cigarettes, is a tiny molecule that passes easily through the placenta into the baby's system. When introduced into the bloodstream of the mother, it affects the unborn infant's heart rate, blood pressure, oxygen supply, and acid balance. The sympathetic nervous system of the infant, which controls breathing and heart rate, appears to be impaired by the drug.

Heavy marijuana smoking, too, can be hazardous to the pregnant mother and her baby. Studies have shown that the chemicals in marijuana do cross the placenta into the baby. Mothers who are heavy marijuana users during pregnancy have been found to be more anemic than normal and to have generally poorer weight gain both for themselves and the babies they are carrying.

Heavy marijuana users are also more likely to have prolonged labors or dangerously fast ones with the possibility of meconium staining, a sign that the birthing baby is in distress. After birth, the babies of heavy smokers have been found to be more trembly and easily startled than normal. They might also have difficulty in being soothed or soothing themselves and are less adaptable to changes in light.

Drugs During Labor

Some drugs, such as anesthetics used on mothers during labor, may have a prolonged effect on baby behavior over a long period of time after birth because of the baby's poor ability to excrete them from his body.

A team of Australian researchers, headed by Dr. David B. Thomas, has found that the epidural, a common painkilling procedure used during labor to numb the mother's lower body, may have a relationship to later baby colic.

Babies of mothers who had epidurals, forty in all, were more trembly, irritable, and had poorer body coordination in the first three days after birth. If the mother had both an epidural and oxytocin, the baby was also likely to show extreme tension and hyperactivity.

Babies in the epidural group cried more frequently by the fifth day of life than those from unmedicated mothers. By one month of age their mothers found them to be less adaptable, more intense, and far more difficult to manage than babies of mothers who had not been administered these drugs during labor.

Thomas's researchers believe that the extreme rise in colicky babies over the past decade may be related to the expanded use of drugs during labor.

Exactly how a mother's high blood pressure, her prolonged labor, or her use of drugs cause a change in her baby's behavior are still unclear. One possible explanation is that all of these factors affect the baby's supply of oxygen, which in turn causes changes in the functioning of his brain and central nervous system.

For most babies the ill effects of oxygen deprivation or drugs are measured in weeks or months, but for other babies the results may be more long lasting. A British study has found that 48 percent of preschool children who have sleeping disorders such as waking up over and over had suffered from anoxia or complications at birth. Anoxia at birth has also been implicated in hyperactivity in school-age boys. A survey of the drug intake of over fifty-thousand pregnant mothers has found that those who took drugs such as Compazine, a potent antinausea medication, had a twenty percent greater chance of their babies becoming hyperactive and impulsive as at school age.

It may well be that for some babies crying and sleeplessness, colic, is a prolonged physical reaction to events that have happened before they are even brought home from the hospital.

The Role of Milk Reactions in Colic

Some babies who cry from bouts of belly pain may be having physical reactions to the substances found in their cow's milk formula. In some cases these babies are unable to handle certain milk sugars during digestion, especially one named lactose. If this is the case, then crying, stomach pains, excessive gas, and diarrhea result. The condition is called "lactose intolerance." (For a discussion of allergic reactions in fully breastfed babies, see Chapter Five.)

Still another form of milk reaction is cow's milk allergy. The baby's immunity system—his defense against disease—goes awry, so that his body fights against a protein found in milk as though it were a disease bearer rather than a harmless food substance. White blood cells mount a reaction by attacking milk particles directly, and others attach themselves directly to the offending protein, preparing to destroy it. Specialized cells, called mast cells, that line the baby's intestines on the inside, release chemical substances to enable the body's disease fighters to leave the blood vessels and enter the area where the body's battle is being waged.

The physical result of milk reactions in babies is a variety of symptoms. The most common symptoms are diarrhea, colic, wheezing (purring in the chest), asthma, vomiting, bronchitis, frequent inner ear infections, and a runny nose. An allergic baby may refuse the nursing bottle or just be generally fussy. Although very, very rare, some babies may even break out in hives from contact with milk on their skins or go into severe, coma-producing shock from drinking cow's milk.

Besides the outward symptoms of a milk-induced allergy, the inner lining of the baby's intestinal walls may be swollen and inflamed and, in some cases, the intestinal tissues may show actual damage, especially if the baby has suffered severe, prolonged diarrhea.

When a baby is allergic to milk, he may have mild bleeding in his intestines, which results in anemia—a lack of sufficient iron in his blood. Anemia in allergic babies is usually seen in a baby over six months old who drinks huge amounts of milk daily and yet is pale. Typically, such a baby looks thin-skinned and has dark circles under his eyes. He may be sluggish and extremely irritable and have a cloudy mucus discharge from his nose.

Half of the babies who are allergic to cow's milk proteins also have problems with milk sugars.

The number of babies who have milk allergies and sugar intolerances is not known. In some ways the milk-allergy bandwagon resembles the hypoglycemia craze of some years back, with nearly every crying bottlefed baby being diagnosed as milk sensitive. True milk allergies are extremely difficult to prove because of the complex nature of milk sugars and proteins and the tremendous variety of symptoms that they create in babies.

Soy Substitutes

The simplest path taken by most doctors when faced with unexplained crying in a bottlefed baby is to take the baby off cow's milk formula and to substitute a soy formula, such as Isomil, in its place. Soy milk is not really "milk" but a liquid synthesized from the protein of soybeans. About 66 percent of the time this will improve a baby's symptoms if he is truly allergic to cow's milk.

Dr. Allan Walker, a pediatric gastroenterologist at the Harvard University Medical School, advises that babies not be given solids for the first six months of life in order to avoid initiating their reactions to food proteins. He states, "I would strongly urge that the pediatrician not repeatedly change formulas containing the same components; that is, not go from one milk-based formula to another. If the child seems to be reacting in the form of gastrointestinal symptoms to a milk-based formula, it makes sense to go to a soy-based formula, primarily because it is a changing from the lactose form of sugar to sucrose."

Twenty-five to thirty-three percent of the time, babies who are allergic to the protein in cow's milk formulas are also allergic to the protein in soy formulas, according to Dr. Walker. When these two feeding alternatives have failed to alleviate the baby's symptoms, then the two remaining alternatives are to put the baby on human breast milk, or to use what is called an "elemental" formula. These formulas, brand names Nutramigen and Pregestimil, are, in a sense, predigested milks that the baby's body can readily absorb. Their proteins and sugars have already been broken down. Parents of these babies find themselves having to pay as much as a hundred dollars a case, or fifty dollars a week for the formulas. Unfortunately, some parents are tempted to water them down to make them stretch further, seriously endangering their baby's nutritional well-being.

Goat's milk, often thought to be less allergy arousing than cow's milk, has many proteins that cause "cross-reaction"—in other words, they produce the identical allergic body reactions as those in cow's milk.

Diagnosis

Pediatric gastroenterologists such as Dr. Walker, or Dr. Alan Lake at the Johns Hopkins University School of Medicine, have a number of sophisticated tests at their fingertips to ferret out the specific milk-digestion problems that a baby may be having. For example, they may measure the amount of hydrogen in the baby's breath, since lactose intolerance raises the hydrogen level. Or, a specialist may decide to feed a tiny tube down into the baby's digestive tract so that a small bit of intestinal lining can be painlessly extracted for testing. The living tissues from the intestines react chemically to the presence of a body's allergic "enemies." Tiny amounts of individual milk proteins may be injected under the baby's skin to see if a body reaction such as swelling occurs. The baby's blood serum may be tested to see if it binds to the protein allergen. A baby's stools may also be tested for the presence of chemical changes or abnormalities.

Most babies outgrow their milk reactions between one and two years of age, although some never do. It is not unusual for some adults to have mild milk reactions without being aware of it. Parents who are allergic to milk usually don't like to drink it themselves. There is evidence that in some cases milk sensitivity is inherited by the baby from one or both parents.

Interestingly, reactions to milk, especially lactose intolerance, are far more predominant in non-white babies. Babies of African or Chinese descent, and the peoples of many other races whose cultures have not practiced the domesticating of cows and the drinking of their milk, are much less able to tolerate drinking cow's milk. The ability to digest cow's milk appears to be most common among infants and adults of eastern European origin where cow raising has been practiced for centuries.

Middle Ear Infection

Your baby's middle ear cannot be seen by looking into his ear because it is located behind the eardrum. It is a tiny canal that drains into the baby's throat behind his palate. The middle ear is often the site of bacterial infections, and once they lodge there the perfect environment is set for repeated infections.

The National Center for Health Statistics reports that middle ear infection is the most commonly found disorder diagnosed in visits to the pediatrician's office. It is second only to the common cold as a disease of babies and children. It has been estimated that as many as one half of all babies and children have middle ear infections in childhood.

Babies often have inner ear infections along with colds. Two surprising causes of chronic ear infections in babies are allergic reactions to cow's milk, which result in continual symptoms that resemble a cold, and smoking by parents. A British survey of a typical group of eighteen-month-old babies showed a significant association between parental smoking and increased ear and respiratory infections.

In another British survey it was found that if neither parent smoked, the incidence of serious respiratory infections in babies during the first year of life was only 7.2 percent. If one parent smoked, the incidence rose to 11.8

What May Be Causing Your Baby's Reaction to Formula

Type of Reaction	Description	Symptoms	Treatment
Carbohydrate	The baby's body has difficulty in digesting the sugars found in cow's milk, most commonly named lactose.	Diarrhea, bloated abdomen, colic, and passing excessive gas	Changing the baby to non-cow's milk formula, such as one based on soy protein.
Protein Intolerance	The baby cannot easily digest certain milk proteins, either because of the inability to chemically process it, or because of the direct damage that the proteins may do to the digestive surfaces of the intestines. Also included in this category are *allergies* to certain proteins such as those in cow's milk, soy milk, corn, wheat, or peanuts, which arouse the body's immune reactions.	Diarrhea, colic, and excessive crying. Frequent colds and rattly breathing or wheezing. Anemia. Milk protein allergy is very difficult to verify scientifically, since milk contains numerous proteins.	Human breast milk is the treatment of choice. Soy milk elemental formulas in which the milk proteins are essentially predigested may be recommended when other milks fail.

Overfeeding	The baby is taking in too much milk or water, perhaps because of other body pain that is temporarily eased by feeding.	Excessive weight gain, sluggishness, and frequent spitting up or vomiting after eating.	Pacifier between meals. Frequent small feeds coupled with direct soothing for crying rather than always feeding.
Malabsorption or Maldigestion	A rare failure of the body to produce certain needed enzymes for digestion, or the result of disease in the lower digestive tract. Included in this category are serious diseases such as cystic fibrosis, an inherited malady characterized by widespread change in the mucous-secreting glands and sweat glands in the body, and celiac disease, the body's inability to deal with vegetable protein, specifically gluten, present in wheat and other grains.	Failure to gain weight, excessive sluggishness, and irritability.	Treatment, including dietary control, will depend upon the disease.

27

percent. If both parents smoked, it was as high as 17.7 percent.

Unfortunately, middle ear infections are often missed in routine physical examinations because a doctor's otoscope—the lighted viewing device that he uses to peer into the baby's ear—may not be sensitive enough to pick up signs of infection, especially if there is wax or debris blocking his view of the ear canal.

Ear infection can be a very subtle disease. Often there is no fever or earache, simply unexplained irritability and sluggishness in the baby. One clinical study found that nearly all of the sixty-six mothers of babies with inner ear infections that were studied had decided that their babies' crying was caused by colic. One specialist found that almost half of his small patients with ear infections had first been treated unsuccessfully by their doctors for digestive problems.

As infection occurs in the baby's inner ear pus and mucus build up inside the tube, putting pressure on the baby's eardrum. When a doctor inspects the eardrum closely with special magnification and light, he can observe the increased fluid pressure and color changes. When the baby's eardrum is tightened up by pressure, his hearing may be seriously impaired.

Now significant advances in technology are helping physicians to diagnose middle ear infections more accurately. The fiberoptic otoscope, an improved viewing device, gives substantially more light and magnification than ever before. Infections once overlooked can now be quickly diagnosed and treated with antibiotics.

Tympanometry is a new technique for testing for middle ear infection. When infection causes fluids to press against the eardrum, the vibrating action of the drum is changed. Short bursts of air are used to measure the flexibility of the drum. When an eardrum fails to vibrate normally, the doctor knows that infection is likely to be present.

If you suspect that your baby may have hearing problems because he doesn't respond to your voice, or because he has had numerous colds and sore throats, you might consider taking him to an ear, nose, and throat specialist, officially called an otolaryngologist (pronounced oh-toe-lare-uhn-jol-uh-jist).

One note of caution: Specialists are becoming increasingly alarmed at the vast number of operations performed to remove children's tonsils when children have recurrent sore throats and inner ear infections. There is convincing evidence that in many cases this surgery is unnecessary. If your doctor suggests a tonsillectomy, which was almost standard treatment in the fifties for chronic colds and sore throats, seek a second opinion. Many children fare the same or better without this procedure.

Sedatives—The Colic Cure-all

When a baby shows signs of irritability and sleeplessness, the most common form of treatment by doctors is to administer sedating drugs to him. One survey of 159 normal 18-month-olds found that 25 percent of them had been given sedatives in their brief lives. Some of the babies had been consistently given drugs for over four months or longer. While such medication makes the baby sleep, restoring temporary peace to the household, the silence may be at too great a cost to the baby's well-being.

The danger of sedating the baby is that he may be overdrugged. His breathing may slow down, his pulse may be affected, and his central nervous system, which oversees the operation of his bodily functions, may be affected.

It is not uncommon for babies to have what is called a "paradoxical" reaction to sedatives. That is, rather than becoming sluggish and sleepy as his parents had hoped, the baby becomes hyperactive, staying awake in a drunken state all night. Babies, too, can have hangovers from drugs. While they are subdued by the drug and sleep, by morning they may become increasingly irritable and inconsolable.

Phenobarbital

Ironically, Phenobarbital, the most commonly prescribed sedative for the treatment of crying and irritability in babies, has been found to *cause* excessive irritability in babies whose mothers have taken it during pregnancy.

In a recent article in *Obstetrics and Gynecology* researchers Frank Witter, Theodore Kinds, and David Blake at the Johns Hopkins University School of Medicine have seriously questioned the use of Phenobarbital for pregnant mothers because of what it may do to their newborns. In some cases it has been associated with newborn bleeding, abnormally low levels of blood calcium, a slowing down of the baby's body reactions, and possible bad effects on the baby's adaptive and learning capacities. When Phenobarbital was given to pregnant rats, in a recent study conducted at the National Institute of Child Health and Human Development, it profoundly affected the maturation of the rat infants. The drug produced smaller offspring, their puberty was significantly delayed, and often they were sterile. In males, male hormones were radically reduced and the descent of the testicles was delayed.

Yet many physicians routinely prescribe the use of Phenobarbital on irritable babies for reasons such as these, reported by a doctor in the professional journal *Australian Family Physician*:

> In the more severe situations, sedation of the infant may be indicated "to take the edge off of him," thereby decreasing his demands. This may be done for up to a few weeks to facilitate the mother's recovery and to enable her to better handle her rather active baby. Mother may also require medication in her own right.

Some physicians may casually recommend giving a baby whiskey, ten drops in a teaspoon of sweetened water, two or three times a day. Alcohol has been the folk remedy for colic for almost a century. It was once given to babies soaked into a "sugar tit," a handkerchief wrapped around a lump of sugar and dipped in liquor.

Alcohol is a potent and dangerous drug for babies—so much so that it is listed in poison control centers across the nation. The baby's body does not react to alcohol in the same way that an adult's does. Severe hypoglycemia, a lowering of the baby's blood sugar, may set in when less than a half a cup of alcohol is administered. The result in the body: tremors, sweating, and possible coma.

> *"Our baby from the time we brought him home from the hospital until he was three and a half months of age cried twelve hours a day. My doctor suggested that we give him Phenobarbital to be taken at five or six P.M. as needed for colic. We gave it to him one time, and he slept twelve hours straight and scared us to death."*

For Better—Or Worse?

Do drugs like Phenobarbital, Atropine, and low doses of alcohol actually make fussy babies get better? Dr. Crossan O'Donovan and pharmacist Alden Bradstock of the Baltimore City Hospitals tested one hundred and ten colicky babies with combinations of these drugs and the standard twenty percent alcohol elixer that is used with them. One fourth of the babies were given only colored water for treatment. Seventy percent of the babies improved regardless of what treatment they received. Seventeen percent got worse.

Benadryl (diphenhydramine hydrochloride) may be prescribed because of its sedating and stomach-relaxing qualities. Its multiple adverse effects on the baby include central nervous system depression, restlessness, changes in the baby's blood, and a thickening of the baby's mucous secretions.

One new therapeutic drug being tested on colicky babies is Mylicon (simethicone), a defoaming agent that breaks down gas bubbles in the digestive system so that they are less painful. Another drug currently being explored in Sweden is *Minifom Emulsion* (polydimethyl siloxane), which absorbs fluids in the digestive system to form synthetic stools. Side effects in babies are yet unknown.

The most widely successful treatment for colic is Bentyl (dicylomine hydrochloride), which acts to relax the baby's intestinal muscles and to inhibit its painful spasms. It has fewer side effects than Phenobarbital and similar sedative drugs, but it still has adverse effects on the baby, including dry mouth, sluggishness, loss of appetite, constipation, rashes, and urine retention.

"When we learn of a four-month-old infant who cries virtually all the time and has never slept through the night, we suggest that his parents discontinue giving synthetically colored and/or flavored baby vitamin drops. Many parents report that within thirty-six hours they have a normal, calm infant who sleeps through the night."

**—Jane Hersey, President,
The Feingold Association
of the U.S.**

Folk remedies for colic are a mild tea given to the baby and made from a teaspoon of crushed fennel seeds that are boiled in a cup of water and strained, a tea made from a boiled bay leaf, or one drop of liquid Asiphiteda (gum of arabic) in a teaspoon of warm milk. Some parents also recommend Hylands Homeopathic Colic Tablets (available in some health food stores and from Standard Homeopathic Co., P.O. Box 61067, Los Angeles, CA 90061).

Even when doctors prescribe medications, parents are often very reluctant to administer them. Out of thirty-five mothers of colicky babies used in one survey, it was found that all five mothers who had consulted their physicians about their babies' crying were in frank despair over their babies' problems. Each was given a prescription for drugs. All expressed ambivalence about employing them. All but one mother promptly discontinued using the drugs after giving their babies only one or two doses.

Some mothers feel that having a drug on hand for their colicky babies is a boon, even if it only stays in the medicine cabinet. As one mother puts it, "I had a tool, so I knew that I wasn't totally at the mercy of my baby's crying. Even though I only used the drug once or twice, knowing it was there for me if I got desperate enough helped me to cope."

Unfortunately, there are no miracle colic cures. Most drugs only serve to cover up the baby's symptoms, not to heal them. Colic is not a single entity, but a complex syndrome arising from a number of possible body problems. Drugs and home remedies all alter the natural balance and operation of the baby's body, and until more is known about how drugs ultimately affect a baby and how they are metabolized by the baby's system, extreme caution in using them should be exercised.

3
Urinary Tract Infection?

One prevalent cause of baby pain that can easily be overlooked is a problem with the baby's genitals or urinary tract. That's because the pain the baby is having seems to be so related to his abdominal area. He slaps his belly with his legs when he cries as if to say, "Here's where it hurts!" Babies and young children generally localize pain coming from other parts of their bodies in their belly button area. *Referred pain* is the term used to describe this oddity of human anatomy when pain is experienced in an entirely different place than from its source.

Dr. Joseph Du of the University of Manitoba Health Center in Canada reports cases of babies who seemed to have colic, yet who really had urinary tract infections, in the August 21, 1976, issue of the *Canadian Medical Association Journal.* He shares excerpts written by a physician that describe a six-month-old colicky baby. The physician was convinced that the baby's crying and sleep problems were the fault of his mother.

The mother is a nervous wreck. Has lost 17 lbs. and looks like a wraith. She is a bundle of nerves and something has to be done to help this poor soul or she will go out of her mind. . . . The baby has been really upset recently, perhaps due to teething, colic, or whatever. Drinks 3 to 4 bottles of milk during the night, and then won't drink a thing during the day. He is healthy and looks absolutely marvelous.

The baby was put on a sedative. Finally, after a series of tests in the hospital, it was found that he had a blocked urinary tube and an inflamed kidney. After corrective surgery the baby's "colic" vanished, and his mother reported that he was like a different child.

Dr. Du reports three other cases of babies with persistent irritability and colic who were found to have urinary tract infections. The babies' "colic" was quickly cleared by treatment with antibiotics.

"Urinalysis is not carried out routinely in infants in the average [medical] office practice," Dr. Du notes, "because of the inconvenience of obtaining a reliable urine specimen. As a result urinary tract infections masquerading as colic may well be missed."

Dr. Robert Jeffs, chief of the Division of Pediatric Urology at the Johns Hopkins School of Medicine, agrees. "The problem with diagnosing urinary tract problems in babies," he notes, "is that a baby won't urinate on command at the doctor's office. It may be minutes or it may be hours before it cooperates."

The usual method of catching a sample of a baby's urine is by using a collection bag—a pouch that resembles a sandwich bag that is fastened around the baby's genitals by an adhesive collar. The baby's genitals have to be very clean—as bacteria-free as possible. If it is a long time before the baby urinates, the urine in the bag may become contaminated with the bacteria that naturally multiply on the skin. This may lead to a misdiagnosis that the baby has bacteria in his urine when the source is really his skin.

The best way to get an accurate urine sample from the baby is to catch it, free-falling, from the baby. That's a much easier trick to accomplish with a baby boy than with a girl, but most mothers can succeed if a nurse shows them how to do it.

Signs of Urinary Tract Infection in Your Baby

The symptoms of a urinary tract infection may be as nonspecific as any of these symptoms: refusal to drink, general fussiness, mild fever, or failure to gain weight. More specific signs are:

- *A sudden change in the usual diaper-wetting frequency of your baby.* Your baby wets much more or much less than usual. (Note: newborns wet as many as a hundred diapers a week. Diaper wetting decreases gradually to about seventy or eighty a week at six months and sixty or seventy a week by ten months of age. Some babies are heavy wetters, others light wetters from birth on.)
- *A stop-start pattern of urinating with the baby trying to hold back to avoid pain, followed by only producing a small amount of urine and crying or fussiness.*
- *A red, flushed face or excessive straining when urinating.* It's normal for some babies, especially girls, to tremble slightly when they urinate. Toddlers with urinary tract problems may squat to urinate.

Once a urine sample is collected from the baby, it is examined under a microscope and the number of bacteria cells present are noted. The presence of pus is also noted, indicating infection. The urine may then be sent off to a laboratory to be cultured, in order to identify more correctly the culprit bacteria so that correct medication can be prescribed for the baby.

To be completely accurate about the presence and type of infection that a baby has, your doctor may opt to do a pubic tap, which is the insertion of a syringe needle directly into the baby's bladder to collect an uncontaminated supply of urine. He may also insert a tiny tube, called a catheter, up the baby's urinary tube (urethra) in order to get a clean urine sample.

"Any boy baby who is proven to have a urinary tract infection should be suspected of having an anomaly in his urological system," Dr. Jeffs from Johns Hopkins explains. Further tests will usually be ordered for him. "Girl babies, on the other hand, may have a simple bladder infection without fever that is caused by a nonserious irritation whose only real sign is more frequent urinations than usual." In that case, no more extensive medical tests may be necessary.

Untreated urinary tract infections and malfunctions may cause more serious problems later in adulthood, such as kidney damage or failure, so testing is important. The choice of tests that your doctor makes will depend upon those that are easily available to him and how much detail is needed in viewing a particular part of the urinary system.

If a problem is suspected, you may want a second opinion from a urologist. Pediatric urologists are small in number and hard to find, and most urologists routinely deal with both babies and children. (Check the reference book *The Best Doctors in the U.S.* by John Pekkanen, published by Seaview Books, for a list of twenty-one pediatric urologists.)

The kinds of tests that are used to discover structural defects and problems with urinary organs include the following:

- *Blood Urea Nitrogen Test* (B.U.N.): An examination of the baby's blood sample for waste products. Not always a sensitive test, according to Dr. Jeffs, and a fair degree of damage may have to have happened before the test indicates a problem.
- *Cystograms (called IVP Cystogram and Radioactive Cystogram):* A tiny catheter tube is inserted up the baby's urinary tract and a dye is put into the baby's system so that the urinary organs can be viewed by X ray. How the baby urinates can also be watched.
- *Nuclear Medicine Scan:* A mildly radioactive substance is injected into the baby's forearm. The baby's urinary functioning is monitored on a film and by a device similar to a sensitive geiger counter that traces the type and rate of excretion from the baby.

Penis Care

If your baby is not circumcised (and there is now a lot of strong, sound medical research to suggest that routine circumcision of boys is unnecessary), his foreskin—the skin covering the penis head—will probably be stuck to the glans—the bulb end of the penis.

Some parents think that they should pull back the foreskin in order to clean underneath. *That part of the baby is not meant to be cleaned inside.* Others fear that the end of the foreskin might get in the way of urination. The true blocking of urine by the foreskin, called phimosis, is a very rare problem. More common is a form of phimosis caused by a parent's trying to retract a baby's or young child's foreskin too early so that the penis tip is strangulated by a tight ring of skin.

Slowly, as the baby matures, the penis head and the foreskin will develop small spaces between them. The spaces enlarge until, by the age of three or four, the child's foreskin becomes loose enough to be pulled back, exposing the penis head.

Sometimes a baby will get a swollen red area on the end of his penis head that is caused by diaper ammonia. This is not a signal that the baby should be circumcised, since then the baby's penis head would only be *more* exposed to irritating chemicals produced by urine and bacteria. The best approach to treatment is to improve diaper washing and changing methods.

There's no need to worry about penis cleanliness in babies, other than the usual rinse-offs. Once your son is old enough to bathe himself—age four or five—then he can be taught, just as his sister would, how to take care of himself.

Circumcision Care

If your baby has been circumcised, Dr. Jeffs suggests keeping the penis area clean with no dressing on top of it. The area should be rinsed off with mildly warm water each time his diaper is changed. Don't use a washcloth for wiping, which may irritate the baby's sensitive penis head and circumcision wound. Some mothers use a well-cleaned plastic squirt bottle to rinse off their babies over the sink. Dr. Jeffs suggests a dip of the baby's bottom into the sink. It's especially crucial, he notes, to clean the area when the baby has had a bowel movement, since this is how bacteria contaminate the penis wound.

Circumcision Danger Signs

The following should be reported to your doctor:

- Increased redness and swelling in the shaft of the penis next to the circumcision wound
- Fever
- Bleeding of more than a few spots on the diaper
- Separation of the wound so that the skin of the penis shaft comes away from the rim of the penis head, as though the incision is coming apart
- Pus in the circumcision areas, or the formation of whitish pustules along the line of the circumcision.

The incision area and penis head are very tender and sensitive. If ammonia builds up in the baby's diapers when they are left on too long, or if the diaper fabric is too rough, your baby's penis may develop redness and a sore spot, called meatal ulcer, which may cause the formation of scar tissue and later problems with urination.

"It's important to protect the delicate skin of your baby's penis tip from long-standing urine or undue diaper roughness," Dr. Jeffs emphasizes.

Treating Diaper Rash

Luanna and Richard Myers were given a one-month subscription to a diaper service as a baby shower present before their baby was born. It turned out to be one of the most time-saving gifts they received, since their baby wet about ninety diapers a week. After one month, when the diaper service stopped, the baby developed a red, sore case of diaper rash that woke him up crying in the middle of the night because when he urinated his skin burned.

Why did diaper rash break out after the diaper service stopped bringing diapers? Diaper rash is commonly caused by the mixing together of soap residues, which are highly alkaline, and the baby's urine, which turns alkaline after being on him for a while. Combined, the two alkalines burn the baby's skin. While the bowel movements of breastfed babies are naturally acidic, the BM's of bottlefed babies are more likely to be alkaline and therefore more irritating to baby skin.

It doesn't matter what brand of detergent is used in the washing machine, what does matter is how well the detergent is rinsed out so that no soap residues remain. Low-sudsing detergents are better for diapers, since they rinse out better than baby laundry soaps that don't work well in hard water. New detergents that claim to contain fabric softeners are to be avoided.

Another cause of diaper rash is ammonia burn. As soon as the baby urinates in the diaper bacteria begin to build up, giving off ammonia as a by-product. Sometimes you can smell it on a diaper that's been used all night. While diaper services can heat the diapers to the point of sterilization, most household water heaters cannot get hot enough to kill bacteria, nor should they, since they could seriously burn a baby. Bacteria remain imbedded in the diaper threads and are carried over from one diaper washing to the next. One solution often used in other countries to kill bacteria is to boil the diapers for ten minutes in a big pot.

Mary Hilton, the nation's diaper rash expert, and author of *The A B C's of Diaper Rash* (available for $1.25 from her at 814 Nola Street, Kalamazoo, MI 49001), offers these diaper-laundering tips:

Rinse the Diapers After Use

First machine cycle: Use ¾ cup of low-sudsing detergent
½ cup *water* softener, such as Calgon
(not *fabric* softener)
½ cup of chlorine bleach to kill bacteria

Start the machine over again with: ½ cup of water softener

On the final rinse add: ¼ cup of vinegar (to make the diaper slightly acidic)

Sunshine and air are good both for drying the diapers and for healing the baby's bottom. Healing can sometimes be helped by keeping the baby completely out of a diaper during naps and after a bowel movement. You can do this by lying him on top of a diaper rather than fastening it on to him. The circulation of air in the diapers can also be helped by fastening them on loosely.

Plastic outer pants are often to blame for diaper rash because they trap moisture and heat—the two promoters of bacterial growth—around the baby's bottom. If you use plastic pants because you want to keep the baby's bed dry at night, then use an extra-large size that has snaps on the sides and then tuck the last snapped part under to allow air in.

A recent study of diaper rash in 1-month-old babies found that 18 percent of the babies who wore only cloth diapers had diaper rash, while 33 percent of those who wore both cotton diapers and plastic pants had it, and 54 percent of the babies who wore disposable diapers had it. *One out of every two babies wearing disposables had diaper rash!* Perhaps you should consider changing over to cloth diapers if your baby is having a problem, or puncturing some holes in the plastic outer coverings of the disposables so that you know for sure when the baby is wet and needs changing, and so air can get in.

New cotton diapers are currently being manufactured that look promising for helping to combat baby wetness. One is called the Curity Day-Night Diaper. It is prefolded and has a polyester sponge embedded in the center to help draw wetness away from the baby's bottom. Another is being manufactured from double-knit cotton, like T-shirt fabric, so that it is very absorbent and formfitting. This prototype diaper is still in the design stage but will soon be available commercially.

Some mothers recommend using old-fashioned knitted wool soaker pants to cover cloth diapers. Wool works like a sponge to draw moisture away from the baby while remaining dry to the touch itself. (Careful, though. If your skin gets itchy and red from wool sweaters, then your baby may have the same reaction.)

Handmade wool soaker pants can be ordered from Marni's Soakers, Box 718, Penngrove, CA 94951. Their price at this writing is $7.50 a pair, 25¢ for more information. "Biobottoms" are machine-made wool diaper covers that come in a variety of sizes with Velcro closures. The price is approximately $11.50 a pair. Write first before ordering from: Biobottoms, 57 Grant Ave., Petaluma, CA 94952.

"The important thing about fighting diaper rash," says Dr. Jeffs, "is to keep the baby dry. If a diaper rash is starting up, change the baby more often than usual." Dampness against the baby's skin softens it and makes it more vulnerable to infection.

Dr. Jeff's basic regimen for diaper rash care is this:

(1) Rinse the diaper area off with water at every diaper changing.
(2) Dry the baby thoroughly. One excellent way to do this is by using a blow-dryer on high flow and low heat for five minutes after each change.

(3) Use a barrier of petroleum jelly or any other over-the-counter diaper cream to protect the reddened skin. Premoistened wipes that contain either alcohol or acetone should be avoided because of extreme dryness they cause on a baby's skin.

Diaper Rash, Thrush, and Sore Nipples

A fiery red diaper rash with a scaly edge that is relatively painless is probably the result of a yeastlike fungus called *Candida albicans.* Candida thrives everywhere; it's in the environment and especially in the mucous linings of the body. Even ordinary diaper rashes quickly become fungus infections, especially in damp climates. Some babies pick up candida when they pass through their mother's birth canal, because it's one of the major culprits of itchy vaginitis, which causes her to have a white, frothy discharge that has a yeasty aroma to it.

Candida is responsible for thrush, a bothersome mouth infection in babies that produces white, raised, curdlike patches on the baby's mouth and inner cheek area. When the patches are wiped away, there's a red, raw sore found underneath. It is probable that candida can play a part in inflamed, painful tissues in the baby's lower gastrointestinal tract, since it is believed that thrush often travels through the baby's system before being excreted in his bowel movements. It sets up shop again in the diaper area, this time causing diaper rash.

Mother and baby may infect each other back and forth. One cause of sore nipples in breastfeeding mothers is candida. Her nipples will be itchy, sore, and cherry-red. The tips will appear scaly. One sure source of candida overrun in both baby and mother is the use of antibiotics such as ampicillin in the treatment of other infections. When the antibiotic cleans out the bacterial colonies residing in the mother or baby, candida runs rampant. Mothers need to be careful about good hand-washing with soap and water so that they don't transfer the candida from their vaginas or after bowel movements to the baby.

Some physicians have found that irritable babies who experience frequent colds and allergylike symptoms have responded very quickly to treatment aimed at candida infections in the lower intestinal tract. Nystatin, a prescription drug, is administered to the babies in carefully controlled oral doses. The drug is also available as a cream or an ointment for the mother's nipples or the baby's diaper area, and as a suppository for vaginal yeast infections. No serious side effects have been found.

The yeast-colic connection has not been proved conclusively, but doctors have been amazed at the quick results of treating babies for yeast infection. Dr. William Crook, a Jackson, Tennessee, physician specializing in the treatment of allergies, believes that toxins created by candida may be partly responsible for the immune system's overreaction to allergies. (Dr. Crook's latest book, *The Yeast Connection*, can be ordered from Professional Books, PO Box 3494, Jackson, TN 38301.)

The home remedy for external treatment of candida is yogurt, an enemy culture to the fungus, applied directly to the nipples or diaper area, or used in diluted form as a douche for the mother. Yogurt is not recommended for young babies to eat, since they aren't equipped to break down unaltered milk proteins, just as they can't handle milk straight from the carton yet.

What's Causing Your Baby's Diaper Rash

A single case of diaper rash may have multiple causes. Anytime that a diaper rash lasts for more than three days, the fungus, *Candida albicans*, probably has also set in to make matters worse. When the baby's skin is damp for more than a few hours, the protective surface of the skin breaks down so that bacteria and fungus can move in and thrive.

Appearance	Likely Cause	Treatment
Tiny red blisters on the baby's body between the belly button and thighs. Baby may also have a rash on kneecaps, cheeks, and neck.	Fabric softener sensitivity.	Don't use detergents that contain fabric softeners, and don't add them to the rinse water. Don't use Bounce or any other softeners or antistatic products.
Fiery red, bumpy rash, sometimes with scaly edges, that is nonpainful yet worsens during the day.	*Candida albicans*, a yeastlike fungus (see p. 44).	Prescription antiyeast agents: Nystatin, Haloprogin, Miconazole, and Clotrimazole. Avoid plastic outer pants and cornstarch-based powders.
Bright red burn encircling the baby's rectum.	Diarrhea burn, milk sugar (lactose) intolerance, or the introduction of a new food to the baby's diet.	Apply a thin layer of solid vegetable shortening as a temporary skin protection. Should be washed off with mild soap and reapplied after each bowel movement, since bacteria can multiply in it.

Symptom	Cause	Treatment
Skin in the diaper area is first red. Then bumps form, followed by white-headed pimples and weeping areas.	Prolonged wetness, especially if the baby sleeps in a wet diaper for ten to twelve hours. Also appears after a cold, sore throat, or ear infection.	Diaparene or Taloin ointments, plus soaking dirty diapers in water containing Diaparene Rinse Tablets. Their chemical, methylbenzethonium chloride, has been found to reduce diaper rash from 29 percent of treated babies to only 4 percent. A 1 percent hydrocortisone cream can be used in severe cases. Steroid creams are not recommended, since they have dangerous side effects, including suppression of the baby's pituitary-adrenal cortex, affecting his growth.
Bright red, painful scald around urine hole.	Acid urine due to too strong a urine or from acidic foods, such as orange juice.	Give the baby a tablespoon of water twice a day to dilute the urine's strength.
Red patches around the baby's waist, and encircling his leg and crotch area.	Allergy to plastic from disposable diapers at the places where it touches his skin.	Change to cloth diapers.

4
Colic and Your Baby's Digestive Organs

Your baby seems ravenous for his evening feed, but a few minutes after you settle down with him, he's arching his back and screaming in pain. It's the same thing that happened last night and the night before that. You can hear his belly gurgling and he doesn't calm down until you place him face down, on your arm while you massage his belly with your free hand or until he passes gas. There's no doubt in your mind that somehow your baby's pain and crying is connected to his digestive system.

One way to better understand baby digestion is to look at how babies mature. The development of body systems in the baby seems to happen for the most part in head-to-toe fashion. Head control comes first, then neck, arms, trunk, thighs, legs, and feet.

In the same way your baby's inner organs mature cephalocaudally—beginning at the head and moving downward. Internally, your baby's digestive system is one of the slowest to mature, especially the lower part.

Look at it this way: Your baby is born in an extremely immature state. Just like kangaroo babies who ride in their mothers' pockets or oppossum babies who latch on to their mothers' tails, the human baby is neurologically incomplete. It may take months before your baby's inner organs, especially his lower digestive tract, function smoothly.

All Babies Have Immature Digestive Systems

Until a decade or so ago, scientists assumed that a baby's digestive system was simply a miniature model of that of a child or an adult. Now research in the newly emerging fields of pediatric gastroenterology and pediatric physiology is totally revising our understanding of how babies process and absorb food.

Like a frog, the baby at birth swallows large amounts of air, expanding its stomach passages. Once the baby begins to take sustenance, the stomach will expand to four or five times its resting state. Its holding capacity will double between the first and second weeks of life and triple by the first month. Even then the baby's stomach's capacity to hold food is ten times less than that of an adult.

In the first months after birth, the baby's digestive tract contains few digestive enzymes, the body's agents for breaking down food substances for use by the body. Gastric glands in the stomach that secrete digestive acids are remarkably sparse—$\frac{1}{25}$ that of an adult. Yet research is now showing that digestive hormones may play a critical role in the contracting and releasing of muscles in the digestive system.

Muscle layers that surround the stomach and the intestinal tract are very thin and weak. The baby's intestines are substantially shorter than a child's or an adult's, and they are not at all the same in appearance. While an adult's intestines have ridges and tiny, hairlike filaments that help in the absorbing and processing of foods, the lining of a baby's intestine is far less well defined.

The graceful squeezings and releasings of peristalsis—
the muscle action of the digestive organs to move food
through the system—is faint or totally absent in newborns.
Instead, in uncoordinated fashion, the baby's stomach and
intestines respond to the stimulation of food by awkward
spasms that may propel their entire contents forcefully forward. Milk may spill backward from the stomach and up
out of the baby's mouth again because of the lack of muscular tone in his esophagus.

**"Positions that really seem to work to relieve gas are
slinging the baby over your shoulder (your shoulder
presses into his intestines), holding him over your arm
while he rests on your hip, and putting him tummy
down on your lap while pushing his knees up to his
chest. It also helps to put the baby in a front pack and
to wear him close to your chest."**

—Jean Marzollo,
9 Months, 1 Day, 1 Year

A baby enters the world with few bacteria, if any, inside his intestines, but within two days his body is inhabit-
ed by rapidly growing groups of them. Some come from the
mother's birth canal, others from the people around him,
the air, and furniture surfaces. Both the "good" bacteria—
those that help in the breaking down of milk for digestion—and the "bad" bacteria—those that can cause dangerous infections and diarrhea—rapidly multiply side by side
in the baby's gut.

Breast Milk Is Important

If a baby is shifted from breast milk to a cow's milk
formula, his intestinal-bacteria colonies rapidly change as
well. Disease-carrying bacteria quickly begin to proliferate,

and certain beneficial bacteria found only in the breast milk die away.

Mounting evidence suggests that human breast milk plays an active role in the maturation and protection of the baby's digestive system. Colostrum, the first substance the mother's breasts produce, and breast milk itself contain a substance that scientists have labeled "the mucosal growth factor." It has been found to speed up the growth of the protective mucous barrier of the intestines—a natural defense against disease infiltration in the body.

Antistaph factors that fight against this potentially fatal invader have also been isolated in breast milk. Lysozyme, a potent antibacterial agent, has also been found three hundred times more abundantly in the stools of breastfed babies than in those of formula-fed babies.

Breastfeeding is emerging as a critical element in fostering the maximum development of the baby's digestive organs and their protective role against disease.

Scientists like Dr. Allan Walker, a pediatric gastroenterologist at Harvard University Medical School, are postulating connections between adult diseases, like chronic liver disease, and the action of bacterial toxins infiltrating the intestines, which occurs in infants not given breast milk's valuable protection. Nonetheless, breastfed babies can still be colicky babies.

A Window in on Painful Baby Digestion

Thirty years ago a Swedish researcher, Sigvard Jorup, conducted revealing research on a syndrome he labeled "colonic hyperistalsis in neurolabile infants." Roughly translated, this means overactive muscular movements of the colon in highly nervous babies. (The colon is the last segment of the intestine before the baby's rectum and anus.)

In a detailed study of 111 frequently crying, colicky breastfed babies, Jorup observed the digestive differences between normal babies and those suffering from colic. He noted that while normal breastfed babies had only one, two, or three bowel movements daily, the highly nervous babies averaged five movements a day, almost every time they nursed.

The usual emptying time recorded for the colon of most babies had been found earlier to be several hours in duration, but for these colicky babies, observed on an X-ray screen, the violent contractions of their colons propelled the contents forward, sometimes in less than half a minute!

Watching digestion in the babies' lower intestines, Jorup found that the moment food substances rounded the S-shaped curve of their sigmoid colons, which empty into their rectums, the colons contracted violently. At that precise moment the babies would raise their legs toward their bellies—a typical behavior of colicky babies. In pain, the babies would abruptly stop nursing to cry. Once the colon contractions had ceased, the babies relaxed and resumed nursing, *unless* the colon muscles remained contracted. If so, the babies stayed fussy and irritable for the entire feeding session.

A more recent researcher into the mysteries of baby belly pain is Ronald Illingworth, England's Dr. Spock, mentioned earlier. After intensive study of fifty cases of "three months colic," sometimes called "evening colic," he described a typical sufferer this way in *The Normal Child:*

A few days after birth, though sometimes only on return from the maternity hospital, the baby, having been perfectly good during the day, has attacks of crying in the evening, mostly between 6 P.M. and 10 P.M. In an attack his face suddenly becomes red, he frowns, draws his legs up and emits piercing screams, unlike the cry of hunger or loneliness. They are likely to continue for two to twenty minutes even though he is picked up. The attack ends suddenly, but sobbing may continue for several minutes. He is just about to fall asleep, obviously tired out, when a further attack occurs. Attacks continue at regular intervals till about 10 P.M., when he lapses into sleep. . . . The attacks recur nightly, but almost always cease by the third month.

> *"Sometimes I found rolling up a cloth diaper and putting it under my baby's tummy helped. When he scooted up his knees, there was at least some support for him."*

From his search for the causes of colic, Dr. Illingworth has concluded that it arises from gas being trapped in the lower loops of the baby's bowel for unknown reasons. Colic for him, as for most researchers, still remains a mystery. "The role of immaturity of the nervous control of the alimentary tract leading to obstruction of gas in loops of the bowels is a likely, but unproven and little understood, cause," he states.

The doctor has found that the drug dicyclomine hydrochloride (see pp. 18, 69), when it is given half an hour before feeding, has been successful in alleviating colic pain for many babies. The drug is anticholinergic, that is, it affects the nerves that signal the baby's intestinal muscles to contract. "If it failed to give relief," Illingworth states, "I would think the diagnosis was wrong."

The Question of Intestinal Motility

Many pediatric gastroenterologists are theorizing, as Illingworth does, that some colicky babies, for whom there is no other explanation for pain, have motility problems. That is, their stomachs and intestines have difficulty in handling food and moving it downward through the body.

One research study on adults has shown that patients who complained of pain from intestinal gas and abdominal discomfort were found to have disordered intestinal motility rather than excessive gas. X rays demonstrated that their intestines allowed gas to move back up into their stomachs. It also took a longer time for gas to be processed in their systems than it did for persons with more normal digestion.

"We discovered several positions that seemed to ease our baby's discomfort somewhat and at least stopped his crying temporarily, although he would still continue to groan pathetically. These positions always involved some pressure on his abdominal area and some sort of jostling of his body. Usually we would carry him with his back to one of our stomachs, his legs doubled up, and firm pressure on his tummy and sort of jiggled him up and down. A second position that also worked was to place him facedown on our arms and to swing him back and forth. One adult hand was between his legs and supporting his tummy, while the other hand supported his upper trunk and head."

Although many cases of colic are outgrown after the first three months of babyhood, some scientists suggest that there may be a connecting link between some types of prolonged colic in infancy, later problems with chronic diarrhea in childhood, and irritable colons in adulthood. Inheritance may play a part. Jorup, the Swedish researcher mentioned earlier, found that almost half of the colicky babies in his study had one or both parents who suffered from chronic digestive disorders themselves, including irritable colons.

It appears that colic, for some babies, is a sign of an extremely sensitive digestive system that has heightened responsiveness to stimulation, perhaps because of a deficiency in the functioning of the nervous system, which oversees the operation of the digestive tract.

Nerves, Not Muscles

The search for an understanding of baby digestion has been spurred on by Hirschsprung's disease, a rare malfunctioning of the infant's colon thought to be due to failure of development of the network of nerves that oversee the smooth operation of the lower digestive tract.

The baby born with Hirschsprung's disease has a massively expanded colon that doesn't work to move wastes along. The symptoms of the disease are constipation, or only small amounts of stool; the swelling of the lower abdomen; and, sometimes, loss of appetite and breathing problems.

If the baby's colon fails to go into action even after medical practices such as drugs and stimulation have been used, then surgery may be necessary to remove the nonfunctioning part of the bowel, reattaching the remaining colon to the rectum.

Recent animal studies are helping to shed light on how intestinal motility works or, in the case of Hirschsprung's disease, why it doesn't.

Eizo Okamoto and his associates at Osaka University in Japan have selectively killed certain nerve fibers that direct movement of the lower intestines of dogs to observe what relationship exists between nerves and intestinal muscle operation.

The researchers found that the *nerves*, not the muscles

of the intestines, cause the abnormal functioning of the intestines. When the myenteric plexus—the executive nerve center, which transmits orders for motion to the intestines—ceases to function, intestinal muscles contract tightly so that the intestines become abnormally narrow or, in some cases, as in Hirschsprung's disease, a section of bowel becomes abnormally expanded. Normal segments of intestine above the poorly functioning, contracted parts showed extremely forceful movements, spewing food matter both backward and forward in the intestines.

The implication of this research for baby colic is that the problems and pains of poor intestinal motility may not be caused so much by the structure of the baby's intestines themselves as by the functioning of the nervous system that directs the intestines.

The unanswered questions still remain as to why some babies have nerve centers that direct digestion precisely, while for others, nerve messages and subsequent muscular reactions appear to be garbled, or even missing entirely.

Structural Abnormalities

Motility problems may be one central cause of baby pain attacks. Another kind of baby digestive pain comes from structural abnormalities that are usually present in the baby at birth, or appear in the months that follow. The medical words for these conditions are *stenosis, volvulus, intussusception,* and *hernia.*

Sometimes a muscle ring at the base of the baby's stomach or in his intestines makes the passage of food matter painful. A partial or complete obstruction may happen when a coil of intestine folds over on itself or loops up inside itself so that its inner passageway is affected.

Typically a logjam is caused, with food matter and gas piling up at the narrow opening. The gurgling of gas may be heard when it squeezes through the small dammed-up spot, and belly rumblings can be watched, pouching out and moving across the abdomen like rolling golf balls.

The baby's pain is cramplike as strong contractions of surrounding muscles try to force food through the unyielding constriction. An adult with a similar condition may describe the pain as traveling across his stomach, climaxing at the point where the food matter reaches the tight ring where the gurgling can be heard.

Obstructions in the baby's digestive system can be "partial," that is, small but passable, or "complete," in which no food is able to pass. Obviously complete obstructions are more dangerous because of the internal pressure, and immediate surgery may be needed to save the baby's life. When experiencing an obstruction, the baby may scream with pain, followed by being quiet, but with a worried look on his face and a marked paleness. The pain comes and goes, sometimes in increasingly more urgent attacks. A doctor should be contacted immediately, especially if the baby is vomiting greenish bile or is showing other serious signs of a problem.

Hernias happen when a baby's stomach, intestines, or other organs don't lie correctly in the walls that normally would contain them, perhaps because the walls of tissue have not been completely formed due to a birth defect. Usually a hernia must be surgically corrected.

These Symptoms Are Possibly Serious:

- Presence of blood in your baby's bowel movements
- Blood or green-tinged bile in the baby's vomit
- Loss of appetite
- Awakening over and over in the night with screaming pain unrelated to feeding
- Conditions that worsen in times: increased vomiting, diarrhea, or constipation

- A change from active interest in the world when awake to sluggishness and indifference
- Severe, long-lasting distention (ballooning out) of the baby's belly

Symptoms NOT to Worry About:

- Excessive passing of gas
- Mild constipation with changes in formula or diet
- Frequent bowel movements in breastfed babies (see p. 68)
- Mild distention (swelling) of the baby's abdomen after meals.

Rectal Problems

Some babies, it appears, have smaller than usual anuses. The result of the too-tight ring of muscles around the baby's rectum is painful, expulsive bowel movements, with the baby struggling in pain to push out fecal matter. The medical term for this condition is "mild anal stenosis."

Some parents have found that using a baby-size glycerin suppository (at the advice of their doctor) eased their babies' discomfort when movements were painful or gas was trapped inside.

Some pediatricians recommend gently dilating the baby's anus hole by inserting a well-lubricated pinky finger (with nail clipped) into the baby's rectum. It may be less damaging to cover your finger with the corner of a sandwich bag, seam side inward, which is lubricated with K-Y Jelly or another lubricant, or to use a rubber cover or a lubricated condom for the job. The result seems to be not only the gentle expansion of the hole, but also the momentary stimulation of the baby's poorly operating colon.

Constipation may also be a cause of bowel-movement discomfort for some bottlefed babies. Some fussy babies who have constipation problems may have *fissure in ano*—a small ulcerated sore on the margin of the anus that makes bowel movements painful. You may see flecks of blood from the ulcer on the baby's bowel movements.

To inspect your baby for an anal fissure, lie him on his back, holding both ankles in one hand, with one finger in between so that they don't knock together. With the other hand, gently spread your baby's buttocks to see if there is a tiny open sore anywhere around the anal ring.

Treatment for anal fissures is as follows:

- Give the baby warm sitz baths, to which a few tablespoons of table salt have been added, three times a day.
- Afterward, gently pat the area dry or use a blow-dryer on high speed, warm setting (not hot), until well dried.
- Apply a nonirritating cream such as a zinc oxide ointment to the sore spot.
- Contact your doctor about altering your baby's formula so that he no longer is constipated, since hard stools are usually the cause of the problem. (Sometimes food allergies are the cause after the baby goes on to solids.)

Maternal Drugs and Baby Digestion— A Possible Link?

Could drugs taken by a mother during pregnancy affect the development and functioning of her baby's digestive tract? There are many drugs that are known to be teratogenic—that is, they cause obvious birth defects in babies—but the more subtle effects of drugs on a baby's body operations are still to be researched. Since the baby's digestive system is one of the last organ systems in the body to mature, it may be more sensitive, more vulnerable, to drug effects in the last months of pregnancy and during labor. This system may also be the most harmed by the lack of oxygen during the baby's birth, but until more is known, these connections are purely speculative.

5
Allergies, Drugs, and Breastfeeding

Eighty years ago an observant physician published a study of fussy breastfed babies who had unusual restlessness, sleeplessness, indigestion, acid stools, gassy distention of the belly, and crying attacks. He surmised that the symptoms of these babies had to have come from within the bodies of the babies themselves, since he observed that a woman breastfeeding two babies at the same time might have one baby who showed the symptoms and another who was perfectly normal.

In 1918 another physician reported the case of a breastfeeding mother who was given a large box of chocolates. The mother helped herself to them, and a few days later her baby developed eczema, a red, itchy, oozing skin condition that is now thought to be allergy related. The mother put the box of chocolates away, and the baby's eczema disappeared. Later she ate more chocolates, and the baby's eczema reappeared.

In the 1920s doctors began to report that eczema in totally breastfed babies could sometimes be cured by taking certain foods out of the mother's diet, such as milk, eggs, or codfish. Now it has been clearly demonstrated that a breastfeeding mother's diet may affect her baby, especially if he is sensitive to certain allergens.

Researchers have discovered that a few hours after a mother eats chocolate, her breast milk contains traceable amounts of theobromine, a substance found in chocolate that stimulates the heart, dilates arteries, and causes the muscles of the internal organs to relax.

Something You've Eaten Can Affect Your Baby

Swedish scientists Irene Jakobsson and Tor Lindberg have tested the relationship between sudden stomach pains and severe crying in totally breastfed babies and their mothers' intake of cow's milk and its products. Of the nineteen colicky babies in the study, thirteen promptly became much better when the mothers took cow's milk out of their diets. The babies' crying and pain quickly reappeared in twelve of the babies when cow's milk was introduced once again into the mothers' diets.

> *"My son was totally breastfed and also very colicky. The doctor recommended that I eliminate milk and other dairy products from my diet. The baby's colic disappeared. I discovered that I could drink about a cup of milk each day without affecting the baby."*

There are two ways that a baby's allergic reactions to something the mother has eaten are thought to be triggered. Extremely tiny particles of cow's milk protein or other food elements—smaller than can be detected by a microscope—are thought to travel to the baby directly through the mother's milk. In addition, a mother's antibodies—which fight against disease and toxins—are constantly being rushed by her body directly into her milk glands to offer protection to her baby. The mother's antibodies may cause an allergic reaction in her baby against food substances that put her body at war.

When an allergic reaction takes place in the mother's or the baby's body, it appears that the body has falsely defined a substance as being harmful when, in fact, it may be benign. Nonetheless, the body acts as though something toxic has entered it, and its alarm systems go off to conquer the seemingly harmful intruders.

Often a breastfed baby showing coliclike allergic symptoms has a father or a mother or another family member who has allergies that are genetically based. Some parents have hidden allergies. A mother may hate to drink milk, unaware that she is avoiding milk because of the diarrhea, runny nose, or other symptoms that set in soon after drinking it. In the study of colicky breastfed babies by Jakobsson and Lindberg, mentioned earlier, eleven of the eighteen mothers had a history of allergies themselves.

> *"My breastfed baby had colic, and I found that sometimes things I ate consistently caused gas pain at a certain time of day, depending on when I ate it. Eggs were one of the* worst. *I gave them up, and it made a big difference. I had to even avoid things that had eggs in them. It was like getting a different baby, but it took about two days to see the change, and it can take longer."*

Some scientists even suspect that a baby may become allergic to specific food proteins while still in the womb. Japanese researchers have recently discovered the evidence of hen's egg antigens—microscopic fighters against egg proteins—in the fluid of infants' amniotic sacs, in the blood of their umbilical cords, and in the dark, sticky meconium stools of the newborn.

The severity of a mother's allergic reaction to foods or toxins varies from one person to another, and how permeable her breasts are to allergic substances—how well they succeed in filtering out food proteins and toxins such as drugs—seems to vary among individuals.

Obviously, if a baby is showing allergic responses to the microparticles of cow's milk proteins in his mother's milk, then introducing cow's milk directly into his system at an early age may only make matters worse. Though rare, some babies have had a severe reaction, called anaphylactic shock, triggered by a sudden, profound allergic reaction to the introduction of cow's milk into the diet.

Conduct Your Own Test for Food Allergies

One way to find out whether your baby is reacting to something in your diet is to stop eating each suspected food, one item at a time, to see if your baby responds by becoming less fussy within the week. Then it is important to reintroduce the food substance into your diet in quantity to see if the baby's irritability returns. That way you will know for sure what the problem really is.

Some mothers recommend removing *all* of the offending substances at once for ten days, followed by a gradual reintroduction of the possible culprits one at a time in order to see what happens to the baby's behavior. Ten days is more than enough time for your milk to be cleared of a bothersome substance. If allergies are the problem, the baby should calm down, cry less, and sleep better.

A Temporary Milk-Free Diet

Since cow's milk is thought to be one of the central causes of allergic responses in solely breastfed babies, you may want to conduct a milk-free test of your own to see if, in fact, the milk you are ingesting is causing your baby to react.

TYPE OF FOOD	FOODS YOU CAN EAT	FOODS TO AVOID FOR THE TEST
Milk	None	Milk: fresh, dried, condensed, evaporated; yogurt, buttermilk
Meats, fish, Poultry	Beef, lamb, veal, chicken, turkey, liver, pork, ham, fish, tuna, organ meats	Creamed or breaded meats or fish, frankfurters, processed meats
Eggs	Prepared any way except with milk	
Cheese	Limit to 2 oz. per day of blue, Camembert, Cheddar, colby, cream, Gouda, Swiss, Limburger, Parmesan, American	Cottage
Breads and Cereals	Any whole-grain or enriched milk-free bread and rolls, Italian and French bread, soda crackers, cooked cereals, some prepared cereals (check labels)	Bread or rolls with milk added, quick breads, prepared mixes containing milk, French toast, zwieback, instant cereals containing milk, lactose
Soups	Broth, meat, vegetable	Cream
Potatoes and Substitutes	White and sweet potatoes, noodles and macaroni, spaghetti and rice	Cream sauces or milk in preparation, instant potatoes
Vegetables	Any fresh, frozen, or canned except those to which milk or milk sugar is added	Cream sauces or milk in preparation

TYPE OF FOOD	FOODS YOU CAN EAT	FOODS TO AVOID FOR THE TEST
Fruits	All kinds except canned and frozen to which milk or milk sugar is added	
Desserts	Gelatin pies, cakes and cookies made without butter or milk, and fruit ices made without milk	Ice cream, sherbet, custard, any dessert made with milk, commercial sweet rolls, prepared mixes containing milk or lactose, whipped cream
Fats	Margarine, lard, peanut butter, vegetable oils, mayonnaise, butter, cream, whipped cream toppings	Milk-based salad dressings, butter, or margarine/ butter combinations
Beverages	Fruit juices	Milk, milk shakes, ice-cream sodas, hot cocoa, coffee or tea with cream
Sweets	Sugar, pure jellies and jams, honey, syrup, sugar candies	Candies containing milk (chocolate, creams, caramels)
Miscellaneous	Salt, spices, vinegar, cocoa powder, olives, pickles, nuts, popcorn, mustard, catsup, chili sauce	Cream or cheese sauces, milk gravies, cocoa mixes

Reprinted with permission from *The Whole Pediatrician Catalog,* McMillan, Stockman and Oski, W. B. Saunders Co., copyright © 1982.

Additional Foods That May Cause Reactions in a Breastfed Baby

Many mothers have found that their babies respond to specific things that they have eaten by becoming colicky and fussy. After having tried the milk-free diet, you may want to examine your eating habits to see if there are other food substances causing a reaction in your baby.

Often the key to a good breastfeeding diet is moderation and frequent changes in protein sources such as meats, nuts, lentils, and cheese, because overeating in one food area makes the chances of reactivity in your baby much more probable.

- Eggs
- Wheat (especially whole wheat)
- Fish (especially shellfish)
- Chicken
- Citrus fruits or juices (strawberries)
- Oats
- Corn
- Chocolate (see pp. 61–62)
- Foods containing caffeine (see pp. 74, 76–77)
- Nuts (especially peanuts)
- Gas-producing vegetables such as cabbage, broccoli, lettuce, onions, and green peppers.

Is My Baby's Diarrhea an Allergic Reaction?

Diarrhea is one symptom of an allergic reaction going on in the baby's body. It can also be a red flag for the presence of an infection. Usually the symptoms of allergy come in clusters. Some other common signals are extreme fussiness and irritability, digestive upsets such as frequent vomiting, stuffy nose, rattly breathing or wheezing, and skin reactions such as eczema. Diaper rash is usually caused by the laundering techniques you use on diapers, or a reaction to the plastic liners on disposable diapers, as mentioned earlier. Sometimes, though, a bright red diaper rash around the baby's anus can be allergy related.

> *"Sometimes I found that eating too much fruit, cabbage, or beans, and drinking too many juices could cause an attack with my baby. I love fruit and did not realize that it would cause colic in a breastfed baby."*

It's not unusual for first-time mothers to think that their breastfed babies have diarrhea when they really don't. The stools of a breastfed baby are usually loose and runny-looking and can be yellow, yellow-green, or brownish in color, and it's perfectly normal for a breastfed baby to have as many as six to eight bowel movements in a day. The aroma of the stools is quite mild and inoffensive.

If your baby has diarrhea, on the other hand, he may have as many as twelve to sixteen stools a day that smell bad and contain mucus or even tiny flecks of blood. The time to worry about your breastfed baby's stools is when they increase suddenly and become almost nonstop, if they smell foul, and if he acts sick or has a fever. *Any baby under two months of age who has a fever should be seen by a doctor.*

Dehydration

The danger of diarrhea in babies is dehydration—the severe loss of body fluids. Signs to watch for:

· Your baby will go for many hours without urinating.
· His mouth may seem dry instead of being moist.

These signs combined with fast, heavy breathing mean you should seek medical care immediately.

Medically, diarrhea is not a sign to discontinue breast-feeding in favor of other fluids. Most medical authorities are convinced that breast milk is by far the most balanced, readily absorbable liquid your baby can have during illness. Fortunately, severe, life-threatening diarrhea is very rare in totally breastfed babies.

Drug Effects Are Still Not Completely Known

There are multiple complex problems in determining how much of a drug is passed on to a baby through his mother's milk. Surprisingly, few research studies have been designed to isolate all of the factors involved in deciding whether or not a drug is safe for a breastfeeding mother. Certain drugs are clearly known to be unsafe or to cause reactions in nursing babies, but most drugs fall into a "gray area," with various research studies finding different amounts of the drug in the mothers' milk, which have different effects on the babies.

Two Kinds of Milk

Mothers secrete two different kinds of milk at each feed—foremilk and hindmilk. If a researcher measures drug amounts only in the foremilk, the drugs that characteristically bind themselves to the fatty, creamy part of hindmilk may be missed.

Milk's Different Components

Researchers have studied the solid parts of the milk that have been sifted out from the liquid components. One study recently found that vitamin D was being carried in the water part of the breast milk. This had been missed by all earlier studies.

Drug Dosage Makes a Difference

How much of a drug is in the mother's milk at feeding times may depend upon how strong a dose she has taken, how many minutes or hours before the feeding she took the drug, and how well her milk filtration process works. It appears that some mothers filter out drugs better than others for unknown reasons, although heredity and diet are thought to play a part.

Different Baby Reactions

No standards have been set as to what constitutes an adverse reaction in a baby. It is known that babies have different reactions to drugs than do children or adults. For example, some drugs may not be excreted from a baby's body for days or even months due to the baby's poorer detoxification abilities. Some babies may be sensitive to a drug while others may not show any reaction at all.

Delayed Effects

Certain drugs, such as hormones or steriods, may have effects that aren't evident until many years later. For example, DES—diethylstilbestrol—which was given to mothers in the 1950s to prevent miscarriages and which was passed to the fetus through the placenta, has been shown to cause the masculinizing of girl babies and the feminizing of boy babies and to predispose female babies to the possibility of cancer of the vagina or cervix decades later. The administration of penicillin to a breastfeeding mother has been linked, in some cases, to the sensitization of her baby to that drug so that later, as a child or an adult, he may have severe allergic reactions to it.

Drugs May Alter the Mother's Breastfeeding Ability

Some drugs, although they may have no noticeable effect on the baby, may affect the breastfeeding act. Certain drugs may alter the protein composition of the milk, interfere in the mother's message system that signals the milk letdown, reduce the quantity of milk produced, or dull her sensitivity to her baby's signals so that she becomes less responsive to him.

Your Milk Supply May Be Affected by a Drug You're Taking

The following drugs listed by chemical names and brand names may impair milk formation and make nursing more difficult when taken in quantity. In some cases these drugs directly affect the body's production of prolactin, a critical hormone in breast milk production and mothering behavior.

"It is widely recognized that nearly all maternally administered drugs and environmental chemicals find their way to the breast-feeding infant."

—"Drugs in Lactating Women,"
Dr. Neil K. Kochenour and
Dr. Maurice G. Emery,
Obstetrics and Gynecology Annual,
1981, 10, p. 107

Stomach Relaxers
Atropine (Belladonna)
    Contac, Donnagel, Donnatel
Dicyclomine
    Bentyl, Nospaz, triacetin
Propantheline
    Norpanth, Pro-Banthine, Ropanth
Tridihexethyl
    Pathilon, Milpath, Pathibamate

Lactation Inhibitors (dry-up pills)
Bromocriptine mesylate
Diethylstilbestrol
Parlodel

Migraine Headache Pills
Ergotamine
    Ergomar, Ergostat, Gynergen, Bellergal, Cafergot

Treatments for Parkinson's Disease
Levodopa
    Bendopa, Dopar, Larodopa, Sinemet

Allergy Medications
Inhiston, Robitussin-AC, Triaminic, Triaminicin, Triaminicol,
    Tussagesic
Tripelennamine
    Pyribenzamine, Ro-Hist
Diphenhydramine
    Benadryl, Ambodryl, Ambenyl, Benylin

"If for the sake of her baby's welfare a mother can put up with a few aches and pains without resorting to drugs, so much the better. It's surprising how many recoveries are due simply to what has been labeled the 'tincture of time.' "

—"Breastfeeding and Drugs in
Human Milk,"
Gregory and Mary White,
Veterinary and Human Toxicology,
Supp. #1, 22, 1980

(Note: *Not* listed are drugs that may have other side effects on your body or the baby, or those that involve radioactive testing. Good sources for further information on drugs and breast milk are: White and White's "Breastfeeding and Drugs in Human Milk," a reprint from *Veterinary and Human Toxicology* (supplement 1, vol. 20, 1980), available for $5.00 from La Leche League, International, 9616 Minneapolis, Franklin Park, IL 60131, and an article by T. O'Brien, "Excretion of Drugs in Human Milk," in the *American Journal of Hospital Pharmacy* (vol. 31, pp. 844–54, 1974), which you may acquire as a photocopy by requesting it on interlibrary loan from your local library.

Common Drugs in Breast Milk That Cause Diarrhea or Irritability

Common drugs are transmitted through the mother's milk and can affect the baby, in some cases giving him diarrhea and in other cases causing irritability and night crying. Take a look at everything you're putting into your mouth or spraying into your nose that might spark a drug reaction in your baby.

Alcohol

It comes through the mother's milk in concentrations similar to that in her blood. In some instances nursing babies show signs of intoxication and high blood alcohol levels when their mothers have drunk heavily. May also affect mother's milk letdown.

Ampicillin

An antibiotic. May cause diarrhea in the baby. Drugs in

73

the penicillin family are thought to sensitize the baby to the drug, possibly causing later allergic reactions. (Ask your doctor.)

Aspirin	Sufficiently high doses may affect the mother's prostaglandin secretion and her platelet formation, and may cause hemorrhaging in the baby.
Caffeine	Excessive caffeine has been associated with baby irritability. (See caffeine chart on p. 76.)
Chocolate	Contains a caffeinelike drug, theobromine, which used medically as a stimulant and diuretic can cause allergic reactions in the baby.
Cold Tablets, Nose Drops, and Cough Medicines	Those containing the chemical phenylpropanolamine are known to cause irritable night crying in breastfed babies: Allerest, Contac, 4-Way Nasal Spray, Sine-Off, Sinutab, Triaminic, Triaminicol, Tussagesic, and other over-the-counter medications.
Cortisone Creams	Avoid using nipple preparations that contain drugs that could be ingested by the baby.

Cyclamates	Artificial sweeteners can cause vomiting and diarrhea in the baby when taken in large quantities.
Environmental Chemicals	Chemicals inhaled or touched by the baby can sometimes cause irritability or body reactions: fabric softeners (especially Bounce), cigarette smoke, hair spray, plastic (especially disposable diaper liners), insect sprays, laundry detergents, and dishwasher steam containing a detergent.
Herbal Teas	Those containing senna can cause diarrhea. Chamomile, in the ragweed family, may cause a reaction in mothers predisposed to hay fever.
Laxatives	May cause diarrhea in the baby, especially those containing phenolphthalein, cascara, or aloe.
Nicotine	Nicotine is present in the breast milk of smoking mothers and can be detected in the milk of mothers who smoke as few as one to four cigarettes a day. Mothers who smoke more than one pack of cigarettes a day have been found to have a decreased milk supply.

Vitamin Pills

Fluoride supplements in the mother's vitamin pills can cause rashes, gastrointestinal upsets, and allergic reactions in the baby. Brewer's yeast, taken by some mothers as a source of B-complex vitamins, may cause gastric distress in their babies. On the other hand, a lack of vitamin B_1 (thiamine) in the mother's diet may cause her to excrete a toxic by-product, methylglyoxal, into her milk.

Sources of Caffeine*

Beverages (by the cup or 12-oz can)

Coffee	146 mg
Tea	50
Cocoa	10
Diet Mr. Pibb	52
Mountain Dew	52
Mello Yello	51
Tab	44
Shasta cola	42
Dr Pepper	38
Diet Dr Pepper	37
Pepsi Cola	37
Royal Crown Cola	36
Diet Rite Cola	34
Diet Pepsi	34
Coke	34
Mr. Pibb	34

Nonprescription Drugs (standard doses)

Stimulants
Caffedrine capsules	200
No-Doz tablets	200
Vivarin tablets	200

Pain Relievers
Anacin	64
Excedrin	130
Midol	65

Diuretics
Aqua-Ban	200
Permathene H_2Off	200
Pre-Mens Forte	100

Cold Remedies
Coryban-D	30
Dristan	32
Triaminicin	30

Weight-Control Pills
Dexatrim	200
Dietac	200
Prolamine	280

*Copyright © 1981 by Consumers Union of United States, Inc., Mount Vernon, NY 10550. Reprinted by permission from *Consumer Reports,* October 1981.

Birth Control Pills

Birth control pills are *not considered safe for breastfeeding mothers.* Some of the effects of the pill on breastfeeding are:

· Diminished milk supply
· Significant reduction of milk proteins by as much as 16 percent

- Possible feminization of male babies
- Marked decrease of all water-soluble vitamins in the milk, such as B_6, B_{12}, riboflavin, and C.

The long-range effects of birth control pills are unknown, but caution is advised.

Marijuana

Marijuana is fat-soluble and is thought to be present in potent quantities in human breast milk. In laboratory animals it has been found in sufficient quantities in the mother's milk to bring about temporary, and possibly permanent, structural changes in infant brain cells. It impairs the formation of DNA and RNA and proteins essential for normal growth and development.

Marijuana may impair a mother's judgment and her ability to care for and breastfeed her baby by significantly lowering her prolactin—"mothering hormone"—levels.

PART II

Meeting Your Baby's Basic Needs

6
How Fussy Is "Fussy"?

Only a decade ago most doctors and parents thought that new babies were all alike—squirming, unintelligent bundles of life, far from individuals. Now researchers are substantiating what our grandmothers knew from experience: that there are wide differences among babies even in the first days after birth. While some babies are cuddly, alert, responsive, and willing to be comforted—all characteristics that foster pleasant parent-baby relationships—others are fussy, irritable, and unable to soothe themselves or be soothed by others—the kinds of babies that may make parenting seem less rewarding.

The most widely used test for baby differences was developed by Dr. T. Berry Brazelton and his associates at Harvard Medical School. This test, given by trained examiners, is called the Brazelton Neonatal Behavioral Assessment Scale. Remarkably, it can be used on babies as young as one day old.

Here are some of the baby characteristics that are noted on the Brazelton scale:

Alertness	How well a baby reacts to the sound of a bell or rattle and how he pursues it with his eyes.
Habitation	How quickly the baby gets used to repeated sounds, especially when he's trying to sleep.
Excitability	How irritable a baby is, how quickly his skin changes color (a sign of excitement), and how smoothly he moves from sleep to alertness, or from sleep to crying.
Consolability	How much intervention a baby needs in order to stop crying, and how well he can soothe himself.
Body Organization	The baby's overall body tone is assessed, such as how well he can hold his head up when he's pulled up into a sitting position, how well he can remove a cloth resting on his face, or how active and cuddly he is.

"If we can tell a mother what her baby's cry means and how to handle it, we may be able to set the stage for better mother–infant relationships."

> **—Dr. Barry Lester,**
> **Assistant Professor of Pediatrics,**
> **Harvard University,**
> **Reported in *Science Digest*,**
> **February 1982**

Tests such as these will soon be used to help parents, even a few days after their babies' birth, to be more sensitive to the unique needs of their newborns. For example, one baby tested was found to be very tense and wiry. His arms and legs moved constantly when he was being given the assessment. He would rapidly go from sleeping to crying back to sleeping again, with very little time in between. To quieten him, the examiner found she had to swaddle the baby, give him a pacifier, and rock him all at once. When handled this way, the baby immediately became alert and responded to the world outside of himself. She found that his own self-soothing capabilities were very limited. He was overreactive—"hyper"—and quick to cry. The examiner helped the baby's mother to plan for the type of baby he was, showing her the effective calming and soothing techniques to use on him.

A Personality Profile for Your Baby

Here's a simple multiple-choice quiz you can use to determine some personality characteristics of your baby. If your baby is easygoing, you'll probably not need a profile to tell you so, but if your baby is more difficult than usual, it's sometimes helpful to get an objective look at what he's like. To take the test simply put a check next to the behavior that is most like your baby's.

(1) When your baby gets hungry, he:
_____ (a) Sucks on his thumb, fist, or fingers without much complaining.
___✗___ (b) Cries on and off until you get to him.
_____ (c) Goes quickly from crying into inconsolable screaming before you can get to him.
_____ (d) Wakes up abruptly, screaming loudly to be fed.

(2) When you take your baby to the grocery store, he:
_____ (a) Seems to enjoy looking at the shelves and people.
___✗___ (b) Starts out enjoying it but gets cranky if you stay too long.

_____ (c) Cries most of the time.

_____ (d) Can't tolerate the grocery store at all. He goes crazy every time, so now you shop without him.

(3) Your baby's fussy pattern could be described as:

_____ (a) He seldom fusses, and then only briefly.

_____ (b) He fusses for about thirty minutes a day.

_____ (c) He fusses for one to two hours a day.

_____ (d) He fusses almost constantly when he's not asleep.

(4) It's 6:30 P.M. and you're fixing dinner. Your baby is:

_____ (a) Sitting calmly in his infant seat or lying in a nearby playpen, watching you or asleep.

_____ (b) Complaining that you ought to pay more attention to him, but he quiets down when you speak to him.

_____ (c) Crying, and will only be quiet if you carry him.

_____ (d) Screaming inconsolably so that fixing dinner is impossible.

(5) Between midnight and 5:00 A.M. your baby is:

_____ (a) Sleeping.

_____ (b) Awake once or twice.

_____ (c) Awake three or four times.

_____ (d) Awake every thirty minutes to an hour.

(6) The best way, you've found, to stop your baby from crying when he's not hungry is to:

_____ (a) Lift him to your shoulder.

_____ (b) Walk with him or rock him for a few minutes while talking or singing to him.

_____ (c) Actively move with him, jiggling him, raising him up and down, or the *opposite*, taking movement and stimulation away and swaddling him.

_____ (d) None of the above. Nothing soothes him for more than a few minutes at a time.

(7) When and where will your baby sleep?

_____ (a) He'll sleep anywhere when he gets tired.

_____ (b) He'll only sleep in his crib, car seat, or other familiar place.

_____ (c) He'll only go to sleep in your arms after feeding, then you can gently put him down.

_____ (d) He won't sleep unless you're holding him or your body is next to his.

(8) How jumpy is your baby? When he hears a sudden noise or the lights are turned on unexpectedly, he:

_____ (a) Frowns and tries to orient to it.

_____ (b) Jumps slightly, but otherwise it doesn't bother him.

_____ (c) Throws his arms back, or really jerks his body, and may cry.

_____ (d) Reacts with a strong startle and screaming, even to laughter or to lights.

(9) How easy is it for you to make your baby happy?

_____ (a) He's not hard at all to please—he's usually contented.

_____ (b) Usually he's easy to please, but sometimes he has fussy spells.

_____ (c) He's hard to make happy about half the time.

_____ (d) He's very hard to make happy and seems unhappy most of the time.

(10) How easily does he keep milk down?

_____ (a) He spits up a small amount of milk once in a while, especially when he's being burped.

_____ (b) He spits up at every feeding.

_____ (c) He vomits up milk, a real gusher, every day or so.

_____ (d) He vomits up a lot of milk at least once or more a day.

(11) If you gave your baby a cuddliness rating, you'd say
he was:

___ꞁ___ (a) Very cuddly, like a rag doll.

_____ (b) Moderately cuddly, like a firm cushion.

_____ (c) Sometimes (1) and sometimes (2), and sometimes doesn't want to be held.

_____ (d) Uncuddly. He cries to be put down.

(12) How would you describe your baby's reactions to life?

_____ (a) Calm and peaceful.

___ꞁ___ (b) Usually easygoing but sometimes worried.

_____ (c) Usually uptight but able to be soothed.

_____ (d) Tense and high-strung.

To find out your baby's score add up the numbers this
way: For every (a) response, count one point, for every (b),
two points, for every (c), three points, and for every (d),
four points.

Here's how to interpret your baby's score:
12–21 points—very easy and adaptable
22–30 points—moderately easy and adaptable
31–39 points—challenging, requires responsive attention
40–48 points—very challenging, requires a lot of patience
and a great deal of responsive attention.

*"Are you judging your baby by
unreasonable standards? Perfect babies,
content to play alone, regular three- to
four-hour feeding schedule—these babies
exist only on TV."*

Of course, the purpose of a test like this is not to make
you think that somehow you or your baby have failed.
What it can do is help you to see where your baby stands in

relation to the characteristics of everyday baby behavior. The most easy-to-recognize baby personality characteristics are the ability to be soothed, contentment, and closeness tolerance. Take a look at these dimensions and how you as parents can learn to adapt to them.

Your Baby's Self-Soothing Ability

Baby Susanna could be seen through the nursery window just a few hours after birth, contentedly sucking on her fingers and looking around as though she were absorbed in the new world before her. Susanna is what doctors would call a strong self-soother. Most babies soothe themselves with their fingers or thumbs. Others calm down quickly when they are picked up and cradled on a parent's shoulder. A baby's capacity to tone himself down when excitement gets too high seems to be built-in and measurable even in the earliest days after birth.

"Babies who took a long time to calm during the first three months had mothers who spent more time engaging them in social interaction during that time period. The mothers appeared to work hard with their initially difficult-to-console babies, and by three months the babies frequently smiled at and participated in eye contact with their mothers. . . . It seems likely that the mothers' responsiveness and involvement stimulated the infants' subsequent sociability."

—Margaret Fish and Susan Crockenberg "Correlates and Antecedents of Nine-Month Infant Behavior and Mother–Infant Interaction," In *Infant Behavior and Development*, 1981, 4, p. 79

A self-soothing baby can sometimes hold himself back from crying while waiting to be fed. If something upsetting happens, he is able to bring himself back under control again quickly. He can often be put into his crib for a nap without more than a few moments of protest. He settles down easily into sleep with the help of finger- or thumb-sucking, a specially prepared lambskin or a blanket, or by simply focusing on a familiar pattern or object in his crib.

A hard-to-soothe baby doesn't possess such control over how the world affects him. Typically he has trouble stopping himself from crying. Once started, his crying quickly escalates until he "goes over the hill," as parents say. It seems like this kind of baby can't find the switch to turn his motor off once he gets started. During parent-baby play he may surprisingly start crying, when only moments earlier he was cooing and smiling.

Often, when the poor self-soother gets tired, he doesn't get sleepy, he gets more and more hyperactive. Even as a toddler or a young child, the one who can't modulate himself well seldom realizes when he is tired. The letting-the-baby-cry-it-out approach to sleep training may work rather quickly and painlessly for the self-soothing baby, but it is a drastic mistake to use this approach on a baby who can't control his crying. Typically the poor soother will scream for hours, each moment more and more desperately until he vomits, pops a vein in his temple, or crumples, exhausted, into the corner of the crib.

The poor self-soother needs you to modulate his activities for him. He's dependent on you to turn the world off, to wrap him up, and to close down stimulation by your soothing techniques so that he can let go and fall asleep. These babies as they mature seem to need regularity, almost to the point of train-station scheduling, to make eating, sleeping, and other day-to-day life events manageable. Vacations are a catastrophe—the baby doesn't sleep in the car like he's supposed to, and sleeping patterns become totally erratic after a weekend trip to Grandma's.

Later on you'll find yourself developing a second sense about when your tot is going to overextend himself, and you'll know to take control before he collapses in pitiful wails from fatigue, hunger, or too much excitement.

The Contentment Dimension

Robbye is what most mothers and grandmothers would call a "good" baby. What they're talking about is the contented disposition in a baby that makes him a pleasure to be with. He is calm, good-natured, and willing to wait for his mother to go to him. He could charm the socks off even the most reserved of fathers. No wonder his mother and father are planning to have at least three more children!

Andrew is just the opposite of Robbye. He doesn't seem to be uncomfortable or in acute pain, but he's not happy either. He complains easily at the supermarket, during walks in the shopping center, or at dinnertime. Sometimes a pacifier helps, but most of the time he spits it right back out again. His grandmother calls him "sobersides" because of the worried, discontented expression that he often has on his face. It seems as though Andrew just doesn't like being in the world much. He'll tolerate being here, but only for brief stints.

Just How Fussy Is "Fussy"?

Different mothers have varying ideas. Some mothers think that if a baby fusses for thirty minutes a day, it's worth worrying over, while others seem to tolerate a baby's screaming without ever seeming to get very perturbed. A first-time mother with a baby like Andrew would surely label him as fussy, while if he were child number three or four, his dolefulness might be taken rather lightly—his mother knowing how to talk and cajole him out of his crankiness once in a while.

The middle-of-the-road fussy baby is just unhappy enough to make you feel vaguely uneasy about him. You're not unhappy with him, but you sometimes wonder if there's something wrong with your mothering. "If I could just feel more *positive* about this whole mothering business," you tell yourself, "then maybe everything would get better."

In some ways a baby who is neither happy nor acutely miserable is more of a challenge to deal with than one who definitely has a problem that has to be solved. Self-doubt is sometimes harder to overcome than the undeniable reality of a baby who brings on a crisis that can be met. Mothers of babies like Andrew often reel under a crushing weight of fatigue from a lack of complete satisfaction with their mother-baby relationship. They need support from other mothers and daily plans for self-renewal to keep from being eaten up by lethargy.

In time you will discover, as Andrew's mother did, that your baby has hidden likes and dislikes. You will find that more or less handling and certain positions work best for him. Andrew fell asleep best when he was sitting upright, looking at a table lamp. He responded to being swaddled and laid on his right side when being put to bed at night. He did better in a front pack, because he seemed to respond to the rhythms of his mother's walk, rather than being strapped in a stroller when being taken outside.

Perhaps you'll find peak times in the day when your baby's behavior is more positive and he's more alert than usual. This is the best moment to drop everything in favor of mother-baby play. In time, too, you'll pick up on his cues about what makes him less than amenable.

For most parents of discontented babies it's touch and go until some positive strategies can be worked out. But being around other parents with similar babies can be really energizing.

Closeness Tolerance

Babies differ as to how much intimacy and closeness they need or can tolerate. Most babies need a lot of intimate warmth and enfoldment to feel secure after birth. It is very normal for a baby to cry to be picked up and to prefer being held and rocked to being left to his own devices. As babies mature they develop what has been called "separation anxiety," which is the fear of strangers or of being out of sight of their mothers. There is a natural lifeline that connects mothers and their babies.

Some mothers are all primed to embrace and give body love to their new babies only to discover that their babies don't want to be held! While most babies are cuddlers, some characteristically are not. They seem to dislike physical closeness. You can tell by your baby's body language if he's intolerant of intimacy. He may arch and squirm as if to say he wants to be put down, to be away from the close one-to-one affection that you naturally want to offer your baby.

"It seems like my baby treats me as the enemy. He cries even at my coming close to him. My best efforts are never good enough. I feel so frustrated by my failure to meet his needs and his rejection of me that I get downright angry."

Later on you may find that your uncuddly baby detests restraints of any kind. He seems to be enraged at being placed in a baby carrier that holds his head, or at having to wear shirts or other clothing that binds him or has to be pulled over his head.

Prematurity

It has been found that in some cases premature babies are more likely to be uncuddly than full-term babies. It may be that your preemie grew accustomed to the long days and nights in an isolette with little human contact. He may have "jelled" with the expectations of constant monotony, droning sounds, and limited contact that have become so familiar.

Premature babies may undergo different maturation cycles than full-term babies do. One survey of premature babies in an intensive care center found that when the preemies reached the age of forty weeks—conceptual age, or about one month after they were brought home from the hospital—they suddenly became extremely hard to arouse, and when they were finally aroused, they were very irritable. There were no complaints from mothers when the babies had their one-month checkups, but suddenly, within the next two weeks, the switchboard lines became jammed with calls from anxious mothers whose babies had suddenly become difficult. One theory is that this irritability corresponds to the typical six-week fussiness period of many full-term babies.

Hypersensitivity

Other possible explanations for uncuddlesome babies are that their nervous systems are either so immature, they can't process human stimulation very well, or that their systems are hypersensitive, so that even human touch seems almost painful to them. These babies are sometimes called "skin sensitive." If that's your baby's case, then you will need to temper your baby handling, maybe even resting the baby on a pillow during feeds at first so that he feels comfortable.

Your baby may have an overactive Moro reflex, which

makes him throw his arms and head back every time he's jiggled. He thinks he's falling, cannot stand to be lowered backward onto the diaper table or into the crib. If your motions are tentative and jerky when you hold and carry the baby, rather than firm and smooth, your baby may associate being handled by you with his inborn but overactive fear of being let go or dropped. Most babies seem to prefer direct, firm handling that communicates purposefulness, and motions that are slowed down enough to adjust to changes in body positions.

If human interactions are too potent for your baby, he may turn his eyes or head away from you as though he is trying to avoid direct eye contact with you. He's trying to tell you that you're coming on too strong for his sensitivities. The best approach is to imitate his head turning or side glances yourself when he does it. That way you begin to get into sync with his rhythms. You may find him beginning to watch you, slyly at first and then more boldly.

How to Cope

Babies, even uncuddly ones, need to learn the language of love that goes on between the bodies of parents and babies. Motion, like the kind carried babies feel, has been found to be a potent force in a baby's developing perception of himself and his world. It's sometimes easy to fall into the trap of just leaving the baby alone, since he seems to be asking for it, but physically isolating a baby from your touch and motion can impair his later abilities to relate to others, and may even affect the development of his body skills.

One way to cope with your uncuddly baby is to yield to his demands at first and then to gradually increase the moments of togetherness, especially during feeding times. After all, eating is a powerful, positive experience. As your baby begins to associate the pleasure of the feeding experience with the closeness of your body, he can probably be brought around to liking human contact. Sleeping with the baby in your bed, too, may help to provide body intimacy when the baby's sensitivities are more muted. Touching tolerance will probably increase naturally, too, with your baby's maturation.

The "Colicky Baby" Personality

Researchers of chronically crying, sometimes called colicky, babies have noted that these babies often have similar personality characteristics to each other. Sigvard Jorup, the Swedish researcher mentioned earlier, studied 111 such babies and found them to be far different from the relaxed, average baby.

"They are, in general, impatient and irritable," he states. "They have difficulty in relaxing, are wakened on the least occasion, become fretful and impatient, and take a long time to calm down again. They twist and turn, kick, and display motor restlessness in general. Their sleep is shorter and less sound than that of normal babies."

> *"I've come to the conclusion that a colicky baby is usually a very sensitive one. Our baby always seemed more sensitive to strangers, to noise, and so forth than her peers. Now she is a sensitive toddler, very alert and curious and bright."*

One of the more unusual characteristics of these babies, Jorup observed, was their excessive sensitivity to noises or light. The click of an X-ray machine would deeply startle the babies. The sound of a voice or the scraping of a chair, a creaking door or the sound of approaching footsteps—all were sufficient to make the baby awaken and cry.

Many of the mothers of the babies being observed noticed that their supersensitive children couldn't stand the sudden turning on of lights. The babies would awaken and scream if an overhead light was turned on, and they couldn't even sleep at all if there was any light in a room.

Certain phrases that have been used by researchers to describe these babies include *delicate, highly nervous, overready response to stimulation, overactive,* and *tense.* One researcher described these babies as often having a "lean and hungry look" about them.

When mothers share information about their colicky babies' personalities, they usually discover that there are often two distinct kinds of colicky babies: the ones who "go off the wall" at the least amount of stimulation, as Jorup found, and those who demand constant stimulation to keep from crying. One type seems to want the world to go away, unable to deal with its cacophony; the other type wants his mother to take the pain away, to rock, walk, sing to, and talk to him—to do *anything* to take his mind off the discomfort.

While one type of baby would like nothing better than to be jostled up and down the stairs at 2:00 A.M., as though it were a distraction, the other type would come completely unglued from such jiggling of barely controlled inner balances, as though there were a defect in the ability to screen out or to dampen stimuli. This type of baby, it would seem, reacts not only to any sudden stimuli from outside himself, but he also reacts strongly to stimuli coming from within himself on every level of body functioning.

When Dr. Alan Lake, a pediatric gastroenterologist at the Johns Hopkins University School of Medicine, examines a colicky baby, one of the first characteristics he looks for is an unusual vulnerability to stimulation. "These babies are superaware, sensitive, and aroused by noise," he notes. "Just as they are acutely aware of outside sounds and changes, they are more sensitive to sensations arising from inside their organs." Dr. Lake likens the babies' responses to the way adults suddenly become aware of every stomach gurgle and pain when they are at home with the flu.

In many cases the colicky baby is "a child who has an abnormally low threshold for organic stimulation. The baby is attuned to body processes that most babies are able to ignore," he says. The reason for the lowered awareness barrier is not known, but for the present Dr. Lake attributes it to an immature nervous system.

Do high-strung babies somehow cause their pain, or does their pain make them high-strung? It may very well be that a baby's highly charged nervous system interferes with his ability to ignore digestion, but it is also plausible that a baby experiencing chronic pain cannot relax, trapped constantly into pain-tightened vigilance. Not until actual cures for colic are found will we know the true relationship between colic and personality.

When Mothers Get Turned Off

One of the problems that an irritable, hard-to-soothe, uncuddly baby creates is that he makes you less eager to interact with him. It's not his fault. He really can't help how he acts or how he feels; but, if he's not rewarding to be with, you may begin to loose your eagerness to engage in things with him, anticipating that you'll only feel frustrated by him.

More than ever the reciprocal nature of parent-baby relationships is being researched. Parents react to their babies' personalities, and babies react to their parents'. A lovable, easy-to-manage baby may be able to warm up even the most aloof and unresponsive caregivers. On the other hand, a very difficult, miserable baby may turn off even the most experienced and eager-to-love parents.

"Inside I felt miserable and disillusioned with motherhood and wondered what was the matter that I was so frustrated, while friends hailed parenthood as a mostly satisfying experience. I was caught in the dreadful trap of comparing myself with other women. Instead of wondering what I was doing wrong that my baby wasn't a sleeping, smiling cherub, I needed to accept the fact that he wasn't and to praise my mothering skills despite their seeming ineffectiveness. I needed to trust my judgment that my situation was rough and that I had every right to my feelings. I should not have based my total self-esteem on my lack of success as a mom."

Dr. Susan Goodman Campbell at the University of Pittsburgh has studied the relationship between babies who were rated by their mothers as "extremely irregular, nonadaptable, and negative in mood" and how much the mothers responded to these babies. The mothers who thought their babies were difficult, Dr. Campbell found, spent significantly less time interacting with their babies, talking to them, and responding to their desire to play or to their crying. Babies perceived as difficult by their mothers not only received less responsive mothering when they were three months old, but much later, at eight months of age, their mothers ignored them even more.

One of the critical variables outside of the mother-baby relationship that can influence how well parents cope with their baby is how much positive social support they receive from other family members and other parents. Support from other people can act as a buffer against the stress of a less than happy baby. It can help parents to cope and respond to a baby that doesn't give them much encouragement. (See the appendix for support sources.)

One ray of hope that parents of a baby with a difficult personality can cling to is that the baby may outgrow it. Fortunately, conditions like colic are short-lived and outgrown in a matter of months. In England another name for colic is "three months" colic, because that's the typical time when many babies seem to get better. Even if a baby doesn't outgrow his problems until four, five, or even twelve months of age, many parents report that things do ease up radically as a child becomes older and more independent.

> *"Anyone who has a baby with colic needs all the moral support they can get and the reassurance that they can get through it and that other people do understand and have made it. Unless you've been through it, you can't imagine how difficult it really is. Our baby cried twenty-four hours a day for eight months. Everyone kept saying he'd be well at three months, then six months, then nine months, and then twelve, until it looked like it was going to go on forever."*

While some babies do continue to be handfuls as toddlers and preschoolers, there is scientific evidence to support that personality traits in babies, rather than being solid and enduring, are most often transient and short-lived.

Dr. Richard Q. Bell of the University of Virginia and his colleagues have studied how well baby traits predict personality later in childhood. Interestingly, they found that the extremely active baby may, in fact, turn out to be the calm child. The highly intense baby was more likely to become a child of low intensity in the preschool years. He was apt to be less assertive, less outgoing, and less communicative in later years. Baby personality often made a complete turnabout.

Drs. William B. Carey and Sean C. McDevitt of the University of Pennsylvania Medical School carried on a long-range study of babies from the age of four months until they were seven years old. Only one fourth of the babies labeled as difficult were rated as such by their parents later on. Three fourths of those babies acquired calmer temperaments, and by an odd quirk of justice, sixty-one percent of the babies with easygoing personalities became more difficult in time.

> *"My advice is don't worry. Sometimes that extra TLC you're giving now has carry-over value later."*

You shouldn't take your baby's personality characteristics too seriously, as though they were written in stone. Rather it is better to be as flexible and responsive as you can, seeking out the human support you need, particularly if your baby is more challenging than most.

> *"Our son was difficult until he was about ten months old. Now at close to three years of age we couldn't ask for a child who cries less. My only answer is there is no one answer. Just have patience and don't give up."*

7
The Mothering Minuet

Ellen Grayson is a remarkable person. A tall, large-framed woman, she's the mother of eight thriving children, one of whom just went off to college. All of her babies were nursed in abundance and reared by her. I figured that if anyone knew how to soothe a crying baby, she did.

One day I decided to watch her very closely as she scooped up a red-faced, screaming three-week-old from its distraught mother and began her professional baby-soothing techniques. She planted the tiny baby against her shoulder, holding it firmly by the buttocks in one hand and gently cupping its head in the other.

Then she began a dance that looked like an ancient mothering minuet. She took eight or ten rhythmical paces forward, turned around and took eight or ten paces back to where she had started from: step ... pause ... step ... pause. Her hand slipped down to the baby's back, patting with each pause, and his toes uncurled.

Sensing that the baby was still wound up, she continued her walk, adding sounds that I had never heard used with a baby before. She produced deep guttural groans; the kind of groans that people make when they're having orgasm. The groans welled forth each time she came to a pause in her rhythmical stepping. Groan-pat-pause-walk, groan-pat-pause-walk, the dance went on. The baby's hands uncurled and he let out a huge, chin-quivering sigh that racked his tiny body.

"Some mothers gently rocked the [crying] infant from side to side, others patted his back or rubbed the nape of his neck. Some rocked and patted at the same time. Some massaged the baby. Others jostled the infant, moving him up and down at a fast pace as they held him in their arms. Some mothers accompanied these movements by humming or speaking softly in a soothing voice. Others remained silent. No matter what form the action, the infants were soon quieted. They seemed to respond to their mother's particular technique, to fit to it, and to be calmed by it."

> **—Mary Ann Dzik,**
> **"Maternal Comforting of the Distressed Infant,"**
> ***Maternal–Child Nursing Journal,***
> **1979, vol. 8, no. 3, p. 167**

Ellen continued the dance, firmly holding the baby in place, refusing to move him from her chest even to check on his expression. After another deep sigh from the baby, as if to say "Home, at last!" his eyes fluttered to half-mast. Within ten minutes of her mothering performance the baby fell into a profound sleep that left his body limp.

Ellen had learned the dance, I found out later, from her own mother, who had learned it from her grandmother. So the skill had been passed down from generation to generation. The three components that seemed the most potent in the dance were firmness, rhythmical motion, and the repetitive deep sound that vibrated her chest where the baby was held.

Remarkably, science is rediscovering the importance, too, of those components in its search for a deeper understanding of baby behavior. *Not only are motion and sound potent baby soothers, but they may play a critical role in a baby's development.*

Arguments for Baby Closeness

In an intriguing article published in the *American Journal of Pediatrics* (1979), Doctors Betsy Lozoff and Gary Britten pose the question "Infant Care: Cache or Carry?" The article ponders whether human babies were meant to be cached, that is, left alone in the "nest" while the parents went out in search of food, or carried on the person of the mother or other caregiver.

The researchers examined the composition of human breast milk and found that mammals who leave their babies behind usually have breast milk that is high in protein and fat for feeding their babies only every two to fifteen hours. Those mammals who carry their babies on themselves have breast milk that is low in protein and fat, designed for feeding babies continuously, or every two to four hours. *The authors conclude, from the composition of human breast milk, that our babies are meant to be carried a lot and fed frequently.* Interestingly, in those countries where carrying the baby on the mother predominates, colic is seldom heard of. The !Kung babies of Africa spend as much as 90 percent of their time directly on their mothers' bodies. American babies, with one in five fussy, spend an average of only sixteen to twenty-three percent of their time on their mothers' bodies.

Baby reflexes, such as the toe grasp and the startle response, which end with the baby's fingers closing into a strong clutch, both seem to be built-in reactions intended to keep the baby attached to its mother.

Many mothers, too, report chest and abdominal hunger pains that feel like their bodies are reaching out to pull the baby in toward themselves. Once the baby is drawn in and enfolded against the mother's chest or abdomen, the hunger is eased. Mothers whose babies are separated from them by hospitalization or permanent loss find the body pain, their closeness hunger, to be almost unbearable.

Some parents may be afraid that if they give in too much to their baby's demand to be held or carried, the baby will become too dependent later. They fear they're going to produce a clingy child.

The research of Dr. Mary Ainsworth of the University of Virginia demonstrates that just the opposite occurs. She found that babies who showed the most enjoyment of close body contact with their mothers didn't become addicted to it. Babies who had a lot of holding were the ones who were content to be put down and who, by the end of the first year, were more likely to move off in independent activity.

Motion Helps Baby Development

Twelve years ago Dr. Mary V. Neal, now chairman of the Department of Maternal and Child Nursing at the University of Maryland, conducted research on the motor development of premature babies. She wondered why they were so often underweight and slower in motor development—even months and years after birth—than their full-term counterparts. After watching how preemies stayed motionless in flat-bedded isolettes with only the droning sounds of the life-support systems nearby, she concluded that the full-term babies got significantly more stimulation from the sounds and motions of their mothers' bodies.

To see if motion was an important key to infant development, she designed a small clear plastic hammock that attached to the top of preemies' isolettes and that was set in motion by a special automatic rocking device. She divided the preemies in her study into two groups—those who received only standard hospital nursery care and those who were rocked thirty minutes a day for the first five weeks after birth.

The results of the experiment were remarkable. The babies who were rocked had better body coordination than the babies who were left in motionless isolation. They also showed better visual and hearing responses and had less edema—a swelling of tissues that usually signals that something is wrong.

Seven years later Dr. Lloyd B. Kramer and Dr. Mary Ella Pierpont of the Georgetown University Medical School conducted a similar study on the effects of motion on premature babies. They used incubator-size water beds that gently rocked the babies, and a tape of the human heartbeat and voice was played to simulate the babies' experiences in the uterus.

Once again the results of the research were extraordinary. The babies receiving motion and sound graduated to normal methods of feeding faster than the motionless babies. They gained weight better and they had larger head circumferences by the end of the study.

To determine if motion also helped normal full-termed babies develop, Dr. David Clark and his associates at the Ohio State University College of Medicine devised a rotating chair that would give a baby intense motion stimulation. Babies in the experiment were held in an adult's arms while they were spun in first one direction and then the other. A matched group of babies were held in the adults' arms in the chair but weren't spun.

The babies who experienced the brief spinning episodes over a period of a month seemed to enjoy the motion and showed better body skills. *In a study involving a set of identical twins, the one who had been spun could sit up and had achieved excellent head control, while the other baby lagged behind and still could not sit up by the end of the study.*

Why does motion affect a baby's development so powerfully? It may be that motion teaches the baby about the relationship between his body and the world around him. Some scientists even believe that profound motion deprivation in infancy can cause certain nerve pathways in the baby's brain to degenerate, perhaps just as muscles in limbs that are enclosed in casts weaken when they are prevented from being used.

How the Vestibular System Works

The vestibular system is responsible for transmitting motion messages to the brain. It is buried within a baby's hearing system, just behind his eardrums. We experience the effects of the vestibular system when we feel dizzy after riding on a merry-go-round, flying, or riding in a fast elevator.

The vestibular system is one of the earliest neurological systems to mature in babies. Floating in a tiny gelatin-filled chamber are small pebblelike crystals that tickle tiny hairs. Each time a baby moves his head nearby nerves pick up the tickling message from the hairs and transmit it to the brain. Intricate curving tubes filled with liquid give out other signals that tell the brain when the baby is rocking, spinning, moving up and down, or making other motions.

Like flashing lights on a tiny complex switchboard, the vestibular messages are transmitted by impulses from the baby's eyes, and from sensors buried in the baby's tendons and on skin surfaces. The brain makes a decision about the baby's body position and directs whatever motions are necessary to keep him protected and in balance.

You can easily see how this motion switchboard in the brain works by holding your baby so that his head is upright and he is gazing straight ahead. Slowly tilt his body backward or turn it to one side or the other. You will notice that his eyes stay fixed straight ahead at a single point of reference even though his body changes position. This reaction, called the "doll's eyes reflex," is only temporary and disappears as the baby matures.

Children who are born with damaged vestibular systems are exceedingly slow to crawl and rock. However, we don't yet know how the vestibular system may be related to the self-rocking and self-spinning behaviors so common to autistic children. Self-rocking may be an autistic child's way of providing himself with much-needed motion. Or perhaps autistic children have some crucial disorder in the switchboards of their vestibular systems.

Many blind babies and young children exhibit self-rocking patterns that have been thought to be a normal part of blindness. Professor Selma Fraiberg of the University of California Medical School has carefully observed blind babies in their homes and has concluded that many of them live in a profound sensory void. They often don't get the carrying, rocking, and sensory stimulation that most sighted babies get from their parents.

Professor Fraiberg feels that part of the problem may be that blind babies do not give their parents the eye-to-eye contact that encourages the parents to pick the babies up. Blind babies who receive large amounts of motion, touch, and loving contact become as outgoing as their sighted peers and don't exhibit any self-rocking patterns.

Swings and Other Soothing Motion Devices

For hundreds of years motion has been used as a form of therapy for mentally ill patients. In the 1800s rotating swings were widely used to soothe and treat schizophrenics. One psychiatrist even noted that his unruly and uncooperative schizophrenic patients became as calm as kittens when they had to take a train ride to a new hospital. He decided it was the rhythmical side-to-side motion of the train that had changed their behavior.

Babies, too, are remarkably soothed by being rocked. In his motion research on babies, Dr. David R. Pederson at the University of Western Ontario in Canada tested different rocking speeds and directions to see which were the best soothers. He found that it didn't matter whether the baby was sitting up or lying down, and that the most effective speed, interestingly, was very close to a mother's rhythmic walk.

> *"Our colicky baby liked: being rocked*
> *in a rocking chair with a not-too-hot*
> *water bottle against his belly, dancing*
> *with us to music, going for a walk or a*
> *ride in the stroller outside while we*
> *talked to him about things we saw, and*
> *swinging in an automatic baby swing."*

"Motion is important in the maintenance and development of all motor and neurological systems in a baby's body," says Dr. Neal of the University of Maryland. She encourages mothers to get rocking chairs and to rock their babies, and she recommends that hospital nurseries consider rocking chairs as standard equipment.

> *"Not a single thing worked all the*
> *time, and we spent many nights just*
> *rocking, walking, and soothing a very*
> *unhappy baby."*

Hundreds of mothers of fussy, hard-to-soothe babies have found that the Snugli, a soft corduroy front carrier pouch that keeps the babies close to their mothers, is the only device that seems to work for them. The carrier has shoulder padding to make the job easier on the mother and it comes with changeable bibs that can be snapped out. The entire carrier is machine washable and can be let out as the baby grows. (For more information you can write to: Snugli Cottage Industries, Inc., Rt. 1, Box 685, Evergreen, CO 80439.)

> *"We couldn't let her cry. We would walk her for hours or rock her. The Snugli would help. As soon as we tried to lie her down, she would cry. She needed walking. She just wanted to be close."*

Automatically rocking cradles and swings have often been helpful for babies who are nearly always fussy at dinnertime. The mothers I talked to suggest that you choose the swing model with the longest running time, since the baby may be jarred from relaxation by your stopping everything to recrank the device. Caution is advised for small babies, who should be secured by a sash or a small belt so that they don't fall forward into the padded front bar of the swing and suffocate because they are unable to straighten back up to breathe.

> *"My baby required motion and constant carrying during his first six months to keep from crying. I finally discovered that a hammock strung up on one side of the kitchen was a great help. I could rock and rest and my hands were freed if I wanted to read or knit."*

Older babies who can sit up may enjoy a doorway jumper that is suspended from the molding by ice-tong-looking hinges. By patting the floor with his feet the baby discovers he can make himself jump up and down. As with all devices, the jumper should be used only under very close supervision, since babies have been hurt by hitting into the doorjamb, and have gotten vertigo—extreme dizziness—from too much action.

You!

No device exceeds the human parent in knowing just how much motion a baby wants or needs. The importance of being sensitive to what your baby seems to be asking for can't be overstressed. While some babies are positively pleased with movement, there are some babies, sometimes premature, who come unglued as the result of movement. These babies may have an overactive fear of falling that causes them to be jumpy and to grasp at things after every change in direction. They need almost complete stillness with slowed-down carrying in the first few months after birth until they feel more calm about things.

Your Voice Is Important, Too

"Why should I talk to my baby when he can't even understand me?" asked Laurel Semper as she sat in the living room, watching the television, while her baby fussed for attention in an infant seat nearby. What Laurel and a lot of other new mothers may not perceive is that babies do indeed hear and respond to the human voice.

In the past it was assumed that babies came into the world as senseless creatures, deaf and nearly blind. The baby's brain was thought to be like a *tabula rasa,* a blank slate, onto which life's experiences were written. The research of Dr. William Condon at the Boston University Medical Center and many other researchers seems to put that notion completely to rest.

Dr. Condon used a frame-by-frame analysis of slow-motion pictures to examine how an adult's voice arouses the newborn baby. He found that babies less than a day old do a rhythmic dance with their arms and legs to the sound of a voice. The babies' motions are so quick that they must be slowed down by film in order for researchers to catch them at all! Babies dance, he found, to English and other languages, but they don't move in rhythm to nonsensical sounds.

> *"Now, at two years of age, our formerly colicky son is a very loving, secure child. I believe the extra care and concern shown during his difficult time has carried over and helped him to be secure and giving.* The time we spent with him trying to keep him from fussing has really given him a boost in language and intellectual development."

French researchers have shown that babies only a few days old recognize and respond to their own names, especially when the names are said to them by their mothers. When a baby is held under his armpits in a standing position by a doctor, and the mother silently enters the room behind the baby, the instant that she speaks his name to him, he turns his entire body, head first, around toward her in an attempt to face her. *No other voice is as potent to the baby as his own mother's.*

> *"Don't let your tiny baby cry alone. Comfort him, speak quietly to him. He needs your presence more when he's upset."*

Parents seem to be preprogrammed to communicate to their babies with exactly the right pitch and slowed speech that the babies understand best, according to the observations of parent-baby "conversations" by Dr. Daniel Stern, a psychiatrist at Cornell University Medical Center. "If you watch how a mother or father talks to a baby, you will see that they raise their voices almost to a falsetto range, and they exaggerate their expressions so that the baby's interest is clearly captured," Dr. Stern points out. He feels that parents naturally train their babies to the rhythms of language from the earliest weeks of life on. A mother says, "You're a cute baby, aren't you?" She then pauses for the exact length of time that the baby needs to answer, if he could speak, "Yes, I am!" Then she echoes his unspoken responses: "Yes, you are!"

A new baby, too, can imitate the facial movements or expressions of persons who come within his foot-and-a-half range of clearest focusing. He sticks out his tongue when someone does it to him, he forms his lips in an *O*, or he makes other facial expressions similar to those of the person in front of him if they are presented slowly enough and at the right moment in his attention span.

What these studies seem to indicate is that a baby has a complex mediating system already at work at birth in his huge elaborate brain, which is uniquely human. How else could a baby who has never seen himself in a mirror make the connection: *his tongue, my tongue . . . he sticks out his tongue, I'll stick out mine?*

It is possible that your baby's sound awareness is formed long before birth. Tiny sensitive microphones have now been used to record the kinds of sounds that babies hear in the wombs of their mothers. The clarity of voices, of rhythms, and of music and other outside noises that come through the mother's body to the baby are astonishing. It is known that a baby's hearing, along with the vestibular system, is one of the earlier neurological systems to mature in the fetus, and there is little doubt now that babies tune in long before they are born.

Parents have convincing stories about their infants' responsiveness to sounds even before birth. One mother of a fussy baby had played the cello all during her pregnancy, especially one passage that took a great deal of practice to master. Finally, a few weeks after the birth of her baby, she once again picked up the cello and began to play the passage. The baby abruptly stilled himself to listen. The mother knew immediately that the baby had recognized the music that had been so familiar to him while in the womb.

Some parents have begun to program their babies with talking and music even before birth. One couple, celebrated in the news media, are graced with three children labeled as geniuses. The couple claims that they began to teach their children months before they were born by exposing them to music and the human voice.

Although these stories of the effect of sound on babies even before birth haven't been scientifically validated, the evidence for the value of motion and sound to baby development and parent-baby relationships *after* birth is convincing.

There may be more to Grandma's rocking chair and lullabyes than we ever realized!

8
Your Fussy Breastfed Baby—
And What to Do

Can a breastfed baby be a fussy baby?

You bet he can!

True, fewer breastfed babies have digestive problems and allergy reactions to the protein in mother's milk as compared to cow's milk, but fussiness has been common to babies throughout human history. The Greek physician Galen described fussy babies back in A.D. 130. Over four hundred years ago, long before bottle-feeding, Thomas Phaire in the *Boke of Chyldren* reported babies with "colike and rumblying in the guttes."

Sometimes a breastfeeding mother is shocked to discover that it doesn't always guarantee a relaxed, "good" baby. Sometimes, too, because a mother is so intimately connected with her baby, his misery seems all the more anguishing. It's as though she's doing all she possibly can do, and yet that's not enough. Those problems lead to self-doubt and questions about whether to continue breastfeeding or not.

Why You Shouldn't Wean the Baby

The first advice that uninformed physicians and nosy in-laws are apt to give a breastfeeding mother with a super-fussy baby is that she should try formula. Let's look at the reasons for continuing to breastfeed your baby even though he's fussy:

> *"Take all magical solutions with a grain of salt. Just because putting Johnny on formula seemed to help somebody doesn't mean you should go out and wean your baby. Relatives are always quick to present the magical solutions that are the least helpful."*

Immunities: Breastfed babies are far less likely to have respiratory infections, diarrhea, and serious life-threatening illnesses because of the natural protection afforded by human breast milk. Immunities continue to be provided not only in just the first few months of breastfeeding but throughout the first year of life or longer.

"It is well known that breast-fed babies have only one fourth to one fifth of the intestinal and respiratory infections of bottle-fed babies."

—**"Are We in the Midst of a Revolution?"**
John H. Kennell, M.D.,
***American Journal of Disease in Children,* Vol. 134, March 1980, p. 303**

Fewer Cavities Later: Studies have shown that breast-feeding produces children with less tooth decay than bottlefed babies with or without fluoridation.

Better Oral Development: Breastfed babies are less likely to have tongue thrusting and jaw alignment problems that sometimes lead to speech impairments.

Fewer Inner Ear Infections: Breastfed babies will run much lower risks of inner ear infections than if they are bottlefed. *Chronic inner ear infection is one of the most frequent reasons for nonroutine visits to pediatricians nationwide.*

Reduces the Possibility of Later Obesity: There is now conclusive evidence that breastfed babies are less likely to be obese in childhood, adolescence, and adulthood.

Natural Intimacy: Babies thrive on body closeness and the physical reassurance provided over and over within the nursing relationship.

Abrupt Weaning Can Be Painful: Bringing breastfeeding suddenly to a halt can be physically uncomfortable for you. Gradual weaning is physically easier and better psychologically for your baby.

Common Fussiness Fallacies

Here's a quick reference guide of responses to the pat answers you may get for your breastfed baby's fussiness.

False	True
"You probably don't have enough milk."	"How much milk my body makes depends on how *often* and how *long* I let my baby nurse and how well he sucks."

False	**True**
"You ought to put the baby on a four-hour feeding schedule."	"Breastfed babies should nurse whenever they signal that they need to. Sometimes my baby wants to nurse a lot, at other times he does not. It's not up to me to decide when he is hungry."
"Your breasts are too small."	"Breast size has no relationship to milk-making capacity. A mother who cannot produce enough milk for her baby because of organ or gland failure is very rare."
"Give the baby formula or cereals to make him sleep through."	"Studies have shown that cereals and other supplements don't help the problem of fussiness or sleeplessness and often they make matters worse, especially if the baby is allergy prone."
"Your nervousness is making your milk go away."	"Stress and tiredness can make my milk letdown slower, and may make my body less efficient, but the problem can be overcome with relaxation and a good diet."
"Bottle-feeding is so much easier!"	"Wrong. I don't have to get up in the night to heat a bottle. I can take my baby with me anywhere in the world without a single can, bottle, nipple, or device. (Breastfeeding's much cheaper, too!)"

False	True
"If you gave the baby formula, then you could get away for a while, because Dad or a baby-sitter could feed the baby."	"My baby needs *me* because I'm intimately aware of him and his signals. I don't want him to have to face his pain and discomfort without me."

The Secret to Making More Milk

Sometimes a breastfed baby fusses because he wants his mother's body to produce more milk.

Milk-making is not an either-you-have-it-or-you-don't proposition. How much milk your body produces is a dynamic process based on your baby's stimulation of your breasts.

The three most important factors that affect how much milk your body makes are:

· How often you let your baby nurse
· How long you let your baby stay at your breast to finish nursing
· How vigorously your baby nurses.

Babies shouldn't be arbitrarily scheduled as to when they can nurse and when they can't. Lindsay Fogg made that mistake. Her pediatrician, who should have known better, told her to nurse her baby only every four hours. The baby couldn't help crying—he was hungry. Every four hours was just not enough of a signal to Lindsay's body to urge it to produce more milk. Because of the long delays between feedings, milk backed up in her breasts' ducts, signaling her body to cut down on milk production rather than to increase it to meet her baby's needs.

Some people think, too, that a baby should be regulated as to how long he is allowed to nurse at the breasts. They will suggest that a baby be allowed only five minutes on each side. A mother's breast milk isn't the same from the beginning to the end of a feeding. The first milk to come out is pearly blue and thin looking. It's called the foremilk. The cream, the hindmilk, doesn't come until the end of long, leisurely nursing. Therefore, feedings should be as long as the baby seems to want to continue, since the baby is still getting milk even after the first rush of his mother's letdown.

The volume of milk that your breasts make builds up gradually over time. Once milk-making is well established, your baby gets as much as nineteen or twenty ounces of milk a day. By the time he reaches six months of age he'll be getting almost thirty ounces of milk a day (and you'll be eating like a longshoreman).

Don't fall for the advertisements that make you think your baby needs a bottle to supplement his nursing. When other foods or liquids are added to your baby's diet, he nurses less and for shorter times, signaling your body to cut down on milk production. Supplements virtually begin the process of weaning.

A baby's sucking strength can sometimes affect how much milk a mother makes. Japanese researchers have found that when mothers who seemed to have insufficient milk for their babies used an electric pump, their milk production jumped up considerably. When they went back to nursing their lethargic or weakly sucking babies, their milk production decreased again. If a baby has a neurological problem that prevents vigorous sucking, he may need special training on how to suck correctly in order to succeed in signaling the breasts strongly enough. It's perfectly normal, though, for some babies to be very polite nursers, while others are barracuda.

Why Is He So Fussy?

It may be that your baby's immature digestive system sometimes chokes up with too massive a feed of breast milk. Frequent small feedings may help to ease him through potentially painful digestive crises.

La Leche League, International, a wonderful support group for breastfeeding mothers, offers the following suggestion in *The Womanly Art of Breastfeeding:*

> Try feeding your colicky but thriving baby from one breast only during a two- to three-hour period. He may want to nurse a number of times during that time span; just keep to the 'empty' breast. After two to three hours, switch to the other breast and again limit nursings to one side.

Some mothers have found that their initial letdown of milk is too powerful for their small babies to handle. The baby sucks and sucks to make the milk come, and then "Bingo!" the milk comes so powerfully that he struggles to swallow without choking. He may take in extra air, too, since his vacuum seal on the breast may not work well in the first month or so, which can result in belly pain. One solution is to take the baby off the breast when you feel the letdown coming by gently breaking the baby's suction with your little finger at the sides of his lips; then let the initial spurt of milk flow into a diaper or a washcloth. This technique frustrates the baby, though. Another answer is to lie on your back at a 45 degree angle while nursing, with the baby on top of you. That way the extra milk dribbles off without choking the baby. In time your baby will adapt to your body's letdown style.

One study found that as many as fifty-six percent of breastfed babies cried regularly in the evenings when they were two and three months old. One explanation for evening fussiness in breastfed babies is that the composition of breast milk is different at various times of the day. Mothers produce the most milk with the highest fat content in the morning, and milk quantity and composition shift to their lowest peak in the early evening. With proper nutrition you can assure that your body has adequate milk-making materials and enough energy to buffer itself for coping with predictable evening crying spells and cycles of night waking.

Normal Fussiness Days

Expect fussiness in your baby at these ages:

- First three weeks of life
- Six weeks
- Twelve weeks

"Oh, you're just having your period!" husbands say accusingly when their wives blow their stacks. Whether you want to admit it or not, there are real physical cycles that can affect how you react and feel. Your baby, too, naturally goes through fussiness cycles in the first year of life. The purpose of the fussiness appears to be milk-building immediately prior to real growth spurts.

Be forewarned that you may have three to four days of day-and-night nursing sieges during these times that may leave you tired and upset. Just at the very point when you'll feel ready to be committed to an institution, your baby relaxes and even begins to sleep a little.

Teething pain and oncoming illnesses can also spark nursing binges. It's easy to get short-tempered about suddenly being so much in demand, but it's better to be flexible and to yield to your baby's body's wisdom about what's needed. As you'll discover later, during toddlerhood, nursing at the breast is one of nature's most potent painkillers for your baby.

Positioning Can Make a Difference

It's not unusual for breastfeeding problems and baby fussiness to be related to each other. "Show me a mother with really bad, sore nipples, and I'll show you a fussy baby who's not really milking the breast properly," remarks Kittie Frantz, a pediatric nurse practitioner and director of the Breastfeeding Infant Clinic at the Los Angeles County branch of the University of Southern California Medical Center.

Mrs. Frantz has found that most of the photographs showing breastfeeding in advertisements and breastfeeding directions in brochures show the baby in the wrong position. People who imitate the pictures may end up with sore nipples and very fussy babies.

"Have you ever tried to eat or drink while facing sideways?" she asks. "That's just the way that many mothers try to make their babies nurse." An important key to successful nursing, according to Mrs. Frantz, who has helped hundreds of breastfeeding mothers, is in correct positioning of the baby at the breast.

Here are her suggestions for breastfeeding success:

- Sit up straight in a chair or on a bed.
- Place your baby's head in the crook of your arm.
- Face the front of your baby's whole body toward you.
- Grasp the baby's thigh or buttock firmly with the hand of the arm that's supporting the baby so that he won't slip down.
- Put your other hand flat against your rib cage under your breast. Then place your thumb on the top of your breast, above your areola—the colored ring of tissue that surrounds the nipple. "Remember to keep your fingers off the areola," Mrs. Frantz warns. That's because the baby needs the areola in his mouth to nurse effectively.

- Now teach yourself how to aim your nipple up or down by how you press your thumb in toward your chest, which makes the nipple go up, or how you press your fingers in toward your chest underneath, which makes the nipple go down.
- Instead of stimulating your baby's cheek or other areas of his face to make him grasp the breast, simply move your breast so that your nipple tickles his lips lightly. This ought to make your baby open his mouth widely.
- Now point your nipple like a gun so that it's aimed right into the center of your baby's mouth.
- Sit back, relax, and pull the baby's whole body toward you so that his mouth "marches right past the nipple and closes down on the colored areola."

Mrs. Frantz is quick to point out that if a baby has good jaw and tongue action on the areola behind the nipple, then the nipple's not all that important to the procedure. Even mothers with flat nipples or inverted nipples that recede backward into the breast instead of protruding outward when the areola is squeezed can succeed at nursing if the baby is getting a good grasp on the areola rather than just chewing on the mother's nipple.

Mrs. Frantz warns mothers about the problems of letting a baby sample the action of a rubber bottle nipple in the early weeks after birth. Sucking on a bottle nipple is an entirely different action than the jaw and tongue movements of breastfeeding. With bottlefeeding, the baby is a passive receiver of milk. With breastfeeding, the baby must actively work the milk from the breast. Although many babies are able to make the transition from the rubber nipple offered in the hospital to the human breast, others are more susceptible to imprinting and are more likely to continue the wrong sucking pattern that they've learned from the bottle. Sometimes even babies with solid experience in nursing will alter their nursing strength and skills after having had one or two bottles.

Some babies have nursing problems because they adopt the wrong kind of mouthing or tonguing actions. If a baby has habitually sucked on his tongue in the womb, he may position his tongue too far back in his mouth when he tries to nurse. While nursing, a baby's tongue should normally thrust forward over the lower jaw, cup at the tip, and then draw up and back and up under the mother's areola and nipple. "One simple remedy for the tongue-sucker is to massage his tongue down and forward with your finger before you nurse him," Mrs. Frantz suggests. "That way the baby's tongue falls forward into the correct position."

Be Kind to Your Breastfeeding Body

Avoid using soaps or creams on your nipples

Your nipples have their own protective oils and antigerm defenses. Washing with soap or other cleansers will lead to dryness, cracking, and soreness. Just use water to rinse. Lubricants such as lanolin only make it more difficult for the baby to hold on. Rubber nipple shields interfere with your baby's sucking stimulation of the breast and can lead to infection. Avoid bicycle-horn breast pumps that can cause severe bruising—except those with very gentle tug-and-rest actions that use only half the bulb's suction power.

Rest

Sleep when the baby does, even during the day. Put the baby in bed with you if it helps you to get more rest. Lie down on the living room or kitchen floor if you need to for five-minute rest breaks.

Maintain a good diet

Be sure to eat regularly. You'll probably be eating more than your husband does for a while. Concentrate on proteins, fresh vegetables, and fruits. Cook dinner meals in advance in quantity and freeze in single-serving portions that can be popped into the oven for yourself.

Drink plenty of liquids

Drink water or a variety of fruit juices. Serve yourself a beverage every time you sit down to nurse.

Exercise

Get out of the house at least once a day. Take long, leisurely walks with the baby in a front carrier. Dance with the baby to your favorite rock music. Do stretching exercises to keep your body in tune. Once your baby's weight begins to near one fourth of your own body weight, be careful to avoid back strain by using your leg muscles rather than your back muscles to lift him.

Breastfeeding and Working

While it presents quite a challenge to both baby and mother, many mothers who find themselves having to return to work are opting to continue the breastfeeding relationship with their babies, even though they must express their milk at work in order to keep their milk supply going. The reasons for continuing to breastfeed your baby even though you are gone for part of the day are the superior nutrition that human milk offers your baby and the opportunity for natural mother-baby intimacy that is present in the hours when you are home.

Continuing to nurse in spite of the separation of work is not an easy task, but many mothers have succeeded through pure determination. The first task that you will need to master is how to hand-express your own milk. One way to learn is by doing it early in the morning before feeding the baby, when your breasts are naturally very full. Collect milk in plastic baby bottles so that they can be frozen if necessary. Human milk will keep for twenty-four hours in a refrigerator, but if it is to be kept longer than that, it should be frozen at 0° F. At that temperature human milk can be stored up to a year. It can be gradually defrosted by being run under warm tap water.

It's not unusual for a baby who is used to nursing to refuse a bottle nipple from either his mom or his dad. You'll probably find that he will accept your milk in a bottle from a caregiver who doesn't have the familiar aroma of the two of you.

At work, you'll need to have a refrigerator where you can store your excess milk, or you'll have to bring your own small cooler with ice cubes for storing the bottles filled with your milk for the next day's feedings.

It's ideal to have the baby near your place of work so that you can nurse during your lunch hour. That gives you and the baby some quiet, relaxing time together in the midst of work pressures, too.

When you're at home in the evenings, you'll find that your baby may nurse quite a bit, as though to make up for lost time. It's important, though, during the daytime on weekends that you follow pretty much the same schedule for nursing that you do for expressing your milk at work. Otherwise you may find yourself painfully engorged every Monday, your body having adapted to the weekend schedule.

Many mothers have found that breast pumps can be helpful at work. (Note: *not* the rubber ball suction cups that you find at drugstores. They can cause bruised tissues and are very ineffective.) Your local La Leche League leader can help you to order a manually operated pump to suit your needs.

Where can you express your milk at work? You should be able to put your feet up and relax without having to worry about someone walking in on you who wouldn't understand what you were up to. One enterprising mother found an unused janitor's closet and locked herself inside for the two times a day she collected milk.

Finally, don't load yourself up with caffeine drinks. You do need a lot of liquids during the day, but you should avoid colas, teas, and coffees, which will only make you more jittery and may give your baby problems, too.

(For more advice about managing working and breast-feeding, write to La Leche League, International, 9616 Minneapolis Ave., Franklin Park, IL 60131, where a new publication is being planned on this subject.)

9
When Your Baby Cries at Feeding Times

Many problems with the fussy, miserable baby seem much worse at feeding times than at other times. It may be because something about feeding causes your baby pain, or that tension has built up between you and the baby because you have begun to anticipate trouble when he settles down to nurse.

How experienced you are at baby-handling may affect how you feed your baby. Dr. Evelyn B. Thoman and her associates at the University of Connecticut have found real differences between the way an experienced mother and an inexperienced one feeds her baby. Experienced mothers were apt to be more sensitive and responsive to their babies' cues during feeding than beginners. Inexperienced mothers were more likely to change feeding activities a lot and to stimulate their babies more during feedings; yet these babies sucked less and drank less than babies whose mothers had mastered the knack of baby-feeding.

Other studies of experienced and inexperienced mothers show that experienced mothers are more likely to understand that their babies' cries are from hunger; they are more likely to perceive that their babies must concentrate on the act of drinking; and they hold themselves back from talking or stimulating their babies until the babies naturally break their suck-pause-suck rhythms.

"Basic trust that when you're hungry you're going to be fed is clearly important. But I think one of the things that's most basic and important to a baby is being understood."

> —**Dr. Daniel Stern,**
> Quoted in "The Competence of Babies"
> by Susan Quinn,
> *The Atlantic Monthly*, January 1982, p. 59

Sometimes when a mother realizes that her baby may start screaming soon after he begins to feed, the whole mealtime situation may take on an atmosphere of tension, dread, and emotional strain. It's natural for a mother to feel that way because she cares deeply about her baby and wants things to go well.

How to Relax at Feeding Time

It's not easy to relax when you're so worried about the baby at feeding time. Most babies are very sensitive to tension signals from their mothers. With a little practice you can learn to control your body messages to your baby so that he can relax and concentrate on eating.

Slow Motion

Abrupt handling of your baby's body is quickly read as a signal of danger. Try picking up your baby in slow motion, easing out quick changes in position so that everything is graceful and smooth.

Arm Relaxation	Especially while you're feeding him, your baby reads the tension of your arms as a sign to hurry or to worry. Train yourself to release your arms into cushiony softness, especially where they touch your baby.
Slow, Deep Breathing	Babies seem especially aware of their parents' breathing rhythms while being breastfed. When you consciously slow down and deepen your breathing pattern, regardless of how uptight you feel, your baby may respond by a relaxed release of his own tension.

A soft, comfortable rocking chair or other homey feeding spot that you come back to over and over again can help to set the mood for more relaxed feeding sessions. Get yourself something to drink and put it on the table beside you. Turn on a tape of restful music. *Voilà!* Now you and your baby can relax and savor the moment, rather than feeling rushed, tense, or worried.

Getting in Gear with Your Baby

Recent research may be able to help mothers and babies to have more harmonious feeding times together. More and more mothers and babies are being seen as couples who interact with one another, instead of as two isolated beings.

One phrase that's frequently used is *mutual engagement,* the word *engagement* meaning "in gear." How sensitively attuned they are to each other and how responsive they are to one another can make a big difference in how well feeding sessions go.

Some of the most promising research on feeding techniques has come from Dr. Tiffany Field and her associates at the Mailman Center for Child Development in Miami, Florida, who have conducted careful observations of mothers interacting with their babies. When mutual engagement is working between mother and baby, feedings seem to go smoothly. The baby gazes at his mother while sucking vigorously; the mother watches silently, carefully timing her interactions to coincide with the baby's natural moments of rest.

When engagement goes awry, the baby appears to be fussy and distracted. He may be slow to suck and may seldom look directly at his mother. His mother may seem anxious while constantly coaching her baby to drink more.

Dr. Field has found that some mothers of difficult babies tend to work harder at feeding their babies. They exaggerate their responses to them, caress them more, and even poke at them, as though they were striving to get more normal responses. "It reminds me of when people mistakenly try to communicate with a foreigner by yelling louder and faster rather than slowing down," Dr. Field notes.

Gaze Aversion

The overworking mother sometimes overlooks one very potent signal from the baby, called "gaze aversion." When a baby turns his head or his eyes away from his mother or father, it's his way of signaling that he wants a break. Ironically the *harder* a parent tries to control a baby's turning away, the *more* the baby does so.

To help reengage mothers and their babies, these researchers have developed what they call "interaction coaching." Taking cues from the way that sensitive, experienced mothers feed their babies, the researchers show mothers how to imitate their babies' gaze aversion. When the babies turn away, the mothers are told to do that, too, so that they become sensitive to this important baby signal. Mothers are also shown how to restrain from pushing the babies too much, and how to slow down movements to match their babies' tempos.

Midwife Ina Mae Gaskin, author of *Spiritual Midwifery*, offers this keen observation in her book:

> Sometimes I'll see a mother breastfeeding her new baby and while the baby is sucking, she'll be rubbing her fingers back and forth on his leg, feeling how soft he is, or maybe plucking at his toes, marvelling how tiny they are, and all the time she is fussing with his body she's not realizing that this is the same as tapping on someone's shoulder trying to get their attention while they're trying to make love. I have cured several babies of colic by pointing out to the mother that the way she was handling the baby while he nursed made his stomach and intestines uptight and caused cramps. Once she learned to get a nice firm grip on his thigh or his butt and let him know she was there without touch-talking irrelevent things to him while they made love, which is what breastfeeding is, after all, then the baby would get over his bellyache.

One important part of good baby-feeding management is not to let the baby go over the hill before you feed him. Often baby indigestion can be caused by trying to feed an upset, tense baby who has been on a long crying jag. Ms. Gaskin suggests that a mother try to quiet him down before feeding, because he can't feed well when his stomach is too tight and his breathing has gotten out of rhythm. One simple signal to help your baby learn to tone down is to tap him gently on his cheek, reminding him to relax before you'll give him either breast or bottle. Once he has regained some calmness, you can proceed with feeding him.

Our great-grandmothers had a similar remedy for calming down a hungry baby a hundred years ago. A baby who was likely to have digestion pains after eating was given a teaspoon of lukewarm boiled water about ten minutes before feeding time. It seemed to relax the baby and to get the kinks out of his belly so feedings went more smoothly.

Sometimes it's hard to tell whether a baby is awake or is sleeping in the middle of a feeding. Experienced mothers perceive rather well when a baby has fallen asleep. They either jostle the baby awake or discontinue feeding him altogether. They may take the bottle or the nipple and stimulate the sleeping baby's lips to help arouse him. New mothers aren't so skilled; sometimes they keep right on feeding a sleeping baby or holding the nipple passively while talking to him when he has drifted off. A moment later the baby awakens, spitting up and confused.

> *"At first I had a hard time telling if my baby was awake or asleep. If I jumped up to feed him on his first whimpers, I sometimes would find myself trying to nurse a semiconscious baby who was only halfheartedly trying to eat. An hour or so later he'd be awake and wanting to really nurse. Now I wait to be sure he's* really awake *and* really *hungry first."*

Don't Prop Up the Baby or the Bottle

Every five years or so some enterprising soul comes up with yet another way to prop up a baby bottle. There are clamps that fasten to the side of the crib with a long spring to hold a bottle, or an inflatable bib with snaps to hold a bottle, or myriad contraptions designed to free a mother to do other things.

Don't fall for any of them.

Bottle propping can be dangerous. If a baby chokes or spits up, he may lose control of the inflowing milk so that he breathes it into his lungs, which may cause pneumonia.

Bottle propping has also been associated with increased inner ear infections, especially if the baby is trying to drink milk while flat on his back. In that position, some of the swallowed milk goes into the inner ear area, setting up a perfect medium for bacteria-causing infections.

"Baby bottle mouth" is caused by babies taking milk or sweetened juices into bed with them as an inducement to going to sleep. Undigested milk pools around the baby's teeth, and the acid from it begins to etch into the tooth enamel so that decay virtually eats away his front teeth. The teeth can be extracted so that the decay doesn't move upward into the waiting permanent teeth. A special orthodontic device may be necessary to keep open the space that the permanent teeth will need years later.

The best model to follow is that of the physical intimacy that a baby gets naturally during breastfeeding. Hold your baby close during feedings and then put him into the crib, or into bed with you, once he has fallen asleep.

The Bottle and Thumb-Sucking

Thumb- and finger-sucking in infancy and sucking on a pacifier are natural ways that a baby uses to soothe himself and gain control over his rapidly changing states. They can sometimes help a baby who has stomach pain after eating. But one critical question that has only recently been answered is why some babies persist in thumb-sucking even when they're six or seven years old.

Psychiatrists Ozturk and Ozturk, working in Turkey,

did a detailed exploration of habitual thumb-sucking in children from ages one to seven. The results of the research were reported in the *British Journal of Medical Psychology* several years ago.

When the histories of fifty children who did not suck their thumbs and a similar group who did were compared, it was found that the amount of time that the baby was allowed to suck at the breast or bottle made no significant difference, although more often than not the babies who were to become thumb-suckers as children were more rigidly scheduled rather than being fed on demand.

The researchers decided to examine how the babies were put down to sleep. Groups were divided up by (1) those babies who were left alone in their rooms to go to sleep after having been fed until they were full; (2) those who were breastfed or bottlefed while they went to sleep, either in their mothers' laps or in bed; and (3) those who were rocked in their mothers' laps, in a cradle, or sung to while they fell asleep.

The researchers found an extremely strong relationship between thumb-sucking and the way the babies were put down to sleep. *Ninety-six percent of the habitual thumb-suckers had been left to fall asleep alone after having been fed.* Among the nonthumb-suckers there was not a single child who was left to fall asleep alone, or without the opportunity to suck at bottle or breast while going to sleep during infancy.

The study described several actual family situations. In one family in which there were three children, only the middle child, a girl, became a thumb-sucker. The oldest child was given the breast to suck while falling asleep, the youngest child the bottle. Only the middle child was put into the bed while awake to go to sleep on her own. Similarly, in another family of three children, it was only the child who had had no presleep nurturance who resorted to his thumb in childhood.

The results seem to indicate that babies need to have human contact and a chance to suck off to sleep with company if the habit of thumb-sucking isn't to endure beyond babyhood into childhood. It is in the wakeful loneliness of isolation in the crib, perhaps coupled with leftover sucking hunger, that thumb-sucking becomes most strongly established.

Bottle Problems

One culprit in baby-feeding problems and crankiness is a bottle nipple that doesn't have the right hole size for your baby's sucking skills. If the nipple hole is too tiny, the nipple may frustrate the baby and collapse from the hard suction. On the other hand, if the nipple hole is too large, the baby may adapt an abnormal tongue thrusting pattern to try to keep the excess milk from choking him. He may also swallow a lot of air, which causes belly pain.

> *"Either the nipple hole was always too tiny and the baby couldn't get anything out, or it was too large and he choked. One night we left a nipple boiling by mistake and filled the whole apartment with silicone smoke."*

Probably the nipple shape is not all that significant. Several years ago a nurser was being marketed that exactly resembled a mothers flat, roundish nipple at rest. But when a baby breastfeeds, the mother's nipple stretches out into a thin ribbonlike shape, sometimes as much as an inch long with a small bulb remaining only at the tip.

The Nuk nipple is now being advertised as the closest to the nursing mother's nipple. It is bulbed on one end and slender in the middle, with the standard bottle-nipple base. Unfortunately, rubber isn't like skin. It sticks to itself, and nursing can be made more difficult when the center section of the Nuk collapses and sticks. This is especially a problem when the rubber of the nipple begins to deteriorate with exposure to saliva and heat, and from poor cleaning. When any bottle nipple begins to get sticky, it should be replaced.

How can you tell if your baby's bottle nipple has the right-size holes for his needs? If he's sucking all right and doesn't seem to have troubles with choking and doesn't squeeze the nipple shut or arch back, trying to get the bottle out of his mouth, then the hole is probably not too large. If he's struggling to get milk out, and the milk is moving very slowly in the bottle, then you might suspect that his complaint is from a nipple hole that is too tiny.

Another test that pediatricians and nurses sometimes suggest is to turn the bottle upside down to see how quickly the milk drips out. A rapid, almost flowing drip is far too fast. A slow drip . . . drip . . . drip is more on target.

The way to make a nipple hole larger is by heating up a needle tip with a match until it's red hot and then inserting it into the rubber nipple. It's worth noting that nipple holes may shrink closed with boiling, so test them frequently.

A further cause of feeding problems with bottles may be an allergy to plastic. If your baby has "contact dermatitis," that is, a rash from where the plastic on plastic pants, paper diaper liners, or on teethers touches his skin, then he may also react to the tiny plastic particles that get into his milk from nursers that have plastic bags, or from plastic bottles. It would be wise to shift to rubber nipples and glass bottles to see if the baby improves.

When Your Baby Spits Up a Lot

Some babies spit up frequently, others don't. If yours is a real milky burper, you'll find yourself always having to cover up for protection. No place in the house escapes the baby's overflows. You'll be glad to know that spitting up usually takes care of itself by the time the baby gets up on his own two feet and starts to inch along furniture and to walk.

Projectile Vomiting

Spitting up, which is usually about a swallow or two of milk, and projectile vomiting, in which the baby forcefully expels milk out across the room, are two different things. An overfed baby will vomit projectilely once in a while, but if it is an everyday symptom, it's something to seek medical help about.

Here are some suggestions for the baby who spits up from a very practical book entitled *Pediatric Telephone Advice* by Dr. Barton D. Schmitt:

- *Try giving your baby smaller, more frequent feeds.* It takes about two and one half hours for a baby's stomach to empty, so try using other soothing strategies first rather than putting "food on top of food" if baby's pain seems to have some other cause besides hunger.

- *Burp your baby several times in the process of a meal* when he comes to a natural pause. Be gentle about it. You don't have to whop him across the back. Sit him up and then gently move his upper body forward. Or lie him on his right side for a moment and then bring him into an upright position over your shoulder.

  Air and belly gas are not the same phenomenon. Sometimes fussy babies have a lot of stomach gurgling and the expulsion of gas. These phenomena are not related to the baby's swallowing of air, since the digestive system normally absorbs extra air right into the system. Extra gas in the system and passing gas may be caused by lactose intolerance (see p. 21) or motility problems (see p. 53).

- *Avoid fastening your baby's diaper so tightly that it presses into his belly.*

- *Sit the baby upright in his car seat or an adjustable infant seat for a while after eating.* For safety's sake, put the seat on the floor or someplace where it can't be slid or wriggled off by your baby's motions. It's perfectly all right for a baby to sleep upright rather than lying down. In fact, some babies seem to prefer it.

Rarer Causes of Feeding Difficulties

Sometimes a premature baby may have difficulty in sucking because he has a very weak sucking reflex. Infants who have been exposed heavily to drugs, including alcohol, during pregnancy often have difficulty in coordinating sucking and swallowing. The extremely sluggish baby, because of prematurity, a lack of adequate nurturance from the placenta, or from drugs administered to the mother during labor, may not feed frequently enough to provide his body with needed nurturance in the first weeks after birth. These babies may need coaxing to wake up and take in food.

Some babies appear to have painful muscle contractions in the neck and jaw area, perhaps because of muscle injuries received during the birth process. Signs of muscle problems in babies are when they clamp down and bite a lot, hold their heads in an odd, thrown-back position, or hold their heads to one side.

Some parents have reported that their babies with muscle problems and irritability got better after having an "adjustment" from a chiropractor, or after having what is called "deep muscle therapy," which massages down deep into the baby's injured muscle tissues so that they become flexible once again, rather than remaining rigid and producing painful spasms.

More serious, enduring problems are found in babies who have central nervous system disorders and injuries and who may be showing the first signs of cerebral palsy, or other lifelong disorders involving their development, not only while feeding but later, when talking and walking.

Fortunately pediatric neurologists are able to detect these problems much earlier than ever before so that treatment can be started right away, rather than waiting until the baby is two or three years old, when less change in a baby's functioning can be hoped for.

Over and over again mothers have reported that they were the ones who knew "something just wasn't right" about their babies, even though their pediatricians kept giving them reassurances. If you feel that way about your baby, and he's having sucking problems, then perhaps you should seek the help of a developmental specialist or neurologist to get a second opinion about your baby's development.

PART III

*Crying and Sleep:
The Shifting Balance*

10
Your Baby's Crying and What It Means

Lauren and Ted Watson are awaiting the arrival of their first child in the birthing room of the hospital. The silence of anticipation settles over everyone in the room as the doctor quietly instructs Lauren to hold back on her pushing so that the baby may be eased out of her body.

"After a few struggles, Oliver breathed, sneezed and proceeded to advertise to the inmates of the workhouse the fact of a new burden having been imposed upon the parish, by setting up as loud a cry as could reasonably have been expected from a male infant who had not been possessed of that very useful appendage, a voice, for much longer space of time than three minutes and a quarter."

—Charles Dickens,
The Adventures of Oliver Twist

First the baby's head is gently freed. Its face is mask-like, its eyes shut. In moments its shoulders are maneu-

143

vered out, and almost instantly the baby's glistening, rubberlike body slips out.

The baby, a girl, is a deep shade of blue with streaks of red blood on her skin from her mother's uterus.

Suddenly, with a gulp and then a cough, newborn Jennifer announces her presence to the world by letting out a tremulous cry. She takes a breath and then cries again, this time more lustily. Each high-pitched squeal lasts about a second, followed by silence while Jennifer struggles for more air. As oxygen flows into her lungs and then into her veins, her blue body flushes a rich, deep pink.

"A cry gives a good, immediate assessment of a baby's medical status because it is the result of a complex series of muscular interactions. If any one of those interactions is affected by illness, the cry will change."

> —Howard Golub,
> A researcher at Harvard Medical School,
> quoted in *Science Digest,*
> February 1982, p. 98

To the doctor the birth cry comes as a signal for relief. The baby's respiratory system is intact and hopefully all will go well from there. For Jennifer's parents her cry symbolizes the end of a long wait. Hearing their baby's voice, they are moved to tears. The baby is here! It is born!

Science Looks at the Cry of Babies

Recent scientific research has produced a wealth of information about the cry of babies that will soon be able to help both parents and physicians better understand why babies cry and what crying means.

Cry research is not new. A hundred and fifty years ago a man named William Gardiner published a book entitled *The Music of Nature,* in which he tried to describe the cries of both animals and humans by musical notes. Forty years later Charles Darwin published *Expression of the Emotions,* which examined the various expressions shown on the faces of children. Forty years after that, German researchers used both musical notes and the phonetic alphabet to try to characterize the features of a baby's cries, helped by using the wax cylinders of an early sound recorder.

In the last two decades the study of baby crying has moved rapidly ahead, aided by the invention of sophisticated recording devices and computers. One such device, the sound spectrograph, uses a sound-sensitive recording pen on a revolving drum to make baby "cryprints."

By cross-comparing cryprints, in terms of how low or high a cry is, how fast it is, or how long the pauses are between cries, researchers can analyze baby differences. Cryprints show that crying in babies is a much more complex, well-coordinated vocal act than ever before realized.

The quality of babies' cries may someday be used by doctors for diagnosing physical problems in babies. It has already been found that babies with cretinism, caused by thyroid deficiencies, have hoarse cries. The cry of babies with meningitis is a shrill, piercing sound. A seriously ill baby may whimper oddly rather than cry, and a deep grunt may suggest pneumonia. Deaf babies produce distorted cries with more screeching and fewer emotional variations. Babies born with a rare chromosome disorder called the "cri du chat" (cat-cry) syndrome have high-pitched, mewing cries that are easily identifiable.

Researchers Howard Golub, who is an engineer at M.I.T., and Dr. Barry Lester at Harvard Medical School are using a computer to help in diagnosing abnormal baby cries. They have divided the cry of the baby into eighty-eight variations of pitch, frequency, duration, and intensity. A computer model has been developed to detect differences between babies with respiratory distress, bacterial meningitis, and certain metabolic disorders. In some cases brain damage has been detected.

The research is still in its formative stage, yet currently the cries of five thousand babies are being tested in order for both physical and emotional problems to be diagnosed. Hopefully the computer will help in pinpointing babies more likely to succumb to sudden infant death syndrome (SIDS) or babies more likely to be abused because of the shrill, irritating quality of their cries.

Scientists have also looked at the possibility of using a baby's cry to predict later intelligence. It is known that some babies have more complex cries than others. Initial research has been promising, with a small relationship evident between more sophisticated crying and intelligence, but researchers are cautious about overinterpreting the data until more is known. As science progresses in studying the cries of babies, such predictions may well be possible.

Crying, the Ultimate Signal

A baby cries not just with his voice but with his whole body. His arms and legs are thrown outward and then jerked back inward again. His leg movements, when viewed in slow motion, show the same sophisticated extension thrusts that adults use to walk.

His face is flushed red and drawn into a tight grimace. His eyes may be only partially opened or completely closed. Babies seldom shed tears during the first three months of life. When a baby's in real pain, or extremely frustrated, his mouth may draw into a widened square that seems to turn purple around the edges.

Each baby's cry is not just one sound but a combination of several sounds made all at once, and every baby's cry is uniquely his own and can be identified from the cries of others. Yet each cry noise a baby makes is unique.

As a signal of distress the cry of a baby is unsurpassed. The baby's vocal cords and voice box are very primitive in the way they operate—comparable to those of nonhuman primates like apes and chimpanzees. There is some evidence that the cries of babies in the early weeks after birth are not under voluntary control.

"Even young children may have the capacity to interpret and respond to nonverbal emotional expressions. . . . A toddler coming upon another child in distress will frequently cry in 'sympathy.' Apparently the information transmitted by infant vocalization is such that it can be interpreted at a very young age. Perhaps prespeech infant vocalizations constitute a universal language that is learned quite early in life."

—Kenneth K. Berry,
"Developmental Study of Recognition of
Antecedents of Infant Vocalizations,"
In *Perceptual and Motor Skills*, 1975, 41, p. 400

A baby's crying has a strong effect on his parents. Not only does it register in their conscious brain centers, but it also activates a more primitive, animal-like part of the brain, where basic body responses are generated.

"The cry sound, averaging eighty-four decibels when measured ten inches from the mouth, approaches the intensity of busy street traffic, factory noise, or even the noise levels of a riveter from thirty-five feet. The cry is twenty decibels louder than ordinary speech, which assures its priority over other acoustic signals in communication. Crying easily cuts through the sound of adult conversation and may even mask parts of it. One can now appreciate why a parent must interfere with the baby's crying: this sound is too annoying to be tolerated beyond a short period of time, particularly at close range. Thus a cry *cries* to be turned off!"

—Paraphrased from
Peter F. Ostwald,
Soundmaking, p. 46

147

When parents have to listen to a baby's crying, three things automatically happen to their bodies: their blood pressure shoots up, their breathing speeds up, and their palms sweat. These are identical body reactions for when parents have to undergo totally unpleasant experiences, like going to the dentist.

While the caring part of a parent's personality is thinking "Poor little thing, I'd better go in and help him," another part of the mind is signaling "fight or flight"—"Either stop this crying *now* or *get out of here!*"

Finnish researchers have shown that a baby's cry directly affects the breastfeeding mother's body. Taped cries of babies were played as new mothers stood in front of a device to measure areas of excess body heat on body surfaces. It was found that the breasts of the mothers quickly heated up when they listened to the cries of their own babies.

Mothers differed as to how much their bodies responded. Some mothers reacted weakly, while others had strong responses. How strongly a mother reacted depended on how often she had heard her own baby's voice and how many times she had breastfed him. The babies had trained the bodies of their mothers to react to their signals.

There's no doubt about it: Crying is by far one of the most potent signals of distress available to the human race.

Crying and Child Abuse

Preliminary interviews with abusive parents show that baby crying is often the trigger to baby battering. It has been found that a set of parents may have five children, yet only one of them, by virtue of its high-pitched cry or unrewarding, negative behavior, evokes violence.

Premature, small for gestational age, and retarded babies are far more frequently abused than normal, full-term babies. It is thought that the high, shrill, and unrhythmical nature of their cries is the trigger to the impulsively hostile reactions of some parents.

"Infants 'at risk' [of abuse] due to the mother's complications during pregnancy, prematurely born babies, and abnormal babies typically emit cries that are either higher or lower in pitch than are normal cries, have greater variability, and exhibit temporal patterns marked by either shorter or longer cry durations and cry intervals. These cries are also said to be so unpleasant that they override differences in maternal style."

> **—Ann M. Frodi,**
> **"Contribution of Infant Characteristics to Child Abuse,"**
> ***American Journal of Mental Deficiency,***
> **vol. 85, no. 4, 1981, p. 541**

Ann M. Frodi and her associates at the University of Rochester have examined the effects of the premature baby's face and high-pitched crying on new parents. Videotapes of premature babies, coupled with their actual crying sounds, evoked the same physiological response in the viewers as (1) being asked to imagine the most anger-provoking scene possible, (2) being repeatedly insulted, (3) being given electric shock, or (4) listening to a series of noxious sounds.

Abusive parents appear to have different responses to a baby's crying than do nonabusers. Although both abusers and nonabusers, according to Frodi, show faster heartbeats, have increased blood pressure, and perspire more, the response is more pronounced in abusers. Abusing parents say they feel more annoyance and less sympathy from the scenes of infant crying.

It is now thought that potentially abusive parents may be more reactive to negative situations than normal. It

149

could be, too, that parents can best tolerate and cope with a baby's cry if it is within an acceptable range of normalcy. Once the in-built sound tolerance range has been violated, human restraint begins to wear thin.

In an interview by Dava Sobel, Dr. Barry Lester, director of Developmental Research at Children's Hospital Medical Center in Boston, gives credence to the idea that a baby's crying may play a part in abuse.

"Mothers with a history of child abuse frequently say they couldn't stand the high-pitched, irritating cry of the baby," he states. He notes that conditions in pregnancy, such as mild malnutrition in the fetus or toxemia in the mother, can give a baby a high-pitched cry of seven hundred to eight hundred cycles per second instead of the normal cry of three hundred to four hundred cycles per second.

Dr. Lester feels that a mother with this type of baby needs support. She has to be reassured that "the kid sounds lousy." The crying really is a terrible noise and the baby requires some gentle handling. With help she can pass her energy on to the child, instead of turning it into depression or anger over the fact that "he's not perfect."

Current abuse research is purposely single-focused. It must be remembered that child abuse is a highly complex phenomenon in need of much more research. Not to be overlooked are the many factors in the family and society at large that contribute to baby abuse. Other things besides a baby's crying that are thought to lead to baby abuse are

- Stress on the family
- Isolation and loneliness of the mother
- A severe breakdown in the mother-baby relationship
- The parents' own experiences of being abused
- The implicit condoning of the use of violence in childcare in the name of "discipline" in our culture.

Where to Find Help

If you have begun to hurt your baby because of his crying, or you are afraid you might very soon, you should call this hotline to find support for yourself and to keep yourself from doing physical harm to your baby. (Also look in the back of this book for a parent support organization near you.)

- *Parents Anonymous*—(800) 421-0353; (800) 352-0386 in California: A national organization of self-help groups for parents who either abuse or fear they will abuse their children.

- *National Center on Child Abuse and Neglect*—Department of Health and Human Services, Box 1182, Washington, D.C. 20013: Write for information on child abuse or for the location of your area's resource center.

How to Interpret Your Baby's Cries

Most mothers can recognize the cry of their own baby over the cries of other babies. One study found that mothers could distinguish between twenty different baby's cries on a tape, even if they were only allowed to listen to sixteen seconds of their babies' crying. Many mothers succeeded even though they had heard their babies' cry only once or twice. Long separations of mother from baby because of forceps or cesarean section deliveries did not hamper a mother's ability to tell which cries belonged to her own baby.

Sometimes mothers may feel a bit guilty because they can't tell what a baby is trying to say when he cries. Perhaps they've read that mothers are supposed to be able to discern what a baby is communicating, as though it were a hidden language.

Actually, not even trained scientists using sensitive recording equipment can discern the meaning of babies' cries beyond very simple classifications, such as hunger, rage, or pain. One study asked listeners to divide babies' cries into four causes. The researchers found that the experts were right only 60 percent of the time, while experienced mothers guessed the cause of crying about 90 percent of the time.

What's the secret of knowing one baby cry from another? Most mothers use their inner sense of their babies' daily schedule to help them, along with observing baby behavior in its everyday context.

If the baby's been asleep for three and a half hours and he wakes up crying, he's probably hungry. If the baby's been up for three hours and he seems fitful and keeps batting at his ear and mildly fussing, he's probably ready to nurse off to sleep. If he wakes up in the middle of the night with a loud, piercing scream, he's probably in pain from a diaper pin pressing into his side, a string from his sleeper wrapped around his toe, a bubble of gas trapped in his stomach, or some other inner or outer pain.

Hungry Cries

Hungry cries are more likely to be rhythmical—a short explosive cry, followed by a pause for catching breath and then another cry. A breastfeeding baby will get restless and "hyper," making complaining noises while nuzzling at your chest. Some babies mouth their fists or suck their fingers when they get hungry. As noted earlier, hungry cries can quickly change into pain cries—what parents often call going over the hill.

Pain Cries

Pain cries usually have a sudden beginning. The first cry is loud and long, followed by a long pause that seems like the baby is holding his breath. Then another alarming scream is sounded. The baby's mouth seems so wide open that his arched tongue can be seen easily inside. The baby's chin may quiver from the effort, and his feet and hands are either drawn up or cycle around tensely.

The pain cry is the most intense signal your baby has in his repertoire. Something about its shrillness and urgency sends mothers scurrying to save their offspring.

One experimenter went into the homes of babies to test how mothers responded to their babies' pain or hunger signals. In another room from the mother, with the baby out of sight, the researcher turned on a tape recording of the baby's crying. Mothers turned out to be somewhat slow in answering the hunger cry, but if a pain cry was sounded, they rushed dramatically into the room with a worried look on their faces. When they discovered it was a false alarm, the mothers got a look of relief on their faces, but they were mildly angry at having been tricked.

Fever Cries

Similar to the pain cry is the whiney, nasal cry of a baby who is flushed with fever, usually from a reaction to shots.

On the other hand, when babies are sleepy, their cries are less rhythmical than when they are crying from hunger or pain. A baby may fuss mildly as though to complain. An older baby may finger his hair, rub his eyes or an ear, or alternate between thumb-sucking and brief crying sessions.

Emotional Cries

After the baby is a few weeks of age, sometimes mothers also recognize cries of boredom or rage, or letting-off-steam cries. The bored cry sounds fake, with low, throaty moans, followed by a cry sound or two and more moans. The bored baby wants your attention and will complain until you come into sight or you pick him up for an instant cure.

"No matter how carefully I planned my day with the baby, it seemed that nearly every time my husband and I sat down for dinner, the baby would start to cry. It was impossible to eat while she was crying, and by the time she'd been diapered or burped or just comforted, my husband had finished eating and my dinner was cold. Since dinner was the time I'd counted on for the two of us to relax together, I soon began to feel very frustrated and angry at myself for not managing better."

—Geraldine Youcha,
"First Baby in the House,"
Parents Magazine,
October 1970, p. 62

A baby may become enraged if he doesn't like a position he's in. For example, some babies can't bear to be naked, to be in a baby carrier, to be swaddled, or to have a T-shirt pulled over their heads. A baby will also protest vigorously if the nipple is removed from his mouth while he's trying to nurse, or if his pacifier falls out and he's helpless to replace it.

The letting-off-steam cry usually comes in the evening after a long day of stimulation. The baby appears simply to need to cry for a while in order to discharge built-up tension. Once the baby has had time to howl out his complaint, he settles calmly down for nursing and sleep.

Babies appear to learn about the possibilities of making sounds other than the cries of hunger, rage, or pain through their own experiences. After the second month of life, when a baby is mildly complaining, he may discover that he can make new sounds. Later, when he's not in discomfort, he may try to recoup some of the sounds that he had generated at first stress.

It's not unusual to hear a baby who's alert and relatively content playfully practicing the use of his vocal cords, making gurgling "ga-ga" and "da-da" sounds. After a while, the baby bores of this, too, and sounds build up as loneliness or hunger overtakes him. These practice sessions form the basis of later language learning.

How Much Crying Is Normal?

Researchers Freda Rebelsky and Rebecca Black at Boston University have carefully studied crying babies by going to their homes. They taped small microphones in the shape of silver dollars to the shirts of ten babies during the first three months of life. Their findings are helping to dispel a lot of myths about how much or how little crying normal babies do.

When the babies in the study were between one and three weeks of age, they averaged about twenty-two minutes of crying every day. Crying increased considerably between six and seven weeks of age, usually to about thirty-four minutes a day. It then decreased to a low of about fourteen minutes a day when the babies reached twelve to thirteen weeks of age.

The most frequently crying baby in the group in the first three weeks of life averaged sixty-four minutes a day. At the peak of baby crying, between six and seven weeks, the baby who cried the most averaged a little over an hour and a quarter of daily crying.

There were tremendous variations in how much the individual babies cried on any given day. One baby cried at least a half an hour every day but peaked out one day at seventy-seven minutes. Others had a much lower range of crying, perhaps only one minute of crying in one day and a half an hour of crying on a very fussy day.

During the first three weeks of life these babies could

be found to be crying in every hour of the day or night, but the crying episodes were usually very brief. Later on, as the babies reached twelve and thirteen weeks of age, nighttime crying reduced considerably, but daytime crying was still the norm.

The babies showed crying peaks around feeding times: 7:00–8:00 in the morning, 12:00–1:00 in the afternoon, and between 5:00 and 6:00 in the evening. The most crying was done by these babies between 5:00 and 6:00 in the evening—a time at the end of the day that appears to be the most stressful for babies.

If you think your baby did better in the hospital nursery with trained nurses, you'll be relieved to know that research has shown that babies cry much more in hospital nurseries than at home, averaging almost two hours of crying a day. Babies at home, on the other hand, average between twenty-two and sixty-four minutes of crying a day.

Don't be distressed if your baby cries more than the researched babies do. Dr. T. Berry Brazelton of the Boston Children's Hospital asked eighty mothers to keep twenty-four-hour charts of their babies' crying. While all the mothers in the Rebelsky/Black study mentioned earlier were old hands at baby care, Brazelton's study used both experienced and inexperienced mothers.

All of Dr. Brazelton's normal, healthy, thriving babies started crying for significant periods of time by the time they were three weeks old. Babies peaked in their crying episodes at six weeks of age—some crying two hours, and others as much as four hours a day. He found that crying episodes began to get shorter when the babies started smiling and making other vocal sounds. Crying had pretty much stopped by the time the babies reached twelve weeks of age, perhaps because they had learned how to make alternative sounds for communication by then.

In a similar study Drs. Robert Emde and Robert Harmon and their associates at the University of Colorado School of Medicine have found three basic fussiness patterns in babies. One group of babies were fretful in the early weeks with unexplained tension and crying at about one month of age and continued fussy episodes until about three months, when they declined sharply. The second group peaked in crying much later, at about two months of age, and continued their fussiness until they were five months old. Still another group were fussy from the beginning and continued to be so until they were about four months of age. Crying gradually tapered down for these babies between four and seven months of age. Crankiness after the ending of the fussy cycle in each group usually occurred in the span of three months after it tapered off and only then because of some life change that upset the babies' routines, such as moving or out-of-town trips.

Unlike baby sleep patterns that show definite changes in maturation over time, the nature of crying remains generally the same for the first seven months of life. What happens is that a baby learns, through time, how to cry *better*. From the same amount of breath he learns how to stretch his cries into longer, more precisely targeted wails instead of the uncoordinated explosive sounds of his newborn days. A baby's use of his tongue for sound-making becomes better, so that within a few months the rudimentary beginnings of sounds that will later be speech emerge.

The groundwork is laid for entering into the complexities of human language from a baby's sense of the potency of his answered cries and through his endless practicing with sounds.

The Danger of the Too-Silent Baby

Granted, a baby who cries a great deal is difficult to manage, but a baby at the opposite extreme, who is silent most of the time and doesn't protest much, may be signaling that something is wrong emotionally.

Can a baby be too "good" at the cost of his own survival? The answer is yes for some failing-to-thrive babies. These babies show no apparent reason for their lackluster eyes, their loss of weight, and their weakening, even to the point of death. Sometimes the failing-to-thrive baby is a so-called good baby who demands very little from his parents. The baby's survival is seriously endangered by his lack of strong signaling for his deep need for closeness and intimacy.

Similarly it is considered a danger signal when a baby who is in the hospital for treatment refuses to cry rather than lustily protesting his separation from his mother and family. A serious form of withdrawal may be happening. The baby's mute silence in the face of a threatening environment may cover deep psychological distress that should be taken as seriously as the wails of a responsive, grieving baby.

Of a hundred children between the ages of four and seventeen who were referred to a British psychiatric unit because of severe emotional problems, one half were described as noncrying babies by their mothers. These silent babies who had now become children were much more likely to have serious psychological disorders, such as childhood psychosis, than those children with emotional problems who had a history of lusty protests and crying signals.

Most of the mothers labeled these silent babies as "contented." But Dr. D. S. Vorster of the Child and Family Psychiatry Service, Plymouth, England, who conducted the research, feels that the extreme withdrawal of the baby who refuses to cry is a "false independence," which may be the first sign of serious problems. In his study of teenage suicide Vorster discovered that, with few exceptions, the victims were noncrying as infants, and were typified by silent protest and disengagement from human interaction.

Similarly Dr. Emmi Pickler, a Hungarian psychiatrist, has found that babies kept in orphanages and other full-time care institutions often do not demonstrate the protest that is natural to babies. When these babies are given distasteful food, they mouth it and swallow it rather than spitting it out or refusing it, as the home-reared baby would do. Rather than trying to crawl away from being diapered, these babies lie passive and motionless. The screams of protest and temper tantrums of the eighteen-month-old or two-year-old are absent. Instead, the babies fall silently onto the floor, faces downward, passively waiting to be picked up and rerouted.

Protests and crying, then, may be healthy signs of a strong baby ego that expects prompt responses from a loving mother or father.

11
Help Your Baby to Stop Crying

Is it possible to spoil a baby by answering his cries too readily or by going to him when he wakes up over and over during the night? Some parents who have very demanding and frequently crying babies feel that they are falling into a trap of being manipulated by their babies, perhaps because that's what mothers-in-law think. "Perhaps," the reasoning goes, "we are being too soft on him. Maybe he needs to be shown who's boss."

The work of Dr. Mary B. Ainsworth and Dr. Sylvia Bell at Johns Hopkins University seems to disprove popular you're-going-to-spoil-the-baby ideas. They found that when parents responded quickly to the baby during the first few months of life, the babies cried less often and for shorter periods of time months later than the babies whose parents didn't respond well to them. It appeared that those babies whose cries were answered quickly and responsively were freed to put their energies into finding other, more acceptable ways of communicating and were more likely to show healthy independence when the time came.

"People still believe that it is possible to spoil a newborn baby by picking it up. . . . In most households with a new baby there will be voices suggesting to the mother the dangers of spoiling. A hot, red, perspiring, sobbing baby manifests his distress to all when left to cry for longer than half a minute before being picked up. . . . When a baby finally does cry himself to sleep, the mother's advisors declare a victory for their methods. Usually, however, the mother, hot, red, and perspiring herself, effectively stimulated by the crying of her own baby, is made to merely feel anxious— knowing better."

—Graham Jenkins and Richard Newton,
The First Year of Life,
pp. 94–95

How quickly a parent responds to a baby's cries dramatically influences how quickly and easily the infant can be soothed. Dr. Evelyn B. Thoman and her colleagues at the University of Connecticut have discovered that the longer a parent takes to answer a baby, the longer the baby cries afterward. The critical cutoff point for answering a baby's cries, they have found, is *a minute and a half*! If the mother answers after the first ninety seconds, the amount of time that it takes to quiet the baby triples, quadruples, or in some cases increases to fifty times longer than if she had answered quickly!

> *"I think the most important thing for me was that I did what I knew I had to do, what my baby needed, not what friends or family thought was needed."*

Parents' attitudes about spoiling can make a big difference in how they act, and subsequently how their babies act. Dr. Susan B. Crockenberg at the University of California tested expectant parents to find out about their attitudes toward spoiling the baby. Those who felt they would be hesitant about picking their babies up were more apt to have babies who cried more often and longer than parents who felt babies should be responded to.

> *"The comment that picking him up*
> *will spoil the baby can best be handled*
> *by saying 'We, the family, are much*
> *happier when the baby is happy.' Be*
> *firm on this subject."*

It has been noted that in less developed countries babies' cries are taken very seriously and answered immediately. It is only in industrialized societies, where separation of mother and baby becomes the rule rather than the exception, that there is great concern over spoiling.

In 1938 a book by authors C. A. and M. M. Aldrich, called *Babies Are Human Beings,* summed up what was later found to be true through research:

Most spoiled children are those who as babies never had essential gratification owing to a mistaken attempt to fit them into a rigid regimen. The spoiled child who has missed satisfaction as a baby adopts the efficient technique of whining and temper tantrums to get what he wants. The mechanism of spoiling is the neglect of needs rather than overindulgence. Twenty-five years' experience has taught me that responsive adults breed responsive babies, and that rigid disciplinarians of babies at this age breed spoiled, unhappy children with no confidence in themselves or their parents.

All Babies Cry Sometimes

Quick responding is the number one technique for making crying more manageable. There are times, though, when babies seem to want to cry, as though they are letting off steam.

Dr. T. Berry Brazelton in his column in *Redbook* magazine has observed how babies of the Mayan Indians in southern Mexico would cry as much as two hours a night. The babies had been carried on their mothers' bodies all day and swaddled next to them at night. The babies were allowed to nurse whenever they wanted to and sometimes the mothers kept their breasts in the babies' mouth, like a pacifier. It was rare to hear a baby cry during the day. In spite of such mother-baby intimacy, the babies would have periods of unconsolable crying during the night for as long as two hours. No one worried about it, though. The Indians had a saying for such behavior: "When everyone gets quiet, it's the baby's turn to do the talking."

Ina Mae Gaskin, author of *Spiritual Midwifery*, thinks that parents shouldn't get too upset about a baby's crying either. "All babies cry sometimes," she says. "Act, but don't get uptight about it—it's no big deal."

> *"Sometimes you just have to let a baby cry a bit. After a while, you learn how to tell what some cries mean. You'll find yourself wondering what the cry is saying rather than just jumping up at the noise itself. Perhaps your baby is just tired but too wound up from excitement to go to sleep. He just needs some time to let off steam before falling asleep."*

Both Dr. Brazelton and Ms. Gaskin suggest that once you've responded to your baby and checked out all of the possible causes for crying, let him fuss for a while. It may be that he's collected tension inside himself and needs to vent it, just as adults get tense if they don't let out their frustrations. There's a difference between *not responding* and *responding and allowing,* in which you've used your judgment about what your baby seems to need. Babies in pain should have human comfort, and those screams are different from those of a baby too wound up to go to sleep. Ms. Gaskin describes the situation in her book *Spiritual Midwifery.*

> Sometimes a new baby will get into an uptight energy loop with you and will cry no matter what you do. In a case like this, you can make sure he's fed and dry, put him in his bed . . . tell him to go to sleep, and then leave him alone to do it. He'll probably cry for a couple of minutes and then go to sleep.

She suggests that if the baby doesn't settle down after a while, you put him in a baby carrier and go on about your business.

Don't Try to Train Your Baby Not to Cry

Most psychologists believe that a baby's crying is a potent, built-in signal for help. But there are a few who feel that crying is a learned behavior. They have no doubt studied the work of B. F. Skinner, the first behaviorist, who could radically alter the behavior of animals by giving or withholding rewards, a process called "reinforcement." When animals were given positive rewards—reinforcement—such as food pellets when they were very hungry, Skinner could train them to do all kinds of ornate tricks if each step of the trick was rewarded with food.

Certain psychologists reasoned that perhaps baby crying was a learned behavior—that by responding to the baby with food, parents were training their babies to wake up over and over during the night, crying to eat. If crying was learned, they decided, then it could be unlearned, "extinguished," by parents not rewarding it.

These behaviorists advised parents to ignore crying at

a certain hour of the night, say 4:00 A.M., believing that it would stop. In some cases the approach worked. If the parents consistently refused to go to the baby at 4:00 A.M., some babies stopped crying.

Many baby-development specialists have raised serious questions about the let-them-cry-it-out school of reasoning. More and more it is being discovered that a human baby is a complex, feeling being. The danger is that the baby may adopt a pattern of giving up, or hopelessness, when his cries are consistently not answered. Your not responding, rather than causing the baby to stop crying, may teach the baby that it is hopeless to try—that he is powerless to make things happen for himself.

"Ideally, crying should teach the child optimism about the environment, which he learns when his cries are answered. An infant as young as eight weeks is capable of understanding this, and of appreciating the fact that he can cause things to happen."

—Michael Lewis,
Professor of Pediatrics at
Rutgers Medical School,
Quoted in *The New York Times*,
Nov. 11, 1981

Some parents have found that the cry-it-out strategy, though giving temporary relief, has backfired. The baby gives up asking for parental response for a while, but the old cycle of awakening returns—this time with nighttimes as periods of high anxiety for a baby who now not only must struggle with hunger pangs, but also with the fear of being abandoned by his loved ones when darkness sets in.

As you will see later on in Chapter Twelve, separation from the baby during the day, and the bodily separation of a baby from his mother by the use of a crib, can affect night demands. Assuring your baby of your continual closeness may help the baby to ease into sleep more readily.

"Somewhere along the line my husband and I realized that we did not have an average baby. Our crying baby in many ways is a special child. Once the realization sank in, we felt less threatened by meeting her special needs. We could then more easily turn a deaf ear to well-meaning friends who insisted that we were surely spoiling her. We have decided that we have a beautiful baby who needs lots of extra love and comforting."

The best approach, it appears, from research and from the advice of experienced parents, is to respond quickly to the baby. Give him what he seems to need and then, if he seems to want to cry for a few minutes in order to sleep, allow the baby the space to fall back on his own resources.

Some babies are more resourceful than others. Some grow better in time with their self-management. Others aren't self-managers at all and need a mother's intervention and soothing to let go, even if it's only for a few hours. Ultimately it comes down to your wisdom and compassion— two things that are critical but difficult to muster in the middle of the night!

Your Baby's Shutdown System and How to Use It

In a sense the human baby undergoes an additional out-of-the-womb pregnancy in the arms of his mother and father during the first months after birth. He is at their mercy to provide him with the milk and warmth that he needs to survive. Human breast milk is adaptive to almost continual feedings both day and night. The newborn's temperature regulation system appears to be built to function

Why Babies Cry and What to Do About It

Assuming that your baby has no long-term chronic problems that cause pain over and over, here are the most common reasons for baby crying and what you can do to intervene.

Cause	Symptom	What to Do
Hunger	Rhythmical, brief cries that get more and more intense until they turn into pain cries.	Let the baby establish his own schedule for feeding rather than an arbitrary three- or four-hour schedule. Check bottle nipples to see that the hole is not too small—liquid should drip out when the bottle is inverted. If breast-feeding, let the baby nurse more frequently so that your milk production increases, and allow the baby a long time at each breast if he's eager to suck.
Overfeeding	Frequent spitting up and discomfort soon after meals that seem to be from stomach distension.	A young baby's stomach holds only small amounts of milk. Some irritable babies improve with more frequent, smaller feeds rather than widely spaced, large feeds.

Cause	Symptom	What to Do
Thirst	(Bottlefed babies) Same as hunger cries but unsatisfied by formula. Caused by excessive sodium in the formula. More frequent in hot weather or mid-winter when furnace heat is excessively drying.	Offer the baby water by the teaspoon that has been boiled. To provide air humidity, install a cold air humidifier or an aquarium in the nursery, or keep damp towels over the heating vent. (Keep the humidifier washed out with soap and water so bacteria don't form.)
Tiredness or Overstimulation	The baby fusses and complains sporadically. May bat at ears or look swollen-eyed. Will turn away from adults trying to play or talk to him. May seem to "want" to cry at times as though to let off steam, especially in the evenings.	Nurse the baby to sleep in bed. You sleep, too. You probably need it as badly as he does. If bottlefeeding, give the baby the bottle and let him drink while falling asleep in your arms before lowering him into bed. Hold back from jiggling, loud, jazzy play or other vigorous play in the late afternoon. Put the baby in a Snugli or other fabric carrier and go for a long, soothing walk. Perhaps letting the baby fall asleep in an upright seat or on a quilt on the floor while you pat his back will quiet down a baby who's had too much handling.

Too Cold

Baby is startled and cries when undressed or placed on changing pad; shudders or turns blueish.

Some babies are more cold sensitive than others. The facedown position for sleeping conserves heat the best. Keep towels warming on the heat vent or on top of the hot water heater and use them to cover cold surfaces such as the changing table. Use a specially processed lambskin pelt as a changing table cover. Wipe the baby clean with warm, damp washcloths under a receiving blanket and wait until he's older for actual immersion baths. Warm up the crib with a hot water bottle, using warm water, or a warm electric heating pad before settling the baby down to sleep. Keep booties on day and night. Wet diapers will sometimes make a baby cry if they become cold, but there's no need to wake a sleeping baby to change them.

Cause

Too Hot

Bowel Movement or Urination

Symptom

Irritable, whiny baby is flushed red, may be sweaty, breathes rapidly. (Check for fever if the baby seems sick or has had a shot within three to twenty-four hours.)

The baby turns red and seems to squirm and strain to pass a BM or to urinate; seems fussy as time nears, or screams out in pain.

What to Do

Babies need no more clothing or covering than adults do. Overheating, especially in winter, from blanket sleepers that don't allow the baby to cool off naturally, can cause a serious form of heatstroke and possibly death. Fasten baby's blanket to the crib bars with spring-operated shower curtain rings or specially designed blanket rings (from nursery specialty stores) so that air can get in.

These symptoms should be brought to the attention of your doctor, since they may mean a possible constriction of the baby's urinary passage or anus. Some babies have too small an anus and can be helped by the insertion of your lubricated little finger (clip fingernail as close as possible) or the use of a small glycerin suppository. (Ask your doctor first.)

Internal Pain

Screaming pain from immature digestive system, teething pain, muscle aches, and inner ear infection.

See Part One, especially Chapters One and Two.

External Pain

The baby may wake up in the night with piercing screams or suddenly start intense pain cries for no apparent reason.

Check for the proverbial diaper pin. Crying may also be caused by tight bands on clothing, scratchy leakproof pants, or irritating fabrics. Check each toe and finger carefully to see if they have become strangled by a loose string on a sleeper or blanket or a long hair coil.

Cause

Loneliness or Boredom

Symptom

The coos and gurgles of a three-month-old or older child build up into protests and wails. The baby seems discontent in his infant seat, playpen, or crib, or you've left him in another room and he can't see you any longer.

What to Do

Carry a newborn or young baby on your body with a Snugli or other carrier. Keep the baby near you so that he can see where you are. Try stringing noisy rattles on the playpen mesh so baby can activate them with his feet. Suspend a musical mobile or other colorful objects overhead. Hand him a rattle, teething beads on a string, or a cool, damp washcloth to chew on. Play peekaboo, or put the baby on his stomach on a quilt on the floor with soft toys in sight. Best of all, pick the baby up and carry him around with you, describe what you're doing, show him how the lights turn off and on, or do other conversational things with him.

Air Swallowing

(Breastfeeding) Pain immediately after eating. During feedings, if milk leaks out of the side of the mouth when he swallows, he may have an ineffective vacuum seal of his mouth on the breast; also, too fast a milk letdown in the mother sometimes causes air gulping. Long crying bouts may cause air swallowing.

(Bottlefeeding) A bottle nipple that has holes too small or too large may cause excessive air to be trapped in baby's stomach, giving him discomfort.

If air causes discomfort, burp the baby by either placing him up on your shoulder, patting his back, or bending him forward in a sitting position in your lap while rubbing his back. Keeping a baby upright after feeding in a car seat or sturdy infant seat can sometimes bring relief from stomach congestion, as can lying the baby on his right side for a few moments and then holding him upright again. (Note: Routine burping is not needed for most breastfed babies.)

on the supplied heat of another body besides his own. Unlike most creatures, the human baby is almost totally vulnerable without adult intervention.

One primitive, but very useful capacity mercifully built in to the baby is the ability to shut down awareness when life outside the womb becomes too threatening or overwhelming. How the shutdown system works is not completely understood as yet. Scientists theorize that the baby's primitive nerve pathways can handle only a few incoming signals at a time in the first months. Thus, a young infant cannot suck *and* pay attention to a rattle at the same time.

Certain incoming signals have priority over others, particularly those that travel over the baby's most mature systems—those that require his sense of hearing, his sense of balance, and his sucking reflexes. When strong signals come through these systems, other competing signals are switched off or muted. The only turnoffs under a baby's control are moving his head or eyes away from something—gaze aversion—crying, and sleep. The other closing down mechanisms come from outside of himself.

Here are the basic shutdown signals of your baby's and how you can use them to soothe and stabilize him when he is fussy or irritable. (*Shutdown signals will not make a baby forget he is in pain or that he is hungry, since pain and hunger take precedence over all signals.*)

Sucking

The act of sucking or nursing appears effectively to block incoming signals, including pain. It appears that by focusing on his mouth and tongue area and his sucking, the baby completely turns his attention away from outside stimuli. Babies who are able to master the art of finger- and hand-sucking appear to cry much less than babies who have no self-soothing techniques. A pacifier, too, can be used in the early months to help a baby remain calm and oblivious to discomforts and irritations. *Tip: For much milder response on his part, let the baby nurse while he gets injections.*

Noise

The baby's hearing system is quite well developed at birth and afterward, much more so than his visual capacities. For some reason certain sounds cause the baby to blank out stimuli coming from inside or outside of himself so that relaxation and sleep soon follow. The most effective sounds are monotonous and droning, or rhythmical and repetitive. Here are some sound sources you can try with your baby:

- Vacuum cleaner motor
- Running dishwasher or clothes dryer
- White noise from a radio station off the air
- Recordings of human womb noises
- Recordings of your baby's own crying.

Tip: Make an hour-long tape of the vacuum cleaner to play at naptimes.

Motion

As noted earlier, the baby's vestibular system, the intricate organs that tell the baby where he is in space, is a relatively mature system at birth. Rhythmical motions stimulate the vestibular system, acting as powerful inhibitors of minor discomforts. Here are ways of providing motion:

- Walking with the baby
- Rocking chair or cradle

- Baby carriage with springs
- Wind-up baby swing (some have cradle attachments)
- Snugli or other front fabric carrier that attaches the baby to you as you walk or work
- Moving baby up and down in wide arcs, almost to the point of deep knee bends
- Car rides with baby in the car seat.

Tip: Make your baby carrier, or rebozo, out of a square yard of cloth tied like a sling for a broken arm.

Body Immobilization

Many babies have an overactive startle response that makes them jerk back over and over, throwing their arms outward, followed by clutching forward with their hands as if to grab on to the parent. From the looks of it these babies have a fear of falling. When they are naked, or touch the cold changing table, or have their positions changed rapidly, especially when going down backward, they seem to feel as if they are sky divers in the first few seconds after falling out of a plane. Body immobilization—holding them down—can help these babies to relax and let go. Sometimes just holding down an arm or a leg will be soothing enough.

Swaddling

Swaddling is a time-honored way of dealing with baby skittishness. Put the baby in the center of a receiving blanket with one corner of the blanket positioned over his head, one below his feet, and one beyond each arm. Fold up the bottom corner of the blanket over the baby's feet. Pull in the side corners and wrap them around the baby so that his arms are held still. (A diaper pin can be used to keep the blanket fastened into a cocoon.) The top corner can be used as a hood to cover the back of the baby's head. Stretchy Ace bandages can be used to gently wrap around the baby from the feet upward. Be careful not to wrap so tightly that the baby's circulation is affected, and avoid the baby's neck area, which is very vulnerable to strangulation.

Wedging

Put the baby, wrapped in a blanket, on his right side so that his back is up against the crib's bumpers and his head is touching the top padded corner. Place a firm stuffed toy or small pillow against his abdomen to brace him in this position. (Avoid placing pillows around the baby's face area.) You can also put the baby in a small padded cardboard box so that he feels enclosed (without the lid, though, since the baby needs air). Often babies will naturally gravitate to a corner of the crib because they long for the comfort and security of close head confinement.

12
Why Your Baby Doesn't
"Sleep like a Baby"

In the early 1900s baby doctors claimed that the reason why infants slept so much was because of the lack of oxygen to the brain from drinking too much mother's milk. Later on it was believed that the baby's immature brain got fatigued much faster than an adult's and thus needed more rest. Most people still regard sleep as the opposite of being awake.

Scientists are now peering into the crib with a number of precise instruments in order to find out what baby sleep is really like. What they are finding is that the old phrase "He sleeps like a baby" couldn't be *more wrong* in describing how babies sleep.

Because a baby's brain, like an adult's brain, operates with low-level, detectable electricity, researchers have begun to employ a measurement device called an electroencephalogram, or EEG. By taping flat metal discs called electrodes onto the baby's head, the electrical activity of the baby's brain can be transcribed as jagged waves made by an oscillating pen on a moving sheet of paper. The lines are called brain waves.

The brain waves of babies and their mothers have yielded rather startling information. For example, the rest-activity cycles of babies in the last months before birth correspond to their mothers'; *but* it is not the baby who sleeps more like the mother. It is the mother who, because of profound hormonal changes, becomes aligned with her baby in sleeping patterns! Immediately after giving birth, the mother returns to her more normal sleep patterns, while the newborn's sleep cycle seems to maintain the rest-activity patterns he has established before birth.

The brain wave patterns of newborns show that they undergo three very distinct phases of sleep: active sleep, quiet sleep, and a transitional sleep sometimes called the "basic rest activity cycle," or BRAC. In a given bout of sleep your baby will fall into active sleep, then have a period of BRAC, followed by deep sleep, then will fall back into active sleep over and over in repetitive minicycles.

Your baby will make about nine transitions in the night between active and deep sleep, and it is in these shifts that he is most likely to cry out, lift up his head to look around, turn himself over by mistake, or arouse himself to being completely awake. About an hour after falling asleep many babies predictably cry out briefly as they move into another active sleep episode.

The term *active sleep* is well chosen, for when the amount of physical restlessness that a baby displays during this phase is measured by motion-sensitive, air-filled mattresses, it is found that a baby is often more active during active sleep than he is during normal wakefulness! While observing your baby during active sleep, you'll sometimes see his eyes moving under closed, or partially opened eyelids. He may chew or chomp, or move his mouth like he's nursing. He will probably move around restlessly.

During quiet sleep, on the other hand, the baby is still and his breathing is regular. His eyelids are firmly closed and his face seems totally relaxed. There are few or no mouth movements. If you happen to jar the crib during a period of quiet sleep, the baby may experience a strong startle, yet during active sleep such a movement seems to have no effect.

Another state directly related to baby sleep is drowsiness. When your baby is getting ready to go to sleep, his eyelids seem to get very heavy and turn red. Sometimes his eyes flutter open and closed and his eyes have a dull, glazed appearance to them, as though they are unfocused. His eyes may roll backward in his head. Within one to two minutes your baby will fall asleep. Some new parents even mistake a sleeping baby for an awake one, and may try to make a drowsy, half-conscious baby eat, without much success.

It's much easier for a baby to end sleep than it is for him to begin sleep. The amount of time required to fall asleep decreases over the first three months after birth, with a major shift occurring between three and five weeks of age. It takes an awake two-month-old an average of twenty-seven minutes to get to sleep, but it takes a six-month-old only about sixteen minutes to accomplish the same feat.

Babies don't sleep the same way that their parents do. Parents usually fall directly from drowsiness into deep sleep. It takes an adult about an hour and a half to get around to an active sleep episode. A baby normally falls from drowsiness directly into active sleep. He will spend about one half of his total sleeping hours, nine or more hours, in active sleep. His parents will spend one-fourth of their sleeping time in this phase, only about two hours in all.

Surprisingly, brain waves show that there's very little distinction between a baby's active sleep pattern brain waves and the brain waves of the awake baby when he sucks, fusses, or cries. Adults, too, have been found to have brief active sleep episodes in the process of the day even when they are fully awake. Scientists believe they are seeing in the brain waves of both babies not a clear-cut division of asleep and awake states but a twenty-four-hour brain rhythm. In other words, sleep isn't really sleep, and wakefulness isn't really wakefulness. Both are portions of a larger, overriding brain cycle.

The Purpose of Baby Sleep Cycles

The reason why babies require so much more active sleep than adults do will still remain a mystery until more precise brain studies can be carried out, but the theories themselves are intriguing.

Premature babies are known to spend as much as 80 percent of their time in active sleep. This corresponds directly to the period when the baby's brain is growing at its most rapid rate. The firing rate of electricity in the adult's brain is as high in active sleep as it is in wakefulness, though more irregular in patterning. Animal studies have shown that during active sleep oxygen intake increases, the blood pressure in the brain rises, and the circulation of blood to the brain increases as much as 50 percent over other sleep states.

Active sleep, then, seems to be directly related to brain growth and development.

While active sleep is a chaotic and unpredictable happening in babies, the phase called quiet sleep is sophisticated and becomes stabilized by as early as the second week after birth. It appears to be instrumental in body growth and the repair of tissues. Human growth hormone (HGH) is only secreted during this phase in children and adults.

As the baby matures active sleep declines rapidly and quiet sleep increases. For some unknown reason a changeover in baby sleep takes place sometime between two and three months of age. Quiet sleep takes domination over sleep cycles in a sudden jump that is marked by the baby now falling directly into quiet sleep from wakefulness, as his parents do. The brain stimulation from active sleep now appears to be less necessary.

Brief Facts About Baby Sleep

- Baby sleep-wake patterns begin to form even before birth.
- The typical sleep pattern for newborns is to sleep during the day and be awake at night—the very opposite of their parents' cycles.
- Most newborns sleep for two to four hours at a time. The average is three and a half hours.
- The range of sleep needed by young babies varies from twenty-three out of twenty-four hours, to ten hours out of twenty-four.
- Babies' sleeping patterns seem, for the most part, to be biologically determined.
- The phrase *sleep through the night* used by mothers usually means that the baby has one long span of sleep between midnight and 5:00 A.M.
- In rare instances a baby may sleep through the night as early as ten days after birth, but the typical age for doing so is three months.
- Waking up once, twice, or three times during the night is very common. Between one third and one quarter of all babies continue to wake up during the night even after one year of age.
- Feeding the baby solid foods appears to have little effect on sleep length.
- Erratic sleeping cycles in babies have been associated with prolonged labors, lack of oxygen, and other birth complications.
- Exposing the baby to light-dark cycles and gently paring off the ends of a baby's naps appear to be the most effective methods for slowly altering a baby's day-night sleeping rhythms.
- Some babies awaken in the night because of their fear of separation from their mothers. Taking the baby into the parents' bed can sometimes help.

Your Baby's Master Clock

For decades researchers have known that plants and unicellular animals are profoundly affected by the day-night cycles of the earth, but the study of sleep rhythms in humans, and especially babies, is very recent.

The bodies of most animals and human adults exist on a circadian rest-activity pattern, which means that there are predictable ups and downs of body energy and functioning over each twenty-four-hour period. Grown-ups also have daytime—(diurnal)—and nighttime—(nocturnal)—cycles. For example, the adult body temperature troughs between 4:00 and 5:00 in the morning. Temperature rises slowly, reaching the pinnacle of warmth between 4:00 and 5:00 in the evening. Other body functions that show periodicity are growth and development, blood pressure, cell division, and hormonal changes.

"Don't make any decisions in the wee hours of the morning, such as weaning, giving the baby away the next day, or leaving for Tahiti by yourself. You're not fully awake and aware, and often things will look different in the morning."

The development of rest and activity cycles in the baby seems to depend a great deal on maturation. There appears to be a master synchronizer in the baby's brain that determines when organ systems are ready to begin following the twenty-four-hour cycles typical of more mature organisms.

Interestingly, the most mature organ system in the baby is his skin, and it is already into twenty-four-hour, day-night rhythms at birth. The body temperature regulators, the excretion patterns of urine, and the secretion of other body chemicals and hormones lag behind by months until the baby's inborn master timer decides to set the internal clocks.

A German researcher, Theodor Hellbrügge, and his associates have examined the sleep/wake patterns of hundreds of babies over more than a thousand hours of sleep and wakefulness. What they have found is that not only do newborns not have day-night body cycles, but they are *much more likely to be awake at night than during the daytime.* In other words, their typical sleep-wake cycle is exactly the opposite of their parents'.

It is not until around the fourth month of life that the cycle of being awake mostly during the day and sleeping mostly during the night settles for most babies. Then, too, the baby's body temperature, his heart rate, his urine excretion, and other bodily functions show the more adultlike peaks and troughs.

Most researchers now agree that babies do not *learn* to sleep at night in the sense that their parents teach them. Rather, sleeping patterns appear to emerge as a form of biological adaptation on the part of the baby's body, intimately related to the maturation of many other systems.

> *"If you're up a lot at night, try not to look at the clock. It can be very depressing to know that you've been up three times in one hour, or you've been up for two hours, or you've only got two hours of sleep left until the older children wake up for school."*

The reason for delayed day-night predictability in babies appears to be a biologically sound one. This prolonged irregularity signifies a final elaboration of neural organization in the baby's body. Babies are given, by nature, a period of plasticity while a very complex nervous system elaborates and unfolds.

Is He a Good Baby? Does He "Sleep Through the Night"?

Nosy Aunt Clara leans down to look over the baby in his stroller. She asks the age-old question that relatives always ask: "Is he a *good* baby?" which is followed quickly by "Does he sleep through the night yet?"

By now you've learned to hedge a bit. "I think *all* babies are good, don't you, Aunt Clara? *Why*, pray tell, do you ask?" Score one victory for the little people of the world.

If your baby doesn't sleep through the night yet, don't be concerned. Researchers have discovered that when most mothers use the phrase, it is a euphemism for a baby sleeping for one long period, say, between midnight and 5:00 A.M. So your baby may not be doing as badly in the sleep department as it seems when you're having conversations.

> *"There were days when I cried when my friends talked about their babies taking three-hour naps!"*

There are rare babies who, indeed, adapt to clear daynight rhythms by as early as ten days after birth. More typically a young baby sleeps one and a half to three hours at a stretch with an occasional freak doubling up of two sleep periods.

The sleep needs of any group of babies show wide variations, indeed. Some newborns may sleep as much as twenty-three out of twenty-four hours (especially if they've gotten a dose of the mother's drugs during labor). Others appear to only need ten or twelve hours of sleep. Some babies show a period of initial sluggishness and heavy sleep in the early days, only to be followed by tremendous irritation and wakefulness weeks later.

Some babies may sleep through the night after the second or third week of life and then begin to wake up during the night again. Those babies who do wake nightly usually show patterns of gradually decreasing frequency of arousal. For others the transition into long sleep is almost overnight, as though the babies forget to wake up. Still others simply sleep increasingly longer in the mornings. Another group are completely erratic in their night waking patterns, with no seeming predictability at all.

For most babies it's not until the third month of life that sleep begins to show longer, more adultlike patterns. One study found that seventy percent of the babies observed sleep from midnight to early morning by the age of three months. By six months of age eighty-three percent had "settled." Once babies settle into regular sleep patterns, *approximately half of them will go back into night-waking again in the months to follow. Ten percent of the babies—one out of every ten—never sleep through the night during the first year of life!*

The Infant Sleep Disturbance Syndrome

Why do some babies never sleep through the night, showing erratic, unpredictable sleeping patterns that may not settle until after the preschool years? One study has shown that as many as thirty percent of all babies at four months of age and seventeen percent of all babies at six months of age fail to sleep through from midnight to 5:00 A.M.

In a survey of toddlers twenty-three percent of the babies were found to wake up one, two, or three times in the night at fifteen months old, twenty-two percent did at twenty-one months, and twenty-eight percent did at twenty-seven months of age. Thus, it is clear that night-waking in babyhood is extremely common.

Whether a baby's waking during the night is considered a serious problem seems to depend upon how the mother or the father feels about it. For example, when one group of mothers was asked how long they would like their babies to be awake during the daytime, most expressed a preference for about eight hours. In reality, their babies were awake eleven hours. Over and over again mothers wanted their babies to sleep at least three more hours than they really did. As the babies grew older, the number of hours the mothers wanted their babies to sleep increased—perhaps because of their own fatigue and the sense of being caught up in the baby's cycles.

> *"Not knowing how long a baby's nap will be is as exasperating as their lack of length. When my baby does sleep, it's hard for me to decide whether to eat or to sleep. Taking a shower is the impossible dream."*

In some instances the night-waking baby is a superactive, very sensitive child. At least one research study has found a connection between the need for less sleep and higher intelligence in some babies. The very alert, always-moving baby sleeps less, demands more, and crawls, walks, and talks sooner than his more sluggish counterparts. He whisks through the developmental stages at breakneck speed, often at the cost of being sedentary at night.

A few researchers seem to feel that there may be a connection between a baby's weight, his subcutaneous fat, and his sleeping regularity. The popular notion is that babies begin to sleep better when they reach about twelve pounds, and that heavy, plump babies tend to be more regular sleepers than thin, wiry babies. Mothers seem to confirm this notion, but research doesn't show any relationship between sleep differences and baby size.

The cycles of quiet and active sleep are totally disorganized in babies who have been severely damaged during birth. Since quiet sleep is the state with the most degree of balance, it is usually the first to show alterations in pathological conditions. Babies with milder degrees of birth trauma, and those of diabetic mothers and heroin-addicted mothers, also show altered quiet sleep patterns.

"My baby didn't want to be held when he was trying to go to sleep. I found out that if I just put him down, he would fret for a few minutes and then fall quickly off to sleep. If I held him, he got restless and more and more unhappy until he was crying. He seemed to want to go to sleep on his own."

Dr. Judy Bernal, a British psychiatrist, in a study of seventy-seven night-waking toddlers, found that many had experienced longer than normal labors at birth. The labors of the mothers of night-wakers lasted twelve to thirteen hours, but only six to nine hours for the normal sleepers. These babies also had more difficulty in established breathing immediately after birth, and they had significantly lower ratings for skin color, muscle tone, and reflex irritability.

Dr. Thomas Anders and his associates at Stanford University have now developed a computer profile of baby sleep patterns that precisely defines ninety-four different sleep characteristics using EEG's. The purpose of the Infant Sleep Profile will be to diagnose brain damage in babies days after birth, since they usually have poorer sleep-organizing capacities then. Researchers believe that soon it will be possible to predict with a high level of success which babies will sleep well and which ones are destined to be night owls.

Solids and "Sleeping Through"

A survey of baby-feeding has been carried out in England and on a hundred mothers with babies between six weeks and six months of age, to find out if feeding the baby solids influenced the babies' waking up during the night. Forty-nine babies gave up the nighttime feeding before getting solids, fourteen long after solids had begun, and eighteen soon after solids had been started. The researchers conclude that there is little evidence to sustain the belief that feeding a baby cereal will make a baby sleep through the night. Dr. R. M. Robertson states, "Perhaps these findings may help to counter some rather persuasive advertising and avoid sowing some of the seeds of later infant obesity" (*British Medical Journal,* Vol. 1, Feb. 2, 1974, p. 200).

The Connection Between Sleep and Separation

The nightly sleeping rhythms of infant monkeys may help researchers to get a clearer understanding of the sleep of human infants. Monkeys have been used because their environments can be so easily controlled and their patterns of sleep come closest to human patterns.

It has been found that each monkey species—and the individual monkeys of the given species—has its own unique sleeping patterns. However, the basic, laid-down cycles seem unaltered by the environment. For example, there is little difference between the sleep of monkey infants reared in the stress of total isolation from that of infants reared in the constant companionship of their mothers.

One notable exception to this finding is the sleep of infant monkeys who belong to a species that is characterized by close mother-infant bonding from birth onward. If infants in this species are reared with their mothers and then must endure separation during the night, their sleeping patterns show profound alterations with a marked shortening of quiet sleep episodes.

Separation of the monkey mother from her offspring seems to affect her behavior as well. Her capacity for precisely synchronizing her interactions with her infant—her attunement to her baby—breaks down during the separation. For a period of time after reunion with her baby she is unable to carry on the relationship quite as well as she could before the separation.

"No other society prepares its children for independence as we do. We feel that the first step in building an independent character begins with early nighttime separation from parents. Many children find this a harsh lesson. Most adults forget that sleep is lonely. Children express their loneliness by crying. They're trying to say, 'I want to be with you. I don't want to be abandoned.' In other societies and in other animal species families sleep in the same room. In our cultures youngsters are put in a room by themselves, the light is turned off, the door is shut, and that's all."

**—Dr. Wilse Webb,
Research Professor of Psychology,
The University of Florida,
Quoted in "Good Night, Sleep Tight, Please,"
Ruth Winter, *Parents*, December 1978,
pp. 57–58**

It would be a mistake to overdraw the connection between monkeys and humans, since humans have been found to be much more adaptable than monkeys, but it is known that long-term separations of mothers and their babies can cause a separation syndrome in human babies as well.

First the baby seems very distressed. He then moves into a stage of despair, followed by apathy and detachment. When the baby appears to accept the separation, say, in a hospital setting, it may be at the cost of his emotional tie with his mother and his ability to sustain relationships for a time. After the separation is over and the baby returns to his parents, he may seem detached and treat his mother as though she were a stranger. Later he may go to the opposite extreme for a time, becoming overly dependent and clinging, refusing to be left alone.

Such behavior is more predominant in the baby of six months of age or older, when separation appears to be more stressful than earlier. Yet it is plausible that the enforced nightly separation of mother and baby that so characterizes our society may play a part in long-term sleeplessness of separation-sensitive babies. *Judging from the history of humankind and baby-rearing practices worldwide, separation of mother and infant during the night is an abnormal pattern of behavior.*

The stages of distress, despair, and apathy occur more often on nights when parents are under stress and become hostile toward the baby, threatening physical punishment when he doesn't cooperate by falling off to sleep quickly in his crib. It's the very fear of separation that may be keeping the baby aroused, since deep sleep for all creatures is predicated on a sense of safety and security from dangers, real or imagined.

The human baby is somewhat unique in his prolonged dependency after birth. He is unable to move himself physically to where his parents are in the months following birth. Rather, he is dependent upon his signaling capacity, his crying, to bring his parents to him.

All of the baby's existence needs are tied up in the responsiveness of his primary caregiver. The baby is not mature enough yet to console himself with the concepts of "safe bedroom," or "safe crib," because for him safety is a body feeling that comes from the sense of warmth and enfoldment of an adult.

Ironically the very thing that most parents do to get more sleep causes them to get less sleep. Here's the typical logic that is involved: A parent feels (s)he can sleep better if the baby is in another place, and so the baby is put into a crib in a separate room. The baby becomes frightened by the isolation and cries out to bring the parent close. The parent, who is sleeping, becomes aroused by the crying, a built-in, unavoidable reaction. The parent gets up and gives the baby food. The baby goes to sleep in the parent's arms. The parent returns the baby to the crib and goes back to the bedroom to sleep. The baby sleeps until hunger pangs and loneliness rearouse him. The baby cries, the parent is aroused . . . and so the night passes. Both the parent and the baby are unnerved and frustrated.

If separation is what is bothering your baby the most (other than his natural nightly needs to be fed), then reuniting him with your body closeness during the night should markedly improve his night-waking symptoms. One way to test if this is true is to take the baby into bed with you for a week or two to see if his night-waking decreases. (You may find that you get more sleep as well.)

"You don't put a baby who doesn't sleep well in a crib, you put him in the bed with you. Just throw your crib away and buy a new dress. Once he's asleep, don't move him. Once you move him, that's it!"

Bed-sharing may be more manageable when the mattress is put on the floor so that your fears of the baby's falling out of bed are eased. Other parents have found that lowering one side of the crib, and the baby's mattress, to the last position may enable it to fit flush against the side of the parents' bed so that the baby can be easily transferred back and forth.

Common Objections to Sleeping with the Baby

"He will turn out to be a homosexual."

If that were true, then 90 percent of the world's population would be homosexual—since it is rare in most human societies for babies to not sleep with their mothers. Virtually all mammals with young bed down with them.

"He will smother in the blankets."

Research has shown that bedding has totally adequate air ventilation for an infant's survival needs. Babies also have built-in face-protection reflexes, and they use their hands to bat down face coverings.

"My husband will roll over onto him."

Some fathers, perhaps, are not as aware as others while asleep, but babies have the self-saving capacity to cry, kick, squirm, and move themselves if they have to. Put baby on the other side of yourself if Dad worries you.

"The baby will spoil our sex life."

Most couples find other places for their togetherness when they allow the bed to belong to the family.

"The baby will mess up the bed and spit up on it."

Probably true. You can use a waterproof mattress cover or a waterproof pad, and waterproof diaper covers, and you can keep towels handy. Everything can be washed, anyway.

"I can't sleep with the baby next to me. He keeps me awake."

It may take awhile to get used to your small nighttime companion, but most mothers report that the luxury of waking up with their babies is very sweet and memorable.

"My husband doesn't want it. He needs his rest to get up to go to work."

Caring for a baby is equally as demanding as any salaried position, if not more so. You need your sleep in order to give to the baby during the day. After all, the baby belongs to both of you, and by giving in to the baby's inborn need for closeness, you are insuring the conservation of his body energies for emotional as well as physical growth.

Shaping Baby Sleep

Are there techniques that parents can use to help their babies sleep more at night? Very little research has been done on altering baby sleep behavior; nonetheless, there are some very intriguing small studies that look to be promising in altering a baby's day-night sleep habits. Since the number of babies studied is so small, and factors such as natural sleep changes are not controlled, the studies must be taken simply as examples of possible, but not thoroughly tested, approaches.

Light and Darkness

The alternation of light and darkness appears to be a possible influence for inducing daytime wakefulness and nighttime sleeping in babies. In a study done in France two babies were kept in continuous light from the eighth day of life onward. Similar to babies under normal conditions, these babies' sleep patterns and demands for food were quite irregular in the first few weeks of life. By the eighth week of life the babies developed a definite sleep rhythm, but due to the lack of exposure to light and darkness, the rhythm appeared between 5:00 A.M. and 1:00 P.M. When the babies were exposed to the light of day and the darkness of night at three months of age, within nine days their rhythms had altered to sleeping between 7:30 P.M. and 5:00 A.M.

There may, in fact, be great wisdom in the practice of Swedish and Russian mothers of letting their babies sleep in the outdoor sunshine. Even in the middle of winter these babies are swaddled soundly, except for their faces, and then placed outside in their carriages for their naps. Not only is the air more healthy than the stale air inside heated buildings, but the strong in-pouring of light probably helps to influence the babies' inner clocks toward more nocturnal sleeping patterns.

Reward

A second promising study has used the principle of positive reward to alter a baby's night-waking patterns. Rita McGarr of Byron Union School and Melbourne Hovell of the Stanford University School of Medicine report their approach in the *Education and Treatment of Children* (1980, vol. 3, pp. 73–80).

The parents in this study had tried letting their three-month-old baby "cry it out," only to have the baby scream for two hours. They had added solid foods to the baby's diet and had tried other strategies to promise sleep, none of which worked.

Rather than having the parents punish the baby for not sleeping by ignoring her cries, McGarr and Hovell devised a way that the baby could be reinforced for sleeping. The results showed that the technique worked, since rewarding positive behavior is far more powerful in changing how babies and children behave than punishment is.

First the parents of the baby kept a detailed record of her night-waking patterns for two weeks, so that they knew when and for how long their baby usually slept during the night.

The baby was then awakened from sleep fifteen to thirty minutes prior to her usual spontaneous waking and crying times. Awakenings were planned to be especially rewarding to the baby. A music box was played, the mother cuddled and responded to the baby, changed her diapers, and then nursed her back to sleep.

Each night the baby was awakened fifteen to thirty minutes later than the night before. The baby showed a clear-cut pattern of sleeping until awakening, with sleeping time gradually lengthening. Two exceptions were when the baby regressed back to earlier waking patterns due to illness.

At the end of the study, which lasted approximately two months, the baby was sleeping for approximately six hours and awakening spontaneously at 5:30 in the morning, when the baby's father got up to go to work.

The authors conclude that (1) artificially awakening a child prior to the expected awakening time and (2) awakening the child at gradually lengthening intervals are two effective ways of shaping a baby's sleeping behavior.

How to Use the McGarr-Hovell Approach to Alter Your Baby's Sleep Schedule*

The basic principle of this method is to reward the baby for sleeping rather than waking and crying.

(1) Keep a record of your baby's sleeping and waking times from the time you put him down in the night until he awakens in the morning. Do this for a week and a half to two weeks. Once you have a lead on your baby's night sleep-wake patterns, you are ready to begin.

(2) Starting with your baby's first sleeping episode for the night, awaken your baby fifteen to thirty minutes *before* he is expected to wake up.

(3) Use a music box or another pleasant sound, and then gently change his diaper, if needed, and offer loving cuddling and nursing or a bottle until the baby falls back asleep. In this way you are rewarding the baby for sleeping behavior rather than for awakening and crying episodes.

Be sure to record when you wake the baby up so you can refer to it the next night.

(4) The following night increase the time you awaken the baby by fifteen to thirty minutes longer than the night before. Use the same music and rewards as earlier. If you awakened the baby at 3:45, then awaken him the second night at 4:00 instead. Do this for each expected awakening.

Again, keep a record of when you awakened your baby.

(5) On each proceeding night continue to lengthen your awakening times by fifteen to thirty minutes later than the preceding night.

(6) If the baby awakens earlier than his scheduled time, record the time and respond to him immediately as usual. On the next night awaken him fifteen to thirty minutes earlier than his unscheduled awakening of the night before.

If the method is working for you, your baby's sleep pattern will show stepwise increments of sleep time so that within a period of ten days the baby's sleep will become almost normalized. Fallbacks to the baby's old patterns are to be expected, especially during illnesses or other times of stress. If your baby is awakening because of physical pain, the method may not be as effective for you.

*Copyright © 1980 by Rita McGarr and M. F. Hovell, *Education & Treatment of Children*, vol. 3, "In Search of the Sandman: Shaping an Infant to Sleep." Reprinted by permission.

Frequent Feedings

A similar approach of paring off the end of sleep episodes in the daytime has been suggested by some pediatricians. The baby should be fed frequently during the day, awakened from naps, if necessary, to feed so that the baby nurses or drinks, say, every two and a half to three hours during daylight. Then, during the night, let the baby sleep as long as he wishes.

It is felt that feeding the baby more frequently may help the baby to sleep longer at night. The approach is based on the fact that most babies, if they are picked up at reasonable intervals during the daytime, are willing and able to take in more nourishment.

The value of all of the aforementioned approaches is that they are basically positive and rewarding to the baby, rather than negative or punishing. Letting the baby cry it out, on the other hand, is an extremely negative maneuver that may only make the baby more upset and anxious.

"My baby slept a little and cried a lot. Even as a newborn she slept only a half an hour at a time, and when she was awake, she cried if she wasn't nursing. In time things were much better. By the time she reached six months of age she began to improve. Now by age four she is making up for lost time; she sleeps nine to ten hours, plus she still takes a two-hour nap every afternoon."

198

PART IV

*Strategies
for Survival*

13
Shattering the "Perfect Mother" Myth

"To *hell* with housework," declares one mother of a colicky baby in Frances Wells Burck's *Babysense.* "It takes all of your energy, mental as well as physical, to help the poor thing through the night."

This mother, like most mothers of less than easy babies, has had to confront the "perfect mother" myth that is pervasive in our society. The myth is used to ruthlessly divide the "sheep" from the "goats"; those who "succeed" from those who "fail" at their mothering roles.

Magazine ads and television commercials portray the supermom, who presides over an immaculate home, dresses like a fashion model, sings to a sweet, joyous Gerber baby, and who has all the time and energy in the world to devote to the needs of her spouse and baby.

How successful a mother is, according to the myth, is defined by the reactions of her role-complements—her husband and baby. As with any role, she is dependent on feedback to determine how effectively she's measuring up against the standards of perfection meted out to her by society. If she's capable of soothing the fretful infant, then she feels competent. If he continues to cry, then she determines that she has failed. If she is able to keep her husband happy, then she has succeeded; if he is discontent, then she has failed.

When asked to state who is the most important member of their family, mothers who believe in the perfect mother myth are more likely *not* to list themselves first, according to a study by Mariann Lovel and Dorothy Fiorino, reported in the journal *Advances in Nursing Science,* July 1979. The researchers feel that this subordination of the self is one of the major stresses of motherhood. By attempting to conform to the perfect mother image, many women undergo a tremendous sense of powerlessness, a part of the overall oppression of women, according to the authors.

Implicit in the myth is the assumption that the mother is responsible for the reactions and behaviors of her baby and husband—that somehow she is in *control* of them. If the baby cries, it's her job to stop him. If the baby won't sleep, then it's the mother's task to find a way to *make* him sleep. If the father is fatigued, jealous, or unhappy about the new baby, then it's the mother's job to placate him. Like the little Dutch boy with his finger in the dike, the mother finds herself trying to remedy what often cannot be remedied.

A vicious cycle ensues. The baby cries, and the mother conscientiously tries to soothe him. She fails, and the baby continues to cry. The father gets aroused and angry. The mother tries to placate the father. The baby is handled more in an attempt to stop the crying. The increased efforts fail again. The mother becomes anxious, depressed, and exhausted. The relationships between mother and baby and mother and husband become more insecure and eroded as the baby cries more and the husband withdraws further.

At some point it must be realized that a baby can't be *made* to go to sleep, nor can he be *made* not to cry. A discontented husband can't be made to be happy. The perfect mother myth and its illusion of control are not only erroneous but destructive to the emotional well-being of the mother and the entire family.

Mothers who break away from the myth of perfection must then set about to redefine what is happening to them and their roles on more realistic terms. Husband and wife are forced to come to grips with the fact that they must stick together through the stress of the baby, or stay separately in energy-sapping loneliness.

> *"Stop blaming yourself for what is going wrong. Redefine your role in a more realistic way. Find activities besides baby care that are meaningful to you, even if it's a single daily thing that makes you feel that you have some control over your life. It's critical not to adopt the attitude that your needs do not count."*

Ellen Forrester tells what happened between herself and her husband, Chris, this way: "The baby was getting me up over and over in the night. Chris decided that there should at least be one person who got sleep in the night, and that was him. He moved downstairs to the living room couch, leaving me to cope with the baby alone. Whether I wanted to admit it or not, I developed deep resentment toward Chris for abandoning me to deal with our baby all by myself."

Finally at eleven o'clock one night, when Chris was showered and ready to bed himself down for the night, Ellen confronted him with her anger at being appointed as odd man out to take total responsibility for the baby's needs. At first Chris was angry. He had missed the body-touching that had been the mainstay of their affection for each other. He felt like the baby was an unwanted intruder that had shattered their otherwise good marriage.

*"Our baby had colic the first three
months. It's a very frustrating
experience for new parents as well as for
the baby. There are a whole range of
emotions, including anger and guilt. A
few times I cried with her out of
helplessness. I think parents need to be
reassured that these are normal feelings
and not to feel bad about them."*

Even though the baby was crying, Ellen and Chris
tearfully realized that they had to come back together again
if they were going to see their way through this crisis. They
went down to the kitchen and put on a pot of coffee, calling a temporary work stoppage while together they talked
out the ways they could cope better with the baby's needs,
and their need for each other.

"One thing we decided," Chris remembers, "is that our
baby was not like other babies. He was special. He had special needs. And that meant we were having to give more to
him than other parents were asked to give."

*"Be good to yourself. Your ego may be
wobbly because you are fulfilling
someone else's needs twenty-four hours
a day. You may find yourself exhausted,
obsessed with the baby, and feeling
something less than a human being.
What you need is mothering yourself."*

Ellen was able to admit her own hunger to be moth-
ered, to be fed, instead of trying to be the wellspring, all
giving and no receiving. Chris admitted his loneliness, his
deep desire to be a good father, but his frustration at not
knowing what to do or how to cope.

Miraculously the baby fell off to sleep on his own.
They tiptoed upstairs to be sure that he was still breathing.

He was. He looked so peaceful and angelic lying there. The precious words "I love you" were spoken once again. "We love you, too, even if you are a monster," they said to their sleeping baby, as they half-cried and half-laughed. That night they slept together.

The next day Ellen felt happier and more relaxed, even though she had gotten up three times during the night to nurse the baby. Somehow his cries didn't invoke the same exhausted sighs that they had the day before. The following evening Chris fixed dinner while Ellen relaxed on the couch with the baby. While they were eating Chris reached out and squeezed Ellen's free hand. Somehow they were going to get through it together.

That was three years ago. The colicky baby, Daniel, is now a robust, outgoing preschooler. His high energy level still makes him a challenge, but not as much as when he was a baby.

"Chris can't wait to get home to play with Daniel," reports Ellen. "They've got a very special relationship going." That's fortunate, because baby number two is due any day.

Ellen is praying that this baby will be "good," but if he's not, she knows that she and Chris will manage together somehow.

Notes to Dad

- Please be home on time. Things can crumble in those last few minutes.
- Take baby away from the house for an hour or two so Mom can nap or take a leisurely bath.
- Talk to baby and say positive things about him. Mom wants to know there is something lovable about him.
- Lend a listening ear; colic can't be cured but there is much relief in understanding.
- Offer to take Mom on an outing. She might not want to go be-

cause of being tired, yet she needs adult companionship almost as much as sleep. (Don't take no for an answer.)
· Make a run for take-out food or cook dinner yourself.
· Take over the baby right after dinner or at some other definite time each evening for fifteen minutes or more.

Debbie Bosnos,
CEA Newsletter, Tucson, Arizona
June–July 1980

The Problem of Learned Helplessness

Learned helplessness is a recently coined term that is used to describe how people react when they are confronted with a situation over which they feel they have no control. The theory behind learned helplessness is that when people are confronted with uncontrollable events, such as the continual demands of a difficult baby, they soon learn that responding brings no change, which then undermines their incentive and their capacity to respond.

> *"Just complaining about your rotten life with your baby doesn't help. It leads to self-pity. And that flows over you and you want to just sit in it. It doesn't get you anywhere and it doesn't solve problems."*

When mothers are faced with a laboratory situation in which they cannot escape the taped cries of a baby, they pay less and less attention to the cries. This study conducted by Wilberta Donovan at the University of Wisconsin appears to confirm the notion that when a caregiver is faced with an inescapable situation, the tendency is to turn off and respond less. Lack of success is followed by a stronger sense of helplessness that then affects the mother's readiness and ability to act constructively to bring about changes on behalf of her baby.

Donovan's study seems to change the old adage "success breeds success" to the opposite—"failure breeds failure." A mother's past success in controlling the crying episodes of a baby can be used, according to this psychologist, as a reliable indicator of how well she will be able to cope with her crying baby in the future.

A person's environment may affect whether a person becomes depressed or gets sick. A study by Abigail Steward and Patricia Salt at Boston University has found that women undergoing family stress are likely to become depressed, while career women with no family responsibilities are more likely to develop physical symptoms in the face of stress. The researchers feel that the housewife's sense of lack of control over stressful events and her narrow range of response alternatives are more likely to lead to a sense of helplessness and depression.

> *"It is the loss of control, more than anything else, that makes me so frustrated and anxious. My not being able to count on anything. But that's a fact of life in living with an infant for the first couple of months."*

The sense of learned helplessness can be the breeding ground of serious depression, according to psychological research. But not everyone who experiences a seemingly helpless situation becomes depressed. Those mothers who view their experiences with loss of control as proof that they are *totally helpless individuals* are much more likely to become depressed than those who are able to perceive that their helplessness relates only to very specific situations.

Depression Is Linked to Your Attitudes

How positively or negatively a person perceives himself and his situation can affect whether or not help-lessness leads to more serious depression.

Here are three critical attitude factors found to be associated with depression, and how they can be turned into positive attitudes.

Associated with Depression

Defining the problem "globally"

"My baby's crying just demonstrates how inadequate as a mother and a wife I am."

versus

Not Associated with Depression

Defining the problem specifically

"My baby's crying is caused by something very specific that has nothing to do with my adequacy as a mother or my value as a wife."

Believing that the problem has no limits

"My baby will always be a severe stress to me, even when he gets older. This stressful crying will never end."

versus

Seeing the limits of the problem

"I know that this painful situation is bound to come to an end."

Seeing the problem in a narrow perspective

"Surely I'm the only mother who's suffering like this."

versus

Seeing the problem in a broader perspective

"There are many other mothers who must be having an experience like I'm having. I am not the only one trying to cope."

The Baby You Wanted—The Baby You Got

During pregnancy most mothers have gloriously idealized dreams about what their babies will be like. This sense of romantic expectancy seems to be the way that people mentally prepare themselves for making deep life changes. The same process happens when teenagers dream about careers, or lovers dream about marriage. Dreams of babies pave the way for the life commitments and involvements that parenting will soon bring.

What do you do, then, when your romantic visions of what your baby was going to be like are exploded before your eyes by a crying, fretful, sleepless baby who doesn't in any way resemble your hopes and dreams?

"We had feelings of anger and bitterness toward our colicky baby and often thought there ought to be an organization for people with children like him. I'm sure hearing others talk about their same feelings would have alleviated some of the guilt. Looking back now, I know they were normal feelings, but at the time I didn't know that. Even people with normal babies get frustrated and angry. How can you help it, then, listening to a screaming child all day and night while you're worn to a frazzle?"

Instead of the pudgy-cheeked Ivory Snow baby you expected, you got a tiny, screaming mogul who seems to be taking over your every waking moment. Instead of standing wistfully in front of the living room curtains in your nightgown, with a smiling cherub beaming up at you, you find yourself exhausted, disheveled, and covered with baby spit-up.

Psychologists have found that when people's dreams are shattered, the natural reaction is rage—boiling, seething rage. This kind of anger results from what is called "the violation of expectancy."

> *"It seems to me a big part of dealing with the fussy baby or a whining two-year-old or whatever is in dealing with one's own needs and expectations. Everything interlocks so."*

It's a rare mother who doesn't feel some sense of being violated when a baby fails to match her deeply held and cherished dreams, and the rage that comes from the violation of expectancy can be one of the most potent roadblocks to a mother's dealing constructively with her present reality—her real, live baby.

Eileen was unaware of the depth of what she was feeling. Her baby, Lisa, was a sleepless, colicky baby almost from day one. Eileen halfheartedly joined a mothers' support group that met in different homes once a week. When she went, she seldom shared any negative feelings about her baby, but rather talked about how badly she and her husband had wanted to have a child or what a blessing it was to have a baby.

> *"If I could focus my attention on doing one thing that I was trying to do at a time, it was tremendously helpful. When I diffused my own energy of what I was wanting to do, or thinking of how many things I had to do, it made my baby be much more hyperactive."*

At home, Eileen felt tired and lifeless. Her husband came home to a wife who, once energetic and life-loving, was now surly and irritable. Eileen found fault with every little thing that he did, and all the while Lisa cried and cried with neither parent knowing what to do. During the night Eileen would have bad dreams about dying in an accident and leaving the baby behind, or about the baby falling onto train tracks or over a balcony. The dreams always ended with Eileen feeling deeply anguished and lonely.

Eileen began to lose contact with the friends she had had before Lisa was born, mostly because she felt they wouldn't understand what it was like to live with a baby like hers. She found herself resenting other mothers who seemed to be too perfect to be real. She felt that they were self-centered and on an ego trip over their babies.

Eileen became more and more withdrawn as three months came and went, with the baby still crying. Her husband would return home at night to find the apartment totally in disarray, and Eileen looking as though she hadn't had a bath or combed her hair in days.

Finally he convinced her to seek the help of a counselor at a nearby family services center. It wasn't until after several months of counseling that Eileen's deep rage against her baby began to surface.

One day she exploded. With gritted teeth and screams of anger, Eileen at last vented her pent-up rage at having been given a baby who demanded so much of her.

The result of Eileen's confrontation with her deeply held anger was an immediate clearing of the air. Her energy began to return. Her old sense of humor started popping up. She jokingly apologized to Lisa, her baby, when she realized that the baby couldn't help the day and night demands and the crying.

In the weeks to follow the counselor explored the fact that Eileen was really trying mentally to deal with *two* babies—her dream baby and the *real* baby that fell far short of her expectations. In a sense, Eileen had been going through the stages of grief that one would experience as the result of a lost loved one—denial, despair, rage, and, finally, acceptance. She had to release her claim on a baby that never existed.

When her energy-sapping conflict was resolved, Eileen began to interact more with her baby. She noticed Lisa's bright blue eyes. She rejoiced in her smiles. She started to play mother-baby games. She began to make contacts with other mothers in the mothers' support group whose babies were more like her own. Eileen became more hopeful, and life began to become more balanced. Once her idealized baby and her idealized version of herself as that baby's mother were laid to rest, Eileen could then take up the task of reaching out to her challenging, *real* baby.

> *"During this time it is really hard to cope with your feelings. Most important is not to feel guilty about wanting to leave. Everyone needs to get away for a few hours or more. This really needs to be stressed, as I could hardly pry myself out of the house and was just making matters worse on myself. Your baby will survive with a baby-sitter, and it will make a new person out of you."*

When You Have to Go to Work

It's natural to feel guilty about leaving your baby to go back to work. Your baby *will* miss you, even more so if he cries a lot and has sleeping problems, because you have become his anchor in a period of intense turmoil and possible pain.

Many mothers-to-be are now insisting on having adequate maternity leave—even up to a year—in order to allow their relationships with their babies to stabilize and to assure that their own bodies have had time to return to normal, rested functioning.

There will probably never be a period in your life, or in the next decade, at least, that is as stressing and fatiguing as the one you're going through right now with your fussy baby. Add to that the stress of finding a reliable sitter, coping with outside schedules, worrying about how the baby is doing, and a sleep schedule more sparse than that of boot camp and you may find yourself quickly in up over your head.

Judith Shaw, a public relations executive in New York, went back to work when her son, Aaron, was four months old. "Many mothers I knew talked about how their babies miraculously stopped crying and slept through the night right before they returned to work," she says. "Well, this didn't happen in the case of *my* son. He didn't even come close to sleeping through the night until he was nine months old!"

Judith's number-one priority before returning to work was to find a loving, responsive caregiver for her son. "It had to be someone I absolutely trusted; someone I knew would have the patience to give Aaron the love, the warmth, and *all the holding he needed*," she noted.

Judith and other working mothers I have interviewed have these tips for making things easier on yourself:

- When going back to work, negotiate for a more humane schedule. Consider working part time for a while, or find another equally skilled worker who will go in with you to fulfill the responsibilities of one full-time slot.
- If the above options aren't realistically available to you, consider asking your employer to allow you to come in a bit later and leave a little earlier each day, so you can have the time to settle the baby and beat the rush-hour traffic. Even if this sched-

ule is possible for only a matter of weeks, it can make your transition to working again a lot easier.

- Ask your caregiver to start work as soon as possible, and stay home with her for as long as possible if she's going to your home, so that you can set up your daily routines together.
- If your caregiver is outside your home, spend some time with her and your baby so that you can see how she responds to the baby. "I was reassured that Aaron spent time with me and the caregiver together. That way he got to know early on that we were working together as a team," Judith notes.
- Plan to have the caregiver fix the main dish for dinner and to stay an extra hour after you get home. Her job, then, will be to keep you and the baby free from phone calls and interruptions so that the two of you can relax together. One mother found that taking a long, leisurely bath with her baby helped her to get back into sync with him. In another family everyone eats a high-protein snack before going home to the family rest hour on a quilt on the living room floor.
- Eat well during the day. Food will help you keep going when a demanding baby and the chronic lack of sleep sap all of your energy. "Look at it this way," Judy says. "If you eat a big lunch at work, you'll be able to go to your baby *first* before hitting the refrigerator when you step in the door."
- Go to bed as early as possible in the evening. Tuck the baby in bed with you. He'll sleep better, and you'll have that important body-to-body contact that you both have missed during the day.
- If your baby needs rocking, walking, and strong soothing measures throughout the night, consider a pact between you and your spouse about who

does what when; i.e.: "I'll soothe the baby before 2:00 A.M., and you take over between 2:00 and 6:00 in the morning. Tomorrow night we'll change shifts so that we each will have the promise of a stretch of uninterrupted sleep."

- When you're home, try to put work out of your mind. This is not easy advice to follow, but critical if you and your baby are to relax with each other.
- Find a nearby parenting center or mother support group to help you make it through the work-with-little-sleep crisis. Some centers have groups especially for meeting the needs of working mothers. "It's a way of meeting people with young children," Judith notes, "and since you can usually bring your baby along with you, it can be a good outing for both of you."

100 Coping Tips for the Less Than Perfect Mother

Laundering and Housework

(1) Use a diaper service for six months.
(2) Store clothes unfolded on open shelves, or buy five or six laundry baskets to keep sorted, unfolded clean laundry in.
(3) When friends ask what they can do to help, schedule them to come in once a week to have tea and do the laundry.
(4) Call the high school to find a teenager to do the heavy housework once a week.
(5) Fill a dishpan with hot, soapy water in the sink in the morning and drop dirty dishes in it for soaking as the day passes, then simply rinse them and let them air dry. Never towel dry dishes.

(6) To control diaper rash, use ½ cup vinegar in the first rinse when washing diapers. The acidity counters bacterial growth.

(7) Don't bother to fold clean diapers. Just throw them into a laundry basket beside the baby's changing table.

Food Management

(8) Eat at least some of your meals on paper plates set inside woven or plastic holders to keep down dishwashing.

(9) Buy frozen entrees such as beef stew, lasagna, or fried chicken for emergency use.

(10) Prepare dinner in the morning when energy is high. Make more than enough and freeze the extra for dinner later on in the week.

(11) Stock up on high-protein snacks: canned or packaged nuts, cheeses, and high-vitamin foods: dried and fresh fruits, vegetables that can be eaten raw, whole-wheat crackers, canned or frozen fruit juices.

(12) Prepare simple, basic meals that require little preparation time—hamburger patties, simple sandwich spreads, foods that can be eaten raw.

(13) Eat like a king for breakfast to have energy for the lows that usually hit around 2:30–4:30 in the afternoon.

(14) Learn how to make nutritious milk shakes from fruits, yogurt, and other natural ingredients for fast minimeals.

(15) Use a crib-shaped mesh playpen with wheels, or a portable small-size crib, and equip it with a musical mobile and other items for baby to watch and play with in the kitchen when you're trying to cook dinner.

(16) Freeze your own TV dinners from leftovers—main course, vegetables, apple slices and raisins—in used trays, cover with foil, and label.

(17) Go out to eat every Friday night—even if it's just to Burger King.

(18) Start a Thursday night dinner co-op with other families who have colicky babies. You can all eat together and commiserate while the babies scream it out.

(19) Take extra vitamin B-complex tablets for more energy.

Soothing Your Baby

(20) Buy a used carriage that has springs so that baby can be jiggled to sleep anywhere.

(21) Tape the noise of the vacuum cleaner to help your baby to sleep, or his own voice, or the white noise from an FM station that's off the air.

(22) Try letting the baby sleep upright in his car seat to ease digestion pains.

(23) Keep booties on a fussy baby twenty-four hours a day. (Some parents say it works!)

(24) Invest in a Snugli baby carrier and keep the baby in it whenever he's fussy.

(25) *Never* wake a baby up to change his diaper.

(26) Once the baby's asleep, *don't* move him.

(27) Provided it's not too cold outside your front door, often a baby can be soothed by standing with him very briefly in a rush of fresh air.

(28) Put the baby across a firm couch cushion so that his legs hang down over the edge of the cushion for naps. (Use a waterproof pad for protection.)

(29) Don't worry about the baby getting cold during the night—let him sleep facedown and he will conserve energy in the critical front and belly areas.

(30) Give your baby sunshine baths even in winter by putting him in his infant seat or naked on a diaper and quilt in front of a window where sun comes into the home.

(31) Put baby belly downward on a "warm" hot water bottle on your lap.

(32) Give the baby a teaspoon of boiled water ten minutes before feeding time if he gets upset when he's hungry.

(33) Try different carrying positions to ease baby's belly pain—the "colic carry" with baby lying facedown across your arm, his cheek at your elbow, or carry him with his backbone against your belly, pressing his knees up against his stomach.

(34) Lying the baby on his right side for a few minutes and then raising him back upright sometimes brings up swallowed air.

(35) Some babies' pain is relieved by passing gas. This can be helped by putting a small glycerin suppository, or your lubricated pinky finger (nail clipped) in his anus.

(36) Put the baby with only diapers on on Dad's bare chest so both can take a nap.

(37) To stop him from crying, raise the baby as high as you can while supporting the back of his head and then lower him down with a deep knee bend, almost to the ground.

(38) Make a fennell tea from one tablespoon of fennell seeds, strained, and give a teaspoon to the baby to ease belly pains.

(39) Let the baby sleep on a specially processed lambskin pelt, then you can take him anywhere and he'll settle down.

(40) Sing soothing songs in your deepest voice, putting the baby's name in every so often. (Try "Old Man River" for a start.)

(41) Try dance-walking the baby (step-pause, step-pause) while rhythmically groaning your most primitive animal sounds.

(42) Stuff your smelliest, most-used T-shirt or nightgown next to the baby when he's sleeping (from the outset), so that he associates it with your being near and feels secure when you're not close.

(43) If the baby seems to be having teething pains, let him chew on your bent finger, or let him chew on a clean, damp cold washcloth.

Diapering and Bathing

(44) Take the baby into a warm bath with you so you can both relax.

(45) One mother I know finds it useful to sit a plastic laundry basket inside the tub, allowing the baby to sit in his bathwater with much less risk of slipping out of control.

(46) Change the baby in your lap so he doesn't get chilled and isn't afraid of falling.

(47) Damp-mop the baby under warm blankets if he's upset by baths.

(48) Cut the baby's fingernails by putting him in your lap, back to you, so that his hands are positioned just where yours would be if you were doing it to yourself. If he's too upset, clip them while he's asleep.

(49) Don't use Q-Tips or put anything up your baby's nose or into his ears to clean them. They are self-cleaning organs.

(50) Double- or triple-diaper the baby at night so wetness won't bother him.

(51) Let your baby push against your hand with his feet when he's struggling to have a bowel movement.

(52) Nail a lightweight bookcase or securely fasten hardware store brackets and shelf panels at eye level di-

rectly beside the baby's diapering area so that you have *everything*, diapers, cream, extra pins, in instant reach without having to bend over or go anywhere, or construct a diaper changing area around the bathroom sink.

R and R (Rest and Relaxation)

(53) Sleep when the baby does, night or day.

(54) Put a mattress on the floor and sleep with baby.

(55) Find a favorite retreat spot—a lake or a meadow or whatever—near your home and go there with the baby every afternoon for an hour.

(56) Make the baby a padded bed out of a laundry basket so you can carry him around with you from room to room, or use a deep drawer or a sturdy cardboard box.

(57) Turn the bedroom clock to the wall so you won't know or care that it's 4:30 in the morning.

(58) Buy yourself a collection of paperback novels that are short, cheap, and easy to get through—perfect for reading in the middle of the night.

(59) Place a book of quotations or inspirational Bible verses next to the toilet for quick pick-me-ups.

(60) Collect a file of colorful inspirational pictures of artwork or of interior decorations—your dream folder for low moments.

(61) Put your favorite sayings on the bathroom mirror, the kitchen cabinet, anywhere eye level, so that you see them as you move around the house.

(62) Take minirests wherever you find yourself with a breather—in the kitchen, under the dining room table, on the living room floor. Whenever the moment presents itself, grab it!

(63) Combat cabin fever—get out of the house once every day, even if it's just to take a walk around the block.

(64) Get a haircut or a permanent, so that even if you're exhausted you can still feel like you look good.

(65) Don't be afraid to unplug the phone if you need to sleep. Even kitchen wall phones can now be taken off the wall by lifting the telephone body up and off.

(66) Trick your body into sleeping during the day by taking off your clothes, or even by putting on pajamas.

(67) Don't plan any trips for the first six months after the baby's born—let your relatives come to you.

(68) Send off for baby clothes catalogs and toy catalogs in winter: Community Playthings, Rifton, NY 12471; "Childworks Catalog," Family Bazaar, 352 Evelyn St., Paramus, NJ 07652; After the Stork, PO Box 1832-G, Bisbee, AZ 85603; Cotton Dreams, 999 Laredo La., Sebastian, FL 32958; Childcraft Education Corp., 20 Kilmer Rd., Edison, NJ 08817.

(69) If you've tried everything, then put the baby in his bed (or in the middle of yours), take a quick warm shower, and come back and take a rest, with the baby lying on your chest.

(70) Take a "leave of absence day" *with* your baby by going to a park or a beautiful spot for the day, or simply stay in bed all day, snuggled up next to the baby.

(71) Buy a small portable tape player and earphones and play beautiful music to yourself when you're awake in the middle of the night.

(72) Have everyone in the family eat a high-protein snack before coming home, and then have an official "rest hour" on a quilt on the living room rug instead of the usual dinnertime frenzy.

(73) Play the most beautiful music you can find on the stereo during baby's fussy hours, between 5:00 and 9:00 at night.

(74) Take family baths together with the baby to make up for lost "skin" time when the baby demands nighttime separation of the parents.

(75) Start a mother-baby support group to meet in people's homes with other new mothers in the neighborhood.

(76) Arrange a one-hour trade-off of baby-caring with another mother for two afternoons a week.

(77) Subscribe to a computerized long-distance phone call company like MCI for the first six months after the baby is born so you can call your distant relatives without feeling guilty about it.

(78) When relatives ask about your baby's crying, tell them he's under a doctor's care and that you hope to find an answer to his pain within the next few months. (He'll probably outgrow it by then, anyway.)

(79) Don't lay a guilt trip on yourself about what your neighbors think about your baby's crying. If they say anything to you, tell them he has a postbirth complication, or some such, and that it's expected to clear up in twelve weeks.

(80) Subscribe to *Mothering* magazine (4 issues a year/$10.00, P.O. Box 2208, Albuquerque, NM 87103) and *La Leche League News,* if you're breastfeeding (6 issues a year plus membership/$12.00, La Leche International, 9616 Minneapolis Ave., Franklin Park, IL 60131), for supportive, inspirational reading. For practical tips subscribe to *Practical Parenting* (6 issues a year/$6.50, 18326-B Minnetonka Blvd., Deephaven, NM 55391).

(81) Inquire about the Foster Grandparents program in your community by writing to: Foster Grandparents, Washington, D.C.

(82) Put a rocking chair and a footstool in the kitchen, if there's room.

(83) Install a hammock in the kitchen or the living room with a wall lamp nearby for rocking and reading with baby.

(84) Keep an aquarium in the baby's bedroom for humidity, light, and a soothing droning sound.

(85) Use black-out shades or heavy blankets on the windows so baby won't be awakened by morning light or sounds.

(86) Build the changing table by mounting a sturdy plywood slab right into the closet so that it lies flush against all sides.

(87) Decorate the baby's diapering area at eye level with miniature paintings, favorite photos, wise sayings, a small mirror, and a variety of eye-pleasers especially for yourself.

(88) Make a nursing nest for yourself out of a lot of cushions that can be arranged for your comfort and body support. Include a foot rest if needed and a table for beverages.

(89) Get an insulated hospital pitcher, fill it with your favorite iced beverage, and put it next to your nursing station with paper cups for refreshments all day.

(90) Buy a sausage-shaped bolster or stuff one yourself to fit under your nursing arm to ease muscle strain.

(91) Place a basket in the bathroom over the john for the daily mail. That way you can pick out what to read, and what to toss out, while you're there.

(92) Try rearranging your environment for a while. Pull your mattress into the living room and make it up on the floor. Have a picnic, play the stereo, recline, and relax for a change!

(93) Drag out the old beanbag chair for real relaxation while nursing.

Massage

(94) When the baby has gas, try giving him belly massages by gently pressing your fingers around and around until the trapped gas is freed.

(95) If your baby's a biter, it may be because his jaw muscles go into spasms. Try gently massaging his cheek, temple area, and directly under his chin bone.

(96) If your baby arches his back shortly after he nurses, massage the back of his neck, his shoulders, and shoulder blades with rotating fingertips. Perhaps he has painfully contracting muscles.

Exercise

(97) Practice deep-breathing exercises and total relaxation whenever you feed the baby.

(98) Disco dance with the crying baby; he'll usually calm down.

(99) Stretch like dogs and cats do, arching your back and reaching for the ceiling at least three times a day.

Dangerous Don'ts

(100) Balloons are dangerous to babies: they suffocate on the rubber if it gets into their throats. Also dangerous are small party-gift rattles and pacifiers that comprise more than one piece that can come off in baby's mouth or get lodged in his throat. *Never* tie a baby's pacifier around his neck—it has caused death from strangulation. Hot water that feels comfortable to you can scald a baby, causing pain, redness, and blisters. Don't use thin plastic laundry bags for protecting anything—tear them up and throw them away, as they have caused numerous suffocation deaths.

These tips have come from other mothers. If you have some tips for busy mothers that you would like to share with me, why don't you write to me in care of Warner Books?

14
When Your Body Goes into "Red Alert"

The stress of a crying, sleepless baby is a *personal* experience. It's not something that's going on outside in the world, but something that's taking place right inside your own living room or bedroom. Whether you realize it or not, the stress is taking place inside your body, too.

How much stress a mother or father can endure and for how long depends upon a number of factors, including individual capacities and attitudes. But too much stress for too long a time eventually begins to take its toll on the body.

Some of the symptoms of prolonged emotional and physical stress are high blood pressure, emotional outbursts, sporadic bouts with illness, failure to fulfill everyday responsibilities, and lapses in memory. A parent may experience unusual pounding of the heart, breathlessness, trembling, perspiring hands, digestive upsets, and frequent urination.

All of these symptoms sometimes lead an exhausted mother to believe that she may have a hidden disease. She wonders secretly if the pain she feels in her chest is a stomach spasm or a heart attack; if the change in her menstrual period is from breastfeeding, tension, or is a sign of cancer. It is not unusual for parents to become fearful about their health.

Parents have the capacity to sustain a relatively high degree of stress for short periods of time, based on the evolutionary need for fight or flight—to confront an enemy or to escape it. Under conditions of extreme stress the human body releases hormones into the bloodstream that increase blood supply to the muscles and slow down the digestive process. The body readies itself for extraordinary physical feats.

When we think we are in danger because we feel besieged by a disruptive life event, our body's natural protective mechanism gets out of balance. There are no saber-toothed tigers to face, yet our systems still react as they did in ancient times: The body goes into a sustained state of "red alert."

Red alert happens when parents are faced with constant alarm and sleep deprivation because of their baby's crying. Its central symptom is the development of extreme alertness and awareness. On the outside, a parent appears to have a smooth veneer of calm, but on the inside, he or she is strung tight. Muscles are tense. The mouth goes dry. The mind races with plans about how to react the next time the baby cries. The stress build-up is cumulative, and usually most parents are unaware of what is happening to them.

Burn-Out

After the initial alarm state has passed, burn-out begins to set in. A parent will feel numb and exhausted. A mother who has taken over the twenty-four-hour job of baby care may feel weighed down with sadness and fatigue, lacking in energy or interest for anything but the baby's cycles and needs. Each daily task seems monumental. It becomes increasingly difficult to respond to even the simplest callings to nurture, eat, or do household chores.

Mothers of fussy babies often find that they can't get tasks completed before the day ends and the baby's night-waking cycles set in. Most days are spent attempting to soothe the baby, using whatever techniques can be summoned up. Disorganization is common, and so are putting away the groceries in the wrong place and being so preoccupied with the baby that hours pass with nothing getting finished. "My brain just turned into hamburger," one mother recalled about her months of trying to cope with a baby who cried around the clock.

Converting Feelings into Positive Action

According to Hans Selye, a world-famous authority on human stress, people can learn how to convert negative stress into a positive event by changing their attitudes toward what is happening to them. Parents can learn to convert their anxieties about their babies into a more healthy attitude that takes into account not only their babies' needs but their own.

In order to deal with the feelings that stress invokes, it is important to affirm these feelings as they are happening. The reality that something is going on at the emotional level right then must be acknowledged.

It helps to label feelings, such as "I feel angry," "I feel hurt," "I feel sad," "I feel afraid," or "I resent this baby," because getting a handle on what you are currently experiencing will help you to find ways to cope with it. Some of the feelings that parents of difficult babies frequently experience are ambivalence, anger, guilt, and unfounded fears.

> *"Get out of the house and do anything. Literally anything. Get out at least once a day, rain or shine. You don't need to get away from the baby as much as from the dust, the dirty bathroom, the laundry, and the dishes in the sink. Go out with the baby. You need a change of scenery. It's worth the effort to get out or else you'll be tensely sitting there waiting for the baby to wake up from his nap."*

Ambivalence

It is normal to feel ambivalence about a less than easy baby. On the one hand a parent may feel a strong drive to escape the baby, and on the other hand he may be driven to be almost constantly on guard and vigilant about the baby, always at his side for fear that something may truly go wrong. A parent may feel an intense surge of love and attachment for the baby at one moment, only to be swept up in a jaw-clamping rage the next that makes him wish he could get rid of the baby.

> *"Verbalize your feelings. Don't keep them boxed in. It's not having bad feelings that's wrong. It's what you do with them that counts. A good session talking out your feelings helps."*

Angry feelings are an inevitable part of coping with a less than happy baby. Parents have natural built-in urges to protect their baby when they think that he is endangered. They are physiologically prepared to launch a direct attack on the agent or threat that is causing a baby's crying, but how can a parent attack colic or fight a baby's sleeplessness? They are left without a way to direct their aroused anger and aggression.

Often a married couple will take out frustrations about a baby on each other. At other times parents will carry the anger inwardly as listlessness and depression. Mothers and fathers sometimes cry with their babies out of sheer frustration, or they will leave a baby to scream in the crib, deriving an odd sense of pleasure that "the baby is getting what he deserves," or that he is "learning who's boss around here."

"Most parents who harbor some negative feelings cannot bear to face them consciously. They may also be afraid that direct expression of such negative feelings would lead to acts of hostility or aggression. So they repress the feelings instead, and this in turn arouses feelings of guilt."

—G. D. Jensen,
The Well Child's Problems,
p. 201

Our society limits the way we can use our bodies to discharge tension and anger. In households electrical energy has been substituted for physical energy. Unfortunately appliances and devices used in cramped living quarters do nothing to reduce built-up tensions. In the same way, our society encourages men to substitute vicarious participation in sports through television viewing rather than by direct physical activity.

Many parents feel secretly guilty about their child-rearing roles and what is happening to them and their babies. A mother may be eaten up with guilt because her mother-in-law advised her not to use a pacifier with the baby, and yet she did. Or she may decide to give the baby a drug to make him sleep, on the advice of her doctor, and then feel bad for doing so. She may have the feeling that she is walking on eggshells—one wrong step and she has committed a grave, lifelong error.

> *"I felt so inadequate as a mother. I felt guilty for my feelings of resentment of my baby. I was a real zombi. It hurt me so to see this little baby of mine crying and screaming in so much pain and not to be able to do anything about it except walk the floors with him day and night."*

> *"There are so many guilt trips laid on parents. You bring the baby into the bed with you, and people say she will be a homosexual. Our baby used to cry so much at night that we were just exhausted from getting up to take care of her. The doctor finally said just to defuse our anger by going to bed with her. It worked."*

There's nothing wrong with a parent having a deep sense of responsibility toward his baby or his family, but at times it can be carried too far. Everyone, from the in-laws to the neighbors to many physicians, has done much to intensify the feeling in parents that they are to blame for everything that goes wrong with their babies. This extreme sense of parental responsibility has made mothers and fathers afraid to admit their humanness, their weakness, in the face of profound family crises.

Unfounded Fears

During the night fears about the baby or desires to escape loom large. Ideas hidden in the darker recesses of the mind are sometimes cloaked with a sense of dread or horror. What is imagined becomes far more fearsome than the reality itself. "Perhaps my baby has a fatal illness. . . . He must blame me for all of his pain. . . . Maybe he's retarded or brain-damaged." Or a mother may make plans to buy an airplane ticket to fly to a far-off city, leaving the baby behind for her husband to discover when he gets home. Such plans and fears seldom survive the rational light of daytime.

"I hope that my baby doesn't suffer psychologically because of the turmoil of these first few months of his life. That's my only nagging question now."

How a Baby's Crying Makes a Mother Feel

Nurse Janet Harris took a survey of thirty-five new mothers that was reported several years ago in *The Canadian Nurse*. About two thirds of the mothers confessed that their babies' crying had been a major concern of theirs within the previous four weeks. Five mothers in the study were in frank despair over it. Here's how the mothers felt about their babies' crying:

Feelings	Number of Mothers
Frustrated	12
Bothered	5
Nervous	5
Sorry	3
Upset	3
Helpless	3
Wonder What's Wrong	3
Irritable	3
Guilty About Feelings	3
Heartbroken	2

Some mothers reported that they felt: "hostile," "violent," "mildly angry," "exasperated," "underconfident," "hurt at first—then indifferent," "uptight at first—then resigned," "afraid," "worried," "anxious," "concerned," "[like they didn't] know what to do," "unloving, unattached," "terrible," "like killing her," "needed," "resentful," "confused," "fed up," and "tearful."

Obviously a baby's crying has a powerful effect on a mothers' sense of order and well-being.

"I think it's important that mothers who have crying, sleepless babies know that they are not alone. That they aren't 'doing it all wrong.' That their feelings, which may include resentment of the baby and guilt for not being a good mother, are normal, and that these feelings will pass after the strenuous months of intense colic pass."

Some feelings are difficult to deal with. If you've been taught that it's wrong to feel anger toward your own mother and father, then it may be difficult for you to manage the anger that you may be feeling toward your baby. Similarly, if you were abused by your parents when you were a child, then it will be very difficult for you to deal openly with the negative feelings that your baby is engendering in you, because they will seem so potent and potentially overwhelming.

"The most important thing is to try not to blame yourself."

The next part of the process is to choose those feelings that you wish to deal with openly. Piece by piece you can begin to unravel the effects of stress on your emotions, you can become increasingly aware of how your baby is having an impact on the deeper levels of your emotions. Once the feelings are expressed, then constructive outlets can be found to siphon off tension so that your life can become balanced again.

Learning How to Relax

The effects of muscular tension and anxiety on the body are exactly opposite from those of relaxation. According to some experts, the two states—tension and relaxation—cannot coexist in the body; when you are feeling one, you cannot be feeling the other.

Relaxation does not take away the external stress of your baby's crying and sleeplessness. What it does is help you feel more comfortable with yourself and more aware of how your body is reacting to your baby. Even though you may not be able to control your baby's crying, you can have some control over your body's response to it.

Relaxation has powerfully positive effects on the body. Tests performed at the Thorndike Memorial Laboratory at Harvard University have shown that meditating on any sound, phrase, prayer, or mantra brings about pro-

Dealing Positively with the Feelings Stress Produces

Symptom	Description	Self-Treatment
Fatigue	You feel weighted down, tired, drained. Just going up the stairs seems like a burden. While diapers and dirty dishes pile up you look in the mirror, thinking that you have a dreaded disease.	Do just the minimum housework that has to be done, or hire someone else, a teenager, perhaps, to come in and help out for a few hours a week. Divide up a dirty room as though it were a clock. Determine where 12:00 is and clean from that spot to 1:00. Then go to 2:00. By the time you get to 3:00 congratulate yourself for having finished one quarter of the room. Focus on looking back at what you have accomplished rather than forward at what is still to be done. Put everything out of your mind except the one thing that you are doing at the moment, and then give that one thing your total

absorption and concentration. You're not sick, you're just exhausted. Sleep when the baby does, even during the day. Take a walk outside at least once a day—rain, snow, or shine. Check your diet to be sure that you're eating properly. Buy foods that can be prepared quickly and learn how to make milk shakes or other quick pick-me-ups.

Bring your fears out into the open with someone who can help you sort them out. That way you can begin to let go of those that are completely unfounded. Other fears may need outside help to be relieved. For example, only your doctor can reassure you that your baby is all right and that his crying and sleeplessness will not be harmful to him and that these behaviors will eventually subside.

Fear

You fear something is dreadfully wrong with the baby, or with yourself. You harbor a secret fear that you're not a good parent. You don't want other parents to know, or your mother-in-law to find out. You blame the problems between you and your baby on the fact that you don't measure up.

Symptom	Description	Self-Treatment
Fear (continued)		A physical exam will help to assure you that you are healthy. Accept the fact that *no one* is adequate in the face of a crying baby. Your baby's problems are not because of you. He needs your loving presence, and although he can't say thank you, his development later as a child will show the influence of your giving.
		Your mother-in-law was no better at parenting than you are—she's forgotten a lot.
		Other parents are secretly feeling the same way you are. They need your companionship and honesty just as much as you need theirs.
Excessive Guilt	You take all the blame for your baby's seeming discomfort. You think you should suffer, too. You worry over not "being" or	Accept that you're only human, not a superbeing. No human relationships, including parent–baby relationships, are altogether

"doing" enough. If your baby gets hurt, it's because you weren't watching. If he gets sick, it's because you let someone who had a germ touch him. His crying is your fault.

free of negative feelings. Your baby's pain is not yours, it's separate from you. Don't waste your energy with needless self-blame when you could be enjoying the simple pleasures of everyday living, i.e. the aroma of a newly bathed baby, the taste of good food, the touch of someone near, or the voice of a person you care about on the phone. Forgive yourself your humanity.

Talk over what you are feeling with other parents who have had experiences similar to yours so that the intensity of your self-reproach is diminished.

Take notice of the numerous times during the day that you do something that fits in with your image of positive mothering. Never miss a chance to congratulate yourself on what you're doing. Whenever you do

Symptom

Excessive Guilt (continued)

Nightmares and Insomnia

Description

You dream that either you, your mate, or your baby are killed in a crash or catastrophe, or that you're being carried away from your baby in an ambulance. At other times you find you can't sleep—your brain is racing and you're tossing and turning but you can't fall asleep.

Self-Treatment

something right, praise yourself for it. Say, "Way to go, self!" and "I really did that well!"

Allow yourself an hour of selfish time a day that belongs exclusively to you: trade off with your spouse, call in a relative, pay somebody to help out; plan your weeks in advance, however you can manage. Accept help with the baby during this hour, even if you stay in the house. Get a haircut, buy a book that you read in small doses, get a rock album you like and dance to it, or go to the library and look at magazines.

Such a nightmare is a normal sign of stress for parents who are suddenly burdened with more responsibility than they feel they can handle. Ancient Indian cultures advised immediately countering the dream with an opposite image in which you picture yourself having power and making the outcome be as you want it, or picture your small family together on a tropical island, everyone smiling and happy.

Use periods of night wakefulness constructively. Pray for other people who could use your loving thoughts. Save a good book just for nighttimes. Buy yourself a small cassette player with headphones and listen to soothing, beautiful music that you've chosen for yourself. Eat if you're hungry, or drink a soothing herb tea with milk in it so you'll relax. Once you turn night wakings into a positive experience, they cease to be a problem.

Symptom

Hopelessness

Description

You wake up wishing you could be someplace else. You feel totally out of control of your life—like a hapless victim. It seems like there's no exit and there's nothing you can do to change matters. It feels like this stage of life will last forever.

Self-Treatment

Find some small part of your life that you *can* control. Do *one* task a day very well.

Develop a self-rewarding inner voice that praises you generously for each gesture of goodwill or donation that you give to yourself, your spouse, or your baby. Realize you are *choosing* to give and to respond.

Buy yourself a large blank artist's tablet and set goals for the coming decade in your life. Rather than just wishing for objects, wish for attainments, as well as good qualities in yourself you hope to develop in time. Draw symbolic pictures of these attainments, so that you can keep them fresh in your mind.

Look forward to the lifelong qualities you hope your baby will develop as he grows.

Enroll yourself in evening courses, even as just an observer, to prove you can still absorb information and learn.

Cultivate a friendship with another parent and converse, even if it's only during a walk around the block or during a two-minute-a-day telephone call.

Buy a book of familiar quotations or inspirational verses and tie it from a string to the toilet paper holder for brief retreats.

Anger

You find yourself blowing up at small irritations. You secretly harbor deep rage toward your mother because she didn't mother you properly in the first place, or toward your baby, which may express itself as oversolicitousness coming through gritted teeth.

Vent explosive feelings at first on a sympathetic listener other than your spouse, so that the intensity of the anger can be relieved by putting it into words.

Write angry letters or a journal. Find a safe outlet for physical expression. Beat it out on the bed or the couch with a hanger or a piece of hose. Knock it out by hitting a stick against a tree. Get it out in scouring, scrubbing,

Symptom	Description	Self-Treatment
Anger (continued)		pounding dough, tenderizing meat, hammering nails, yanking weeds, or shoveling. Play golf, softball, squash, tennis, or other activities that demand a smash, wallop, or a fling, or simply jog, which hurls your body in strong ways. Any less strenuous forms of exercising, such as walking outdoors, skating, swimming, or bicycle riding can be ways of venting off steam. Afterward massage your sore muscles and forgive yourself for it. You have a right to feel anger, but you shouldn't carry it around like baggage. Dump it and be free of it.
Physical Symptoms	Palpitations of your heart, shortness of breath, trembling, nausea, muscle aches, cold sweats, irritability, fits of crying, forgetfulness.	These are all symptoms of stress from a profound life change like giving birth and caring for a baby twenty-four hours a day. When the stress eases up, the symptoms go away.

Get exercise every day—whether indoor dancing and aerobics or outdoor walks and running.

Tactile experiences can often have a soothing effect. Bake bread just for the excuse to manipulate the dough, or buy yourself a child's Play-Doh kit and mold and pound it. Find yourself a sandbox, take off your shoes, and play in it.

Adopt a large "pet rock" that you can hold on to in times of stress until you can collect yourself. (*But, don't throw it at your spouse or at your baby.*)

Find a natural setting, such as a waterfront or a stream, and spend time there with the baby for restoration.

Be kind to yourself. After all, you're the only person you really *have* in your life. Mother yourself. Treat yourself with understanding

Symptom	Description	Self-Treatment
Physical Symptoms (continued)		and forgiveness. You're going through a hard time, so give to yourself in many small acts of kindness.
Serious Problems That Require Professional Help	You have frequent crying spells, both day and night. You experience disabling anxiety that makes you unable to function in essential ways, such as being afraid to go to the grocery store, or to stay alone with the baby. You are unable to drive any longer. The overwhelming urge to kill the baby or abuse him in some way comes over you.	Seek the help of a nearby pastor, call the information and referral service, or look up "Counseling Services" in the Yellow Pages. Sometimes colleges have counseling services available to the community, or the YMCA, YWCA, and other service agencies will help you find counseling. Your pediatrician, childbirth coach, or La Leche League counselor may be able to help you find someone. It is critical to seek out a trained professional rather than using another mother or a neighbor. Most professionals have sliding fees, allowing you to pay according to your income.

found physiological changes within the body. These include decreased oxygen consumption, decreased carbon monoxide elimination, and decreased respiratory rates. People who regularly employ relaxation techniques claim that it helps them to deal more effectively with situations that arouse the fight-or-flight response.

"On the few occasions that our crying baby did fall asleep from exhaustion, I used the time for me. No cleaning, cooking, washing clothes, etc. I soaked in bubble bath, relaxed with a drink, read a fun book, and prayed that she would sleep a little longer!"

The easiest techniques to use in practicing relaxation are the same ones that you may have used in preparation for childbirth.

"Try using the deep breathing that you learned in your childbirth classes: stretching up or bending over and touching your toes. Nurse lying down. Take the phone off the hook. Read a book or magazine. Have your husband rub your back, shoulders, or face. Lie down on the floor with the baby. Just get off your feet."

One important part of learning how to relax is becoming sensitive to tight spots or chronically tense muscles in your body that you need to consciously relax. Anger is often stored in the jaw and neck muscles. Sometimes deep massage directed at the pain spots may be necessary to free up muscles that are chronically tense. In time you will begin to recognize how groups of muscles operate together and flair during a tension attack. Pain in the temples is of-

Steps Toward Relaxation

(1) Lie quietly, flat on the floor, on the couch, or in bed.

(2) Close your eyes and keep them closed.

(3) Take three deep breaths slowly. Inhale through your nose as deeply as you can and then exhale through pursed lips as slowly as you can.

(4) Breathe normally for about one minute as you picture an awesome place of beauty, such as mountains, a meadow, or a seashore.

(5) Take another deep breath and this time clench your left hand as tightly as you can.

(6) Exhale slowly through pursed lips as you hold your hand tightly closed.

(7) Slowly unclench the hand and concentrate on the relaxed feeling it gives you.

(8) Breathe normally with visualizations of beauty for one minute.

(9) Take a deep breath and clench some other part of your body, repeating steps (6) through (8).

---

ten related to jaw-clenching tension. Tension headaches often arise from taut muscles in the neck that are painful and stiff at the points where they join the skull or at the base of the neck. These chronic flarings of pain can be dealt with directly by deep pressure and massage that strums the muscles like the strings on a guitar or pushes them as though they were clay.

By using progressive relaxation of your body, and teaching your mind to concentrate on a single image, you can work to desensitize yourself to the negative aspects of your baby-rearing experiences. Several times a day consciously hold an image of your baby as healthy, smiling, and thriving, even though your baby in reality is distant from this image. Picture yourself and your baby as walking through beautiful meadows together. By doing that you are pulling away from the negative aspects of the experience, replacing them with a more positive, energy-giving outlook.

> "The way we talk to ourselves determines the way that we feel about ourselves and constitutes our personal estimate of self-esteem. If we pay attention to negative ideation, we usually feel bad. If we selectively attend to the positive, creative, and resourceful parts of ourselves, our feeling of esteem increases."
>
> —Ruth Daly Knowles,
> "Coping with Lethargy,"
> *American Journal of Nursing,*
> August 1981, p. 1465

One form of self-therapy and renewal in the face of a continual barrage of baby screams is to provide your body with alternative sounds—ear food. The best sounds are those that arouse intensive feelings of pleasure to counter the feelings of anger and annoyance that are aroused by a baby's distress sounds.

The ideal item you can buy is a small, lightweight, battery-operated cassette player with small foam-tipped earphones. Although parents under stress were *not* the primary market the designers had in mind, the units can be life-savers. The player can be strapped to your waist and worn around the house. The earphones don't close out your baby's signals, they simply mute them to the point that you can tolerate them better. No one else can hear the music but you—which is a perfect answer for 4:00 A.M. feeds. The sound reproduction of these tiny players is exquisite, sometimes more impressive than many stereos. Players are priced between forty dollars and one-hundred dollars and can often be bought at a discount.

Your personal tape collection can be anything you

wish, from hard rock to romantic ballads to Beethoven. The important thing is that you choose music that is rewarding, pleasing, and upbeat enough for yourself. You will be arousing positive feelings in yourself that will overcome the negative feelings that your baby's crying arouses in you.

A Closing Parable

It was the day of the annual baby give-away, where excited couples gathered together to choose the baby that was to be theirs for life.

"I have before me a cherubic, loving baby who makes few demands; a wonderful baby boy," said the rosy-cheeked auctioneer. "Who will have him?"

"Us!" "Us!" "Give him to us!" mothers- and fathers-to-be shouted. Everyone wanted that baby!

The noise was so unbearable that even the long-suffering, patient baby began to whimper. The auctioneer banged his gavel for silence.

After much excited talk and bargaining, it was decided that an eager young couple in the front of the room would be awarded the boy, and they proudly walked out, carrying him home.

Next came a sweet, smiling baby girl with a tiny pink ribbon in her hair. She was awarded to an older, childless couple in the room who had longed for a child for over a decade.

And so the day went with babies being presented and

awarded to the couples that seemed the right match or had the right willingness.

Finally the auctioneer held up a screaming, red-faced little baby. "I have here a little boy who will cry for months after you take him home. You will lose a lot of sleep. He will seem not to appreciate your ministrations, and you will spend many hours of anguish over him. Do I have any bidders?"

No hands went up. In fact, the room became deadly silent. No one wanted to suffer with such a baby.

"Ladies and gentlemen," the auctioneer pleaded, leaning over his podium and peering out into the faces of the couples. "Surely someone wants to have this dear, suffering baby?"

People squirmed in their seats and looked at each other, but no hands went up.

"Whoever takes this baby will grow from him," the auctioneer said, since he was a wise man. "This baby will break a couple's hearts and then remold them to three times larger than they were before. He will teach them, through their compassion, how to truly love."

A young couple in the very back of the room rose slowly and unsmilingly and walked to the front of the room, arm in arm. "We will take this baby, sir," the father-to-be said, a serious look on his face. He reached out tenderly toward the tiny, crying soul and handed him to his wife.

Their faces were solemn, because they knew the path they were choosing would be the hardest of all paths. As they took the baby in their arms and walked from the room, the infant hushed, if only for a moment, as though grateful for their stepping forward.

"That couple will be more blessed than all of the others put together," the auctioneer was heard to say as he put away his gavel for the year. "By choosing to love a baby who isn't lovable, they have surely found the golden path to love."

And so they had.

Appendix

1
Family Support Groups, Agencies, and Hotlines

Here's a list of places where you can go to find support groups for parents or simply to talk out your concerns. Please keep in mind, though, that there are many changes in agencies and groups in a short period of time—too many for a directory like this to keep up with. If you don't have any luck in calling the numbers in your area, look up "Social Service and Welfare Organizations," or "Information and Referral Services" in the Yellow Pages of your telephone directory. (The major part of this list is reprinted with permission from the Family Resource Coalition, 230 N. Michigan Ave., Suite 1625, Chicago, IL 60601 (312) 726-4750, which can help you in locating more recent organizations in your area.)

ALABAMA

CENTRAL UNITED METHODIST
CHURCH
616 Jackson Street, SE
Decatur, AL 35601
(205)353-6941

FAMILY COUNSELING CENTER
6 South Florida Street
Mobile, AL 36606
(205)471-3466

FAMILY SERVICE DIVISION
FAMILY AND CHILD SERVICES
3600 8th Avenue, S
Birmingham, AL 35222
(205)324-3411

ALASKA

ANCHORAGE COMMUNITY
MENTAL HEALTH
Parent Training Center Unit
1844 West Northern Lights
Anchorage, AK 99503
(907)272-1722

CENTER FOR CHILDREN
AND PARENTS
808 East Street
Anchorage, AK 99501
(907)276-4994

FAMILIES IN TRANSITION
FAMILY CONNECTIONS
204 East 5th Street, Suite 215
Anchorage, AK 99501
(907)279-0551

JUNEAU WOMEN'S
RESOURCE CENTER
110 Seward Street, Room 6
Juneau, AK 99801
(907)586-2977

ARIZONA

COMMUNITY INFORMATION
AND REFERRAL SERVICES, INC.
1515 East Osborne
Phoenix, AZ 85014
(602)263-8856;
in Arizona, 1-800-352-3792

INFORMATION AND REFERRAL
SERVICES INC.
2555 East 1st Street, #107
Tuscon, AZ 85716
(602)323-1303;
in Arizona, 1-800-362-3474

JEWISH COMMUNITY CENTER OF
GREATER PHOENIX
1718 West Maryland Avenue
Phoenix, AZ 85015
(602)249-1832

NEW DIRECTIONS FOR
YOUNG WOMEN
376 South Stone
Tuscon, AZ 85701
(602)623-3677

SINGLE PARENT PROGRAM OF
PHOENIX CATHOLIC
SOCIAL SERVICES
1825 West Northern Avenue
Phoenix, AZ 85021
(602)997-6105

ARKANSAS

ELIZABETH MITCHELL
CHILDREN'S CENTER
1723 Broadway
Little Rock, AR 72206
(501)374-6395

THE PARENT CENTER
1501 Maryland
Little Rock, AR 52202
(501)372-6890

CALIFORNIA

APPLE
4 G Street
San Rafael, CA 94901
(415)459-1770

BANANAS CHILD CARE
INFORMATION &
REFERRAL SERVICE
6501 Telegraph Avenue
Oakland, CA 94609
(415)658-7101

BERKELEY-ALBANY YMCA
921 Kains
Albany, CA 94706
(415)525-1130, 848-6800

BIRTHWAYS
3127 Telegraph Avenue
Oakland, CA 94609
(415)653-7300

THE BRIDGE AGENCY
PO Box 2068
Merced, CA 95344
(209)723-7719

CALIFORNIA PARENTING
INSTITUTE
342 Keller Street
Petaluma, CA 94952
(707)762-7254, 762-7371

CHILDREN'S COUNCIL OF
SAN FRANCISCO
3896 24th Street
San Francisco, CA 94117
(415)821-7058
(Parent Support)

CHILDREN'S RESOURCE CENTER
Santa Barbara Family
Care Center
PO Box 74
Santa Barbara, CA 93102
(805)962-8988

COALITION CONCERNED WITH
ADOLESCENT PREGNANCY
2110 East 1st Street, #102
Santa Ana, CA 92705
(714)972-4859

CONTINUING DEVELOPMENT,
INC.
1188 Wunderlich Drive
San Jose, CA 95129
(408)725-1717

DEPARTMENT OF CHILD
DEVELOPMENT/PARENT
EDUCATION
Long Beach City College
4901 East Carson Street
Long Beach, CA 90808
(213)420-4253

FAMILY EDUCATION CENTER
Santa Clara County
Strawberry Park School, #5
730 Camina Escuela
San Jose, CA 95129
(408)255-LOVE

FAMILY RESOURCES
PO Box 935
Bolinas, CA 94924
(415)868-0616

FAMILY STRESS CENTER
1600 Galindo
Concord, CA 94520
(415)827-0212

FAMILY STRESS HOTLINE
115 Liberty Street
Petaluma, CA 94952
(707)763-9866; after 5,
763-2278

INFANT CARE PROGRAM
632 West 13th Street
Merced, CA 95340
(209)723-2031

INSTITUTE FOR CHILDHOOD
RESOURCES
1169 Howard Street
San Francisco, CA 94103
(415)864-1169

THE NURTURY FAMILY SCHOOL
374 West Baltimore Avenue
Larkspur, CA 94939
(415)924-9675

PARENTAL STRESS HOTLINE
PO Box 285
Palo Alto, CA 94302
(415)327-3333

PARENTAL STRESS SERVICE
103 East 14th Street
Oakland, CA 94606
(415)893-5444

PARENT EDUCATION PROGRAMS
1860 Hayes Street
San Francisco, CA 94117
(415)346-2246

PARENTS PLACE
3272 California Street
San Francisco, CA 94118
(415)563-1041

PARENT SUPPORT CENTER
NETWORK
Family Service Agency of Santa Barbara
817 de la Vina
Santa Barbara, CA 93111
(805)965-1001

PEP—POSTPARTUM EDUCATION
FOR PARENTS
5049 University Drive
Santa Barbara, CA 93111
(805)964-2009

PIPS—PRESCHOOL AND INFANT
PARENTING SERVICE
Thalians Mental Health Center
8730 Alden Drive
Los Angeles, CA 90048
(213)855-3500

A PLACE FOR PARENTS
2019 14th Street
Santa Monica, CA 90405
(213)396-5603

POSITIVE PARENTING
640 North Center
Stockton, CA 95202
(209)466-9603

PREGNANCY TO PARENTHOOD
FAMILY CENTER
1036 Sir Francis Drake Boulevard
Kentfield, CA 94904
(415)456-6466

SAN JOAQUIN FAMILY
RESOURCE CENTER
PO Box 4646
Stockton, CA 95204
(209)948-1553

SELF-ESTEEM: A FAMILY AFFAIR
675 Old Jonas Hill Road
Lafayette, CA 94549
(415)283-8142

STEPHEN S. WISE
PARENTING CENTER
15500 Stephen S. Wise Drive
Los Angeles, CA 90024
(213)476-8561

SUPPORT FOR SINGLE PARENTS
Triple F Project
27287 Patrick Avenue
PO Box 2493
Hayward, CA 94540
(415)782-5795

TALK LINE
Family Service Agency of
San Francisco
1010 Gough Street
San Francisco, CA 94118
(415)441-5437

COLORADO

CHILD OPPORTUNITY PROGRAM
3607 East Martin Luther King
Denver, CO 80205
(303)339-0603

FAMILY SUPPORT SERVICES
820 Clermont Street, #210
Denver, CO 80220
(303)394-7624

JEWISH FAMILY & CHILDREN'S
SERVICES
300 South Dahlia Street, #101
Denver, CO 80220
(303)399-2660

THE PARENT EDUCATION
PROGRAM
Presbyterian Aurora Hospital
700 Potomac
Aurora, CO 80011
(303)360-3006

PARENTS PLUS
PO Box 7515
Colorado Springs, CO 80933
(303)471-3238

SELF-ESTEEM: A FAMILY AFFAIR
35308 Aspen Lane
Pine, CO 80470
(303)838-6539

CONNECTICUT

CHILD CARE COUNCIL OF
WSPT-WSNT, INC.
90 Hillspoint Road
Westport, CT 06880
(203)226-7007

CONNECTICUT CARE LINE
Connecticut Child Welfare
Association
Hartford, CT 06117
(800)842-2288 (in-state only)

FAMILY DEVELOPMENT
RESOURCE CENTER
660 Prospect Avenue
Hartford, CT 06117
(203)523-4062

MOTHERHOOD AND ME
Connecticut Health Plan
4000 Park Avenue
Bridgeport, CT 06430
(203)255-5623

MOTHERING CENTER, INC.
235 Cognewaugh Road
Cos Cob, CT 06807
(203)661-1413

DELAWARE

DELAWARE ADOLESCENT
PROGRAM
2113 Thatcher
Wilmington, DE 19802
(302)652-3445

DISTRICT OF COLUMBIA

FACT (FAMILIES & CHILDREN
IN TROUBLE)
Family Stress Services of DC
1690 36th Street, NW
Washington, DC 20007
(202)965-1900

THE FAMILY PLACE
1848 Columbia Road, NW
Washington, DC 20009
(202)265-0149

FLORIDA

FAMILY CENTER OF
NOVA UNIVERSITY
3301 College Avenue
Ft. Lauderdale, FL 33314
(305)475-7471

MOMS (MOTHERS ORGANIZED
TO MAINTAIN SANITY)
PO Box 1401
Seffner, FL 33584
(813)685-9852

PARENT EDUCATION PROJECT
Valencia Community College
PO Box 3028
Orlando, FL 32802
(305)299-5000

PARENT EDUCATION RESOURCE
CENTER
PO Box 1453
Melbourne, FL 32901
(305)725-5056

PARENTING PROJECT
Peace River Center
1745 Highway 17 South
Bartow, FL 33830
(813)533-3141

PARENT RESOURCE CENTER
42 East Jackson Street
Orlando, FL 32802
(305)425-3663

GEORGIA

THE MOTHERS' CENTER
OF ATHENS
Route 2, Box 261
Hull, GA 30646
(404)549-5538

THE MOTHERS' CENTER
OF ROME
Route 1, 313 Haywood Valley
Armuchee, GA 30105
(404)291-9914

HAWAII

KA'A O NA KEIKI
Seagull Schools, Inc.
1300 Kailua Road
Kailua, HI 96734

ILLINOIS

BEVERLY FAMILY CENTER
9300 South Pleasant Street
Chicago, IL 60620
(312)779-1230

CHILD & FAMILY DEVELOPMENT
CENTER
Chicago Child Care Society
5467 South University
Chicago, IL 60615
(312)643-0452

CHILDREN'S HOME &
AID SOCIETY
Viva Family Center
2516 West Division
Chicago, IL 60622
(312)252-6277

COUNCIL ON CHILDREN AT RISK
525 16th Street
Moline, IL 61265
(309)764-7017

C-SECTION EXPERIENCE OF
NORTHERN ILLINOIS
1220 Gentry Road
Hoffman Estates, IL 60195
(312)885-7796

EARLY YEARS PROGRAM
Orchard Mental Health Center
8600 Gross Point Road
Skokie, IL 60077
(312)967-7300

ERIE NEIGHBORHOOD HOUSE
1347 West Erie
Chicago, IL 60622
(312)666-3430

FAMILY CENTER
229 South Bench Street
Galena, IL
(815)777-1560, 777-2348

FAMILY COMMUNITY SERVICES
University of Illinois Hospital
840 South Wood Street
Chicago, IL 60612
(312)996-4875

FAMILY FOCUS
2300 Green Bay Road
Evanston, IL 60201
(312)869-1500

FAMILY LIFE EDUCATION
Jewish Family &
Community Services
One South Franklin
Chicago, IL 60606
(312)346-6700

THE FAMILY SERVICE CENTER OF
WILMETTE, GLENVIEW,
NORTHBROOK & KENILWORTH
1167 Wilmette Avenue
Wilmette, IL 60091
(312)251-7350

FAMILY SUPPORT
248 North Throop Street
Woodstock, IL 60098
(815)338-3590

INFANT CARE PROGRAM
Evanston Hospital
2650 Ridge Avenue, #2206
Evanston, IL 60201
(312)492-6896

JEWISH CHILDREN'S SERVICES
One South Franklin
Chicago, IL 60606
(312)346-6700

LIFE (LAMAZE INSTRUCTION IN
FAMILY EDUCATION)
PO Box 784
Tinley Park, IL 60477
(312)795-1949

MOMS, INC.
PO Box 59229
Chicago, IL 60659
(312)583-7997

NI-ASPO: PARENT COALITION
PO Box 174
Highland Park, IL 60035
(312)433-5550, 429-5367

NILES FAMILY SERVICE
8060 Oakton
Niles, IL 60648
(312)692-3396

NORTHSIDE PARENTS' NETWORK
PO Box 10584
Chicago, IL 60610
(312)871-0453, 477-2839

NORTH SUBURBAN YMCA
Children's Center
1010 Forestway Road
Glencoe, IL 60022

PACES (PARENTS & CHILDBIRTH
EDUCATION SOCIETY)
PO Box 213
Western Springs, IL 60558
(312)964-2048

PACT (PARENTS & CHILDREN
TOGETHER)
15 Croydin Place
Kankakee, IL 60901
(815)932-7288

PACT (PARENTS & CHILDREN
TOGETHER)
405 Wagner Road
Northfield, IL 60093
(312)446-5370, 295-1620

PARENTAL STRESS SERVICES
Citizen's Committee for Children and
Parents Under Stress
59 East Van Buren, Suite 1618
Chicago, IL 60605
(312)463-0390

PARENTHESIS
405 South Euclid Avenue
Oak Park, IL 60302
(312)848-2227

PARENT SUPPORT NETWORK
5600 South Woodlawn
Chicago, IL 60637
(312)288-2353, 241-5164

PUPS (PARENTS UTILIZING
PREKINDERGARTEN SKILLS)
2201 South Morison
Collinsville, IL 62234
(618)345-5350

ROGERS PARK FAMILY NETWORK
1545 West Morse
Chicago, IL 60626
(312)743-2818

SINGLE MOMS, INC.
725 West Wrightwood
Chicago, IL 60614
(312)528-1264

VIRGINIA FRANK CHILD
DEVELOPMENT CENTER
3033 West Touhy
Chicago, IL 60645
(312)761-4550

INDIANA

CATHOLIC CHARITIES BUREAU
603 Court Building
Evansville, IN 47708
(812)423-5456

FAMILY HOUSE, INC.
203 Franklin
Valparaiso, IN 46383
(219)464-4160

FAMILY SUPPORTIVE CARE
Oaklawn Center
Elkhart, IN 46516
(219)294-3551

LISTENING, INCORPORATED
8716 Pine Avenue
Gary, IN 46403
(219)938-6962, 938-4796

PARENTS HELPING PARENTS
3410 West Virginia Street
Evansville, IN 47712
(812)479-8423, 425-5525

PARENTS TOGETHER
Porter City Family Services
2588 Portage Mall
Portage, IN 46386
(219)762-7181

PARENT–YOUNG CHILD
PROGRAM
Family and Child Studies
Department of Home Economics
Ball State University
Muncie, IN 47306
(317)896-5018

PERSONAL COUNSELING SERVICE
1321 Applegate Lane
Jeffersonville, IN 47130
(812)283-8383

IOWA

PARENT SURVIVAL PROGRAM
Florence Crittenden House
1105 28th Street
Sioux City, IA 51104
(712)255-4321

PEOPLE PLACE/FAMILY LIFE
ENRICHMENT PROGRAM, INC.
120 South Hazel
Ames, IA 50010

KANSAS

PARENT EDUCATION NETWORK
3501 West 98th Street
Overland Park, KS 66206
(913)381-3460

KENTUCKY

CHILD & YOUTH PROJECT
University of Louisville
323 East Chestnut
Louisville, KY 40202

COMMUNITY COORDINATED
CHILD CARE OF LOUISVILLE &
JEFFERSON COUNTIES
1355 South 3rd Street
Louisville, KY 40208
(502)636-1358

FAMILY & CHILDREN'S AGENCY
111 South Garvin Place
Louisville, KY 40203
(502)583-1741

LOUISVILLE PARENT-CHILD
CENTER
1809 South 34th Street
Louisville, KY 40211
(502)778-2714

MOTHER TO MOTHER
2409 Timberhill Court
Lexington, KY 40509
(606)269-9831

UNIVERSITY OF KENTUCKY
EARLY CHILDHOOD
LABORATORY
Erickson Hall
University of Kentucky
Lexington, KY 40506
(606)257-3782

LOUISIANA

FAMILY TREE PARENTING
CENTER
PO Box 51394
Lafayette, LA 70505
(318)988-1136

PARENTING CENTER
7343-C Florida Blvd.
Baton Rouge, LA 70806
(504)924-0123

PARENTING CENTER
200 Henry Clay Avenue
New Orleans, LA 70018
(504)895-3574

MARYLAND

EXTENDED ELEMENTARY
EDUCATION PROGRAM
Maryland Department of Education
200 West Baltimore Street
Baltimore, MD 21201
(301)659-2404

PACE, INC.
218 Hawthorne Rd.
Baltimore, MD 21210
(301)235-4753

PARENT AND CHILD, INC.
4905 Del Ray Ave., #304
Bethesda, MD 20914
(301)652-5383

PARENTS WITHOUT PARTNERS
7910 Woodmont Avenue
Bethesda, MD 20814
(301)654-8850 or
(800)638-8078

MASSACHUSETTS

COPE (COPING WITH THE
OVERALL PREGNANCY
EXPERIENCE)
37 Clarendon Street
Boston, MA 02116
(617)357-5588

FAMILY & COMMUNITY HEALTH
THROUGH CAREGIVING
Education Development Center
55 Chapel Street
Newton, MA 02160
(617)969-7100

THE FAMILY NEWSLETTER
Forum for Massachusetts Parents
Box 225
Hardwick, MA 01037
(413)477-8596

THE MOTHERS' GROUP
The Children's Workshop
1963 Massachusetts Avenue
Cambridge, MA 02140
(617)354-1633

THE PARENT CONNECTION
1210 Massachusetts Avenue
Arlington, MA 02174
(617)643-3660

MICHIGAN

THE CHILD & FAMILY
NEIGHBORHOOD PROGRAM
33577 Berville Court
Westland, MI 48184
(313)729-2610

FAMILY EDUCATION
Kennedy Center
1541 North Saginaw Street
Flint, MI 48503
(313)762-1371

FAMILY GROWTH CENTER
215 North Capitol
Lansing, MI 48933
(517)371-4350

FAMILY SUPPORT PROGRAM
High Scope Educational
Research Foundation
600 North River Street
Ypsilanti, MI 48197
(313)485-2000

NEIGHBORHOOD DROP-IN
CENTER
506 Eastern, SE
Grand Rapids, MI 49503
(616)458-0481

NEIGHBORHOOD FAMILY
RESOURCE CENTER OF THE
CENTER FOR URBAN STUDIES
Wayne State University
5229 Cass Avenue
Detroit, MI 48202
(313)577-2208

PROBLEMS OF DAILY
LIVING CENTER
Tabernacle Missionary Baptist Church
6125 Beechwood
Detroit, MI 48210
(313)897-2900

MINNESOTA

MELD (MINNESOTA EARLY
LEARNING DESIGN)
123 East Grant Street
Minneapolis, MN 55403
(612)870-4478

MINNESOTA COUNCIL ON
FAMILY RELATIONS
1219 University Avenue, SE
Minneapolis, MN 55414
(218)331-2275

MOTHERS, FATHERS & OTHERS
Rural Route 1
Lake Park, MN 56554
(218)238-6625

MOTHERS, FATHERS & OTHERS
WHO CARE ABOUT CHILDREN
16535 9th Avenue, N.
Plymouth, MN 55447
(612)473-1840

PAIIR (PARENTS ARE IMPORTANT
IN ROCHESTER)
1312 North West 7th Street, H
Rochester, MN 55901
(507)285-8033

SELF-ESTEEM: A FAMILY AFFAIR
16535 9th Avenue, N
Plymouth, MN 55447
(612)473-1840

MISSISSIPPI

EARLY EDUCATION PROGRAMS
Ferguson-Florissant
School District
655 January Avenue
Ferguson, MO 63135
(314)595-2355

FAMILY DEVELOPMENT
PROGRAM
1901 Francis Street
Jackson, MS 49203
(517)784-6155

FAMILY SUPPORT SERVICES
1004 North Jefferson
St. Louis, MO 63110
(314)436-0441

LADUE EARLY CHILDHOOD
CENTER
10601 Clayton Road
St. Louis, MO 63131
(314)993-5724

THE MOTHERS' CENTER OF
ST. LOUIS
516 Loughborough
St. Louis, MO 63111
(314)353-1558

MONTANA

FAMILY TEACHING CENTER
107 7th Avenue
Helena, MT 59601

NEW HAMPSHIRE

PARENT CHILD CENTER
5 Market Lane
Concord, NH 03301
(603)228-1551

NEW JERSEY

FAMILY LIFE RESOURCES
203 2nd Street
Fanwood, NJ 07023
(201)889-4270

NEW MEXICO

THE PARENTCRAFT PROGRAM
PO Box 6852
Albuquerque, NM 87197
(505)256-1191

NEW YORK

CENTER FOR PARENT
EDUCATION
Bureau of Child Development &
Parenting Education
New York State Department
of Education
Albany, NY 12234
(518)473-8276

EARLY CHILDHOOD
DEVELOPMENT CENTER
Center for Comprehensive
Health Practice
163 East 97th Street
New York, NY 10029
(212)360-7872

FAMILIES FIRST
250 Baltic Street
Brooklyn, NY 11201
(212)855-3131

FAMILY DYNAMICS
1360 Fulton Street
Brooklyn, NY 11216
(212)783-6666

FAMILY LIFE CENTER
101 Kensington Road
Garden City, NY 11530
(516)746-1709

FAMILY SURVIVAL OF COLUMBIA
COUNTY, INC.
61 Center Street
Chatham, NY 12037
(518)392-3911

MERRICK-BELLMORE
MOTHERS' CENTER
United Methodist Church
2640 Royle Street
Bellmore, NY 11710
(516)781-8946

MOMS SERVICES, INC.
500 East 83rd Street
New York, NY 10028
(212)988-8484

MOTHER AND CHILD CENTER
11 Wilmot Road
New Rochelle, NY 10804
(914)235-7917

MOTHERS' CENTER
United Methodist Church
265 Asbury Avenue
Westbury, NY 11590
(516)822-4539

THE MOTHERS' CENTER
United Methodist Church
Nelson & Division Avenues
Hicksville, NY 11801
(516)338-4477

THE MOTHERS' CENTER
DEVELOPMENT PROJECT
129 Jackson Street
Hempstead, NY 11550
(516)486-6614

THE MOTHERS' CENTER
OF QUEENS
Bayside YMCA
214-13 35th Avenue
Bayside, NY 11360
(212)229-5972

THE MOTHERS' CENTER OF
ROCKLAND COUNTY
33 Forest Drive
Gamerville, NY 10923
(914)354-7657

THE MOTHERS' CENTER OF
SUFFOLK, INC.
Unitarian Fellowship Church
Nichols Road
East Setauket, NY 11733
(516)585-0471

NATALIE ROBINSON-GARFIELD
33 Bluebird Drive
Roslyn, NY 11577
(516)621-2162

PARENT-AIDE PROGRAM
Mental Health Association
57 Clinton Street
Plattsburgh, NY 12901
(518)563-8206

THE PARENT CENTER
Mt. Kisco Elementary School
West Hyatt Avenue
Mt. Kisco, NY 10549
(914)666-8215

PARENT GUIDANCE WORKSHOPS
180 Riverside Drive
New York, NY 10024
(212)787-8883

PARENT & INFANT
RESOURCE CENTER
St. John's Riverside Hospital
967 North Broadway
Yonkers, NY
(914)963-3535

PARENTING CENTER
92nd Street YM-YWHA
1395 Lexington Avenue
New York, NY 10028
(212)427-6000 x206

THE PARENTING PLACE
Metropolitan Hospital Center
Department of Pediatrics
1901 1st Avenue
New York, NY 10029
(212)360-7329

PARENT RESOURCE CENTER
Flower Hill School
Campus Drive
Port Washington, NY 11050
(516)883-4000 x 230 or 231

PARENTS ARE PEOPLE
4 Johnson Place
Ardsley, NY 10502
(914)693-1589

PARENTS' PLACE, INC.
3 Carhart Avenue
White Plains, NY 10605
(914)948-5187

PARENTS' RESOURCE, INC.
Box 107 Planetarium Station
New York, NY 10024
(212)866-4776, 362-8661

PARENTS WORKSHOPS
34 Scenic Drive
Hastings-on-Hudson, NY 10706
(914)478-1267

PENNINSULA MOTHERS' CENTER
Temple Beth Emeth
36 Franklyn Avenue
Hewlett, NY 11710
(516)781-8946

PEP (PARENTING EDUCATION
PROGRAM) OF BROOKLYN
PO Box 49, Downstate Medical Center
450 Clarkson Avenue
Brooklyn, NY 11203
(212)270-2176

SETON'S CENTER PROJECT RECESS
240 2nd Street
Troy, NY 12180
(518)274-9245

WEBSTER AVENUE FAMILY
RESOURCE CENTER
148 Webster Avenue
Rochester, NY 14609
(716)654-8673

NORTH CAROLINA

CHILD & PARENT SUPPORT
SERVICES
806A Clarendon Street
Durham, NC 27705
(919)236-7112

FAMILY, INFANT &
PRESCHOOL PROGRAM
Western Carolina Center
200 Enola Road
Morgantown, NC 28655
(704)433-2674

PARENTING PHASES
1018 North Elm Street
Greensboro, NC 27401
(919)373-1442

PRESBYTERIAN COUNSELING
CENTER
PO Box 5638
Greensboro, NC 27403
(919)275-9324

NORTH DAKOTA

LUTHERAN SOCIAL SERVICES
OF NORTH DAKOTA
PO Box 399
Fargo, ND 58107
(701)235-7341

TOWNER CHILD DEVELOPMENT
& FAMILY SERVICES PROGRAM
PO Box 158
Towner, ND 58788
(701)537-5409

OHIO

FAMILIAE, INC.
1600 North West Professional Plaza
Columbus, OH 43220
(614)459-3367

THE FAMILY PLACE
Jewish Community Center
3505 Mayfield Road
Cleveland Heights, OH 44118
(216)382-4000 x 218 or 282

FOCUS ON MOTHERS
Northeastern YWCA
5257 Montgomery Road
Cincinnati, OH 45212
(513)351-6550

INFANT/TODDLER LEARNING:
A Parent Resource Center
U.C. College of Medicine
Department of Pediatrics
231 Bethesda Avenue
Cincinnati, OH 45267
(513)872-5341

MOTHERS OFFERING MOTHERS
SUPPORT, INC.
2578 Queenston Road
Cleveland Heights, OH 44118
(216)321-1550

PARENTING PROGRAM FOR THE
PREVENTION OF CHILD ABUSE
AND NEGLECT
CMGH Department of Psychiatry
3395 Scranton Road
Cleveland, OH 44109
(216)459-4614

SINCLAIR COLLEGE INFANT-
TODDLER PROGRAM
444 West 3rd Street
Dayton, OH 45402
(513)226-2502

TOT-LINE
Center for Human Services
3030 Euclid, 4th Floor
Cleveland, OH 44115
(216)431-8200

UNITED SERVICES FOR EFFECTIVE
PARENTING
Pediatric Department
U.C. College of Medicine
231 Bethesda Avenue
Cincinnati, OH 45247
(513)872-5341

WHOLE PARENT/WHOLE CHILD
76 Bell Street
Chagrin Falls, OH 44022
(216)247-6920

OKLAHOMA

THE ADAMS HOUSE: A FAMILY
SUPPORT PLACE
610 Adams
Stillwater, OK 74074
(405)624-5864

PARENTS' ASSISTANCE CENTER
707 North West 8th
Oklahoma City, OK 73102
(405)232-8227 or 8226

TULSA COALITION FOR
PARENTING PROGRAM
1430 South Boulder
Tulsa, OK 74119
(918)585-5551

OREGON

BIRTH-TO-THREE
1432 Orchard, #4
Eugene, OR 97407
(503)484-4401

YWCA TEEN MOTHERS'
PROGRAM
768 State Street
Salem, OR 97301
(503)581-9922 x37

PENNSYLVANIA

ARSENAL FAMILY &
CHILDREN'S CENTER
3939 Penn Avenue
Pittsburgh, PA 15224
(412)681-4210

BOOTH MATERNITY CENTER
6051 Overbrook Avenue
Philadelphia, PA 19131
(215)878-7800 x651

FAMILY WAY
3421 St. David's Road
Newton Square, PA 19073
(215)356-1497

FAMILY WAY PARENT/CHILD
SUPPORT CENTER
1705 Boston Lane
Villanova, PA 19085

INFANT DEVELOPMENT
PROGRAMS
475 West 4th Street
Lock Haven, PA 17745
(717)748-3928

PEHR (PARENT EDUCATION &
HUMAN RELATIONS) CENTER
7007 Ludlow Street
Upper Darby, PA 19082
(215)734-1120

WORKING PARENTS SUPPORT
PROGRAM
8243 Lincoln Road
Verona, PA 15147
(412)241-0441

RHODE ISLAND

WOONSOCKET FAMILY CENTER
460 South Main Street
Woonsocket, RI 02895
(401)766-0900

YOUNG PARENTS PROGRAM OF
RHODE ISLAND, INC.
5 Harrison Avenue
Newport, RI 02840
(401)846-3100

SOUTH CAROLINA

CHILDREN WITH TEACHERS
AT HOME
District One Schools
Box 218
Campobello, SC 29322
(803)472-2846

SOUTH DAKOTA

DEPARTMENT OF CHILD
DEVELOPMENT & FAMILY
RELATIONS
College of Education
South Dakota State University
Brookings, SD 57007
(605)688-6622

POSITIVE PARENTING
PO Box 2792
Rapid City, SD 57709
(605)348-WARM

TENNESSEE

FAMILY RESOURCE CENTER
1617 16th Avenue, S
Nashville, TN 37212
(615)298-4478

PARENT EDUCATION
DEPARTMENT
Florence Crittendon Agency
PO Box 22504
Nashville, TN 37202
(615)255-2722

PARENT PLACE
Child & Family Services
of Knoxville
1524 Western Avenue
Knoxville, TN 37921
(615)524-9483

PLANNED PARENTHOOD
ASSOCIATION OF NASHVILLE
112 21st Avenue, S
Nashville, TN 37203
(615)327-1095

TEXAS

AVANCE
Raul Jiminez Center
733 West Mayfield
San Antonio, TX 78211
(512)927-5375

FAMILY LIFE EDUCATION
Family Resource Center
102 West Rector, #106
San Antonio, TX 78216
(512)344-1055

HOUSTON ORGANIZATION FOR
PARENT EDUCATION
3311 Richmond
Houston, TX 77098
(713)524-3089, 668-2970

UTAH

FAMILY SUPPORT CENTER
2020 Lake Street
Salt Lake City, UT 84105
(801)487-7778

VERMONT

PARENT/CHILD CENTER
Box 646
Middlebury, VT 05753
(802)388-3171

WASHINGTON

EAST SIDE COMMUNITY MENTAL HEALTH CENTER
1609 116th Avenue, NE
Belleview, WA 98004
(206)455-4357

FAMILY LIFE EDUCATION NETWORK
107 Cherry Street, #500
Seattle, WA 98104
(206)447-3883

FAMILY SERVICES OF KING CO.
107 Cherry Street, #500
Seattle, WA 98104
(206)447-3883

PARENT/CHILD CENTER
PO Box 8
Grandview, WA 98930
(509)882-3349

PARENT COOPERATIVE PROGRAM
Washington Community College #17
Lodge Continuing
Education Center
W. 3410 Fort Wright Drive
Spokane, WA 99204
(509)456-6303

PARENT EDUCATION ASSOCIATES
7750 31st Avenue
Seattle, WA 98115
(206)525-4660

PARENT EDUCATION PROGRAM
Centralia Community College
PO Box 639
Centralia, WA 98531
(206)736-9341

THE PARENT PLACE
1608 North East 150th Street
Seattle, WA 98155
(206)364-9933, 364-7274

PROJECT HOME BASE
Yakima School District #7
104 North 4th Avenue
Yakima, WA 98902
(509)575-3295

RENTON VOCATIONAL TECHNICAL INSTITUTE
Home and Family Life Program
3000 North East 4th Avenue
Renton, WA 98056
(206)235-2470

WEST VIRGINIA

SUMMIT CENTER FOR HUMAN DEVELOPMENT
6 Hospital Plaza
Clarksburg, WV 26302
(304)623-5661

WISCONSIN

CHILDBIRTH PARENT EDUCATION ASSOCIATION
PO Box 4056
Madison, WI 53211
(608)221-8486, 244-6958

COALITION FOR FAMILY SUPPORT NETWORKS
Dane County Mental Health Center
31 South Henry Street
Madison, WI 53703
(608)251-2341

FAMILY ENHANCEMENT
605 Spruce Street
Madison, WI 53715
(608)256-3890

4 C'S OF MILWAUKEE COUNTY
2014 West McKinley Avenue
Milwaukee, WI 53205
(414)933-5999

MILWAUKEE ADOLESCENT PREGNANCY AND PREVENTION SERVICES
4 C's of Milwaukee County
2014 West McKinley Avenue
Milwaukee, WI 53205
(414)933-6432

MILWAUKEE AREA TECHNICAL COLLEGE
Family Living Education
1015 North 6th Street
Milwaukee, WI 53203
(414)278-6835, 278-6219

MILWAUKEE MELD
4385 Green Bay Avenue
Milwaukee, WI 53209
(414)263-2044

PARENTS PLACE NORTHEAST
1601 North Sherman Avenue
Madison, WI 53704
(608)241-3421

WYOMING

WYOMING STATE DEPARTMENT
OF SOCIAL SERVICES
Hathaway Building
Cheyenne, WY 82002

2
A Directory of
Pediatric Gastroenterologists

ALASKA

Clinton B. Lillibridge, M.D.
3831 Hampton Drive
Anchorage, AK 99504
(716)264-2300

ARIZONA

Otakar Koldovsky, M.D.
Department of Pediatrics
Arizona Health Science Center
Tucson, AZ 85724
(602)626-6626

CALIFORNIA

Marvin E. Ament, M.D.
Department of Pediatrics
UCLA Center for Health Sciences
MDCC-24-442
Los Angeles, CA 90024
(213)825-6134

Michael N. Applebaum, M.D.
Permanente Medical Group
2200 O'Farrell Street
San Francisco, CA 94115
(415)929-5040

Robert A. Cannon, M.D.
University of California—Davis
4301 X Street
Sacramento, CA 95817

B. Philip Citron, M.D.
540 North Central Avenue, Suite 205
Glendale, CA 91203
(213)956-7507

Kenneth L. Cox, M.D.
Department of Pediatric
 Gastroenterology
University of California—Davis
4301 X Street
Sacramento, CA 95817
(916)453-3750

David R. Fleisher, M.D.
Cedars-Sinai Medical Towers
8635 West 3rd Street, Suite 960
Los Angeles, CA 90048
(213)652-8031

Stephen L. Gans, M.D.
2080 Century Park East, Suite 1802
Los Angeles, CA 90067
(213)353-3322

Daryl Richard Homer, M.D.
Kaiser-Permanente Medical Center
27400 Hesperian Boulevard
Hayward, CA 94545
(415)784-5019

Martin Joffe, M.D.
Marin General Hospital
97 San Marin Drive
Novato, CA 94947

John A. Kerner, Jr., M.D.
Department of Pediatrics
Stanford University Medical Center
Stanford, CA 94305
(415)497-2300

William M. Liebman, M.D.
Department of Pediatrics
University of California
   Medical Center
San Francisco, CA 94143
(415)378-4265

Richard K. Mathis, M.D.
Department of Pediatrics
University of California
Irvine Medical Center
101 City Drive, S
Orange, California 92668

Russell J. Merritt, M.D., Ph.D.
Director, Nutritional Support Team
Children's Hospital of Los Angeles
4650 Sunset Boulevard
PO Box 54700
Los Angeles, CA 90045
(213)669-2181

Donald M. Mock, M.D.
General Clinical Research Center
Moffett Hospital, Room 1202
San Francisco, CA 94143
(415)666-4655

Jay A. Perman, M.D.
Department of Pediatrics, 650 M
University of California School
   of Medicine
San Francisco, CA 94143
(415)666-1830

Frank R. Sinatra, M.D.
Children's Hospital of Los Angeles
4650 Sunset Boulevard
Los Angeles, CA 90054
(213)669-2181

Jon A. Smith, M.D.
236 San Jose Street
Salinas, CA 93901
(408)758-3838

DISTRICT OF COLUMBIA

Lawrence F. Sorkin, M.D.
Associate in Gastroenterology
Children's Hospital National
   Medical Center
111 Michigan Avenue, NW
Washington, DC 20010
(202)745-3031

Jane L. Todaro, M.D.
Children's Hospital National
   Medical Center
George Washington University School
   of Medicine
111 Michigan Avenue NW
Washington, DC 20010
(202)745-3031

FLORIDA

Joel M. Andres, M.D.
Department of Pediatrics
PO Box 296
University of Florida College
   of Medicine
Gainesville, FL 32610
(904)392-6418

Lorne Katz, M.D.
9600 Sample Road
Coral Springs, FL 33065
(305)752-9220

Douglas H. Sandberg, M.D.
Department of Pediatrics
University of Miami School
   of Medicine
Biscayne Annex
PO Box 875
Miami, FL 33152
(305)547-6511

GEORGIA

Daniel B. Caplan, M.D.
Pediatric Gastroenterology/
  Cystic Fibrosis
Emory University School of Medicine
69 Butler Street, SE
Atlanta, GA 30303
(404)588-4380

Stanley A. Cohen, M.D.
993 Johnson Ferry Road, Suite 335
Atlanta, GA 30342
(404)257-0799

Javad Dehghanian, M.D.
2151 Fountain Drive, Suite 200
Snellville, GA 30278
(404)972-0860

ILLINOIS

Thiru S. Arasu, M.D.
Department of Pediatrics
Peoria School of Medicine
123 South West Glendale Avenue
PO Box 1649
Peoria, IL 61656
(309)672-2570

Lawrence M. Gartner, M.D.
Professor and Chairman,
Department of Pediatrics
Pritzker School of Medicine
University of Chicago
5825 Maryland Avenue
Chicago, IL 60037

Paul D. Goldstein, M.D.
5830 Dempster Street
Morton Grove, IL 60052

Terry F. Hatch, M.D.
Director of Medical Education
Carle Clinic Associates
602 West University Avenue
Urbana, IL 61801
(217)337-3100

Barbara S. Kirschner, M.D.
Department of Pediatrics
University of Chicago
5825 South Maryland Avenue
Chicago, IL 60637
(312)947-5782

Seiji Kitagawa, M.D.
Department of Pediatrics
Naval Regional Medical Center
Great Lakes, IL 60088
(312)688-4560

Jerome R. Kraut, M.D.
Lutheran General Hospital
1775 Dempster Street
Park Ridge, IL 60068
(312)696-7700

John D. Lloyd-Still, M.D.
Children's Memorial Hospital
2300 Children's Plaza
Chicago, IL 60614
(312)649-4354

Ira M. Rosenthal, M.D.
5490 South Shore Drive
Chicago, IL 60615
(312)996-6711

INDIANA

Joseph F. Fitzgerald, M.D.
Department of Pediatrics
Indiana University Medical Center
1100 West Michigan Street
Indianapolis, IN 46202
(317)264-3774

IOWA

M. Kabir Younoszai, M.D.
Department of Pediatrics
University of Iowa Hospitals
  and Clinics
Iowa City, IA 52242
(319)356-2950

Ekhard E. Ziegler, M.D.
Department of Pediatrics
University of Iowa Hospitals
  and Clinics
Iowa City, IA 52242
(319)356-2950

KENTUCKY

Samuel A. Kocoshis, M.D.
Director, Pediatric Gastroenterology
Albert M. Chandler Medical Center
University of Kentucky School of
   Medicine, Room MN 467
Lexington, KY 40506

LOUISIANA

Patricia G. Brannan, M.D.
4534 Fairfield
Shreveport, LA 71106
(318)868-1620

Gordon L. Klein, M.D.
Department of Pediatrics
Tulane University School of Medicine
1430 Tulane Avenue
New Orleans, LA 70112

Allan J. Rosenberg, M.D.
Department of Pediatrics
LSU Medical Center
1542 Tulane Avenue
New Orleans, LA 70112

Po-I Tseng, M.D.
Intensive Care Nursery
Willis-Knighton Medical Center
2600 Greenwood Road
Shreveport, LA 71103

MARYLAND

Van Saxton Hubbard, M.D., Ph.D.
National Institutes of Health
Building 10, Room 8N250
Bethesda, MD 20205
(301)496-4151

Alan M. Lake, M.D.
600 North Wolfe Street
Baltimore, MD 21205
(301)955-8769

William C. MacLean, Jr., M.D.
Johns Hopkins School of Medicine
601 North Broadway
Baltimore, MD 21205
(301)955-2786

Paul A. di Sant'Agnese, M.D.
National Institutes of Health
Building 10, Room 8N250
Bethesda, MD 20205
(301)496-4151

MASSACHUSETTS

Richard J. Grand, M.D.
Children's Hospital Medical Center
300 Longwood Avenue
Boston, MA 02115
(617)735-6062

Aubrey J. Katz, M.D.
Pediatric Gastroenterology Associates
319 Longwood Avenue
Boston, MA 02115
(617)734-2050

Ronald E. Kleinman, M.D.
Pediatric Gastrointestinal and
   Nutrition Unit
Massachusetts General Hospital
Boston, MA 02114
(617)726-8705

John N. Udall, M.D.
Pediatric Gastrointestinal and
   Nutrition Unit
Massachusetts General Hospital
Boston, MA 02114
(617)726-8705

W. Allan Walker, M.D.
Pediatric Gastrointestinal and
   Nutrition Unit
Massachusetts General Hospital
Boston, MA 02114
(617)726-2908

Harland S. Winter, M.D.
Children's Hospital Medical Center
300 Longwood Avenue, Enders 1312
Boston, MA 02115
(617)735-6065

MICHIGAN

Jay Bernstein, M.D.
Department of Anatomic Pathology
William Beaumont Hospital
3601 West 13 Mile Road
Royal Oak, MI 48072
(313)288-8050

William J. Byrne, M.D.
Department of Pediatrics
Division of Gastroenterology
University of Michigan Medical
  Center
Ann Arbor, MI 48109

Arthur R. Euler, M.D.
2101 Bronson Boulevard
Kalamazoo, MI 49001

MINNESOTA

F. Jean Perrault, M.D.
Department of Gastroenterology
Mayo Clinic, West 19A
Rochester, MN 55901
(507)289-2511

Charles A. Rogers
2545 Chicago Avenue, Suite 115
Minneapolis, MN 55404
(612)871-5511

Harvey L. Sharp, M.D.
University of Minnesota Health
  Science Center
PO Box 279, Mayo Building
Minneapolis, MN 55455
(612)373-8484

Richard Stafford, M.D.
Minneapolis Children's Health Center
2525 Chicago Avenue
Minneapolis, MN 55404
(612)927-3593

Robert A. Ulstrom, M.D.
University of Minnesota Hospitals
Mayo Medical Building
PO Box 391
Minneapolis, MN 55455

MISSOURI

Giulio J. Barbero, M.D.
Department of Child Health
University of Missouri Medical
  Center
Columbia, MO 65201
(312)882-4932

Robert E. Hughes, M.D.
6434 Summit
Kansas City, MO 64113
(816)444-8987

James P. Keating, M.D.
Department of Pediatrics
Washington University School of
  Medicine
St. Louis Children's Hospital
500 South Kings Highway
St. Louis, MO 63110

Jeffrey J. Kline, M.D.
Department of Child Health
University of Missouri
  Medical Center
Columbia, MO 65201
(314)882-6991

Joseph L. Portnoy, M.D.
14377 Woodlake Drive,
  Suite 117
Chesterfield, MO 63017
(314)567-4424

Charles C. Roberts
Assistant Professor of Peds/Ped GI
Children's Mercy Hospital
University of Missouri—Kansas City
  School of Medicine
24th and Gillham Road
Kansas City, MO 64108
(816)234-3016

Jerry Lee Rosenblum, M.D.
Department of Pediatrics
Washington University School
  of Medicine
PO Box 14871
500 South Kings Highway
St. Louis, MO 63178
(314)367-6880

Kathleen B. Schwarz, M.D.
Pediatric Gastroenterology
Cardinal Glennon Memorial Hospital
  for Children
1465 South Grand Boulevard
St. Louis, MO 63104
(314)577-5647

Calvin Woodruff, M.D.
Department of Pediatrics
University of Missouri
  Medical School
807 Stadium Road
Columbia, MO 65201
(314)882-3996

NEBRASKA

Dean Lowell Antonson, M.D.
University of Nebraska
  Medical Center
42nd and Dewey Avenues
Omaha, NB 68105
(402)559-7348

Jon A. Vanderhoof, M.D.
Department of Pediatrics
University of Nebraska College of
  Medicine
42nd and Dewey Avenues
Omaha, NB 68105
(402)559-7348

NEW JERSEY

Harold Grotsky, M.D.
New Jersey College of Medicine
174 North Woods Drive
South Orange, NJ 07078
(201)702-3961

Stephen F. Wang, M.D.
Department of Pediatrics
Morristown Memorial Hospital
100 Madison Avenue
Morristown, NJ 07960
(201)540-5316

Preston Zucker, M.D.
301 Beech Street
Hackensack, NJ 07601

NEW MEXICO

Donald J. Boon, M.D.
4509 Oahu, NE
Albuquerque, NM 87111
(505)296-6473

NEW YORK

Harvey Aiges, M.D.
Department of Pediatrics
Gastroenterology Division
North Shore University Hospital
300 Community Drive
Manhassett, NY 11030
(516)562-4642

Babu S. Bangaru, M.D.
Pediatric Gastroenterology
1300 Union Turnpike
New Hyde Park, NY 11040
(516)437-2808

Marilyn R. Brown, M.D.
Division of Pediatric
  Gastroenterology and Nutrition
University of Rochester
  Medical Center
601 Elmwood Avenue
PO Box 667
Rochester, NY 14642
(716)275-2647

Arno Buiumsohn, M.D.
Pediatric Gastroenterologic Group
Bronx-Lebanon Hospital Center
1650 Grand Concourse
Bronx, NY 10457
(212)588-7000, ext 555

Michael I. Cohen, M.D.
Division of Adolescent Medicine
Montefiore Hospital and
  Medical Center
111 East 210th Street
Bronx, NY 10467
(212)920-4045

Janna C. Collins, M.D.
Albert Einstein College of Medicine
1300 Morris Park Avenue
Ullmann Building, Room 123
Bronx, NY 10461
(212)430-2225

Fredric Daum, M.D.
Department of Pediatrics
North Shore University Hospital
300 Community Drive
Manhassett, NY 11030
(516)562-4642

Murray Davidson, M.D.
Director of Pediatrics
Queens Hospital Center
82-68 164th Street
Jamaica, NY 11432
(212)990-2261

William C. Heird, M.D.
Columbia University College of
  Physicians and Surgeons
630 West 168th Street
New York, NY 10032
(212)694-2976

Melvin Hollander, M.D.
Department of Pediatrics
Misericordia-Fordham Hospital
600 East 233rd Street
Bronx, NY 10466

Philip G. Holtzapple, M.D.
Department of Medicine, Room 6408
Upstate Medical Center—SUNY
750 East Adams Street
Syracuse, NY 13210
(315)473-5728

Lyn J. Howard, B.M., B.Ch., M.R.C.P.
Director, Clinical Nutrition and
  Pediatric Gastroenterology
Albany Medical College
Albany, NY 12208
(518)445-5299

Abraham Jelin, M.D.
Department of Pediatrics
Brookdale Hospital Medical Center
Linden Boulevard at Brookdale Plaza
Brooklyn, NY 11212
(212)240-6453

William J. Klish, M.D.
Chief, Division of Pediatric
  Gastroenterology and Nutrition
University of Rochester
  Medical Center
601 Elmwood Avenue
PO Box 667
Rochester, NY 14642
(716)275-2647

Emanuel Lebenthal, M.D.
Children's Hospital of Buffalo
219 Bryant Street
Buffalo, NY 14222
(716)878-7793

Neal S. Leleiko, M.D., Ph.D.
Chief, Pediatric Gastroenterology
Mt. Sinai Hospital and School of
  Medicine
5th Avenue and 100th Street
  (ANN17-80)
New York, NY 10029
(212)650-6931

Joseph S. Levy, M.D.
College of Physicians and Surgeons
Columbia University
630 West 168th Street
New York, NY 10032
(212)694-5903

Fima Lifshitz, M.D.
Department of Pediatrics
North Shore University Hospital
300 Community Drive
Manhasset, NY 11030
(516)562-4636

Richard L. Mones, M.D.
401 West 118th Street
New York, NY 10027
(212)666-4610

Leonard J. Newman, M.D.
Department of Pediatrics
New York Medical College
Valhalla, NY 10595
(914)948-0466

Cecelia N. Ores, M.D.
Babies Hospital
Columbia Presbyterian
  Medical Center
3775 Broadway
New York, NY 10032

Jacqueline S. Partin, M.S.
Health Science Building, T-11
SUNY at Stony Brook
Stony Brook, NY 11744
(516)246-7909

John C. Partin, M.D.
Health Science Building, T-11
SUNY at Stony Brook
Stony Brook, NY 11744
(516)246-7909

Philip Rosenthal, M.D.
Pediatric Gastroenterology
Columbia University College of
   Physicians and Surgeons
630 West 168th Street
New York, NY 10032

Arnold Schussheim, M.D.
23-25 Bell Boulevard
Bayside, NY 11360
(212)225-6464

Mervin Silverberg, M.D.
Department of Pediatrics
North Shore University Hospital
300 Community Drive
Manhasset, NY 11030
(516)562-4630

Judith M. Sondheimer, M.D.
Department of Pediatrics
Upstate Medical Center—SUNY
750 East Adams Street
Syracuse, NY 13210
(315)473-5831

Sergio L. Vaisman, M.D.
Department of Pediatrics
Albert Einstein College of Medicine
1300 Morris Park Avenue
Bronx, NY 10461

NORTH CAROLINA

Martin H. Ulshen, M.D.
Department of Pediatrics, 229H
University of North Carolina School
   of Medicine
Chapel Hill, NC 27514
(919)966-3134

OHIO

William F. Balistreri, M.D.
Children's Hospital Research
   Foundation
Elland and Bethesda Avenues
Cincinnati, OH 45229
(513)559-4594

Robert C. Bobo, M.D.
St. Vincent's Hospital and
   Medical Center
2213 Cherry Street
Toledo, OH 43608

Michael K. Farrell, M.D.
Department of Pediatric
   Gastroenterology
Children's Hospital Medical Center
Elland and Bethesda Avenues
Cincinnati, OH 45229

Thomas C. Halpin, Jr., M.D.
Chief, Pediatric Gastroenterology
Rainbow Babies and Children's
   Hospital
2101 Adelbert Road
Cleveland, OH 44106
(216)444-1765

James E. Heubi, M.D.
Children's Hospital Medical Center
Elland and Bethesda Avenues
Cincinnati, OH 45229
(513)559-4415

Robert H. Judd, Jr., M.D.
Pediatric Gastroenterology
St. Vincent's Hospital and Medical
   Center
2213 Cherry Street
Toledo, OH 43608
(419)259-4392

Benny Kerzner, M.D.
Department of Pediatric
   Gastroenterology
700 Children's Drive
Columbus, OH 43205
(614)461-2187, 461-2296

H. Juhling McClung, M.D.
Children's Hospital
561 South 17th Street
Columbus, OH 43205
(614)461-2187

William M. Michener, M.D.
Cleveland Clinic Foundation
9500 Euclid Avenue
Cleveland, OH 44106
(216)229-2200

Stephen L. Newman, M.D.
Department of Pediatrics
Wright State University School
of Medicine
Children's Medical Center
1735 Chapel Street
Dayton, OH 45404
(513)226-8411

Fred C. Rothstein, M.D.
Rainbow Babies and Children's
Hospital
2101 Adelbert Road
Cleveland, OH 44106
(216)444-1765

William K. Schubert, M.D.
Department of Pediatrics
Children's Hospital Medical Center
Elland and Bethesda Avenues
Cincinnati, OH 45229
(513)559-4411

Robert C. Stern, M.D.
Department of Pediatrics
Babies and Children's Hospital
Cleveland, OH 44106
(216)444-3268

Robert T. Stone, M.D.
300 Locust Street, Suite 200
Akron, OH 44302

OKLAHOMA

Sean J. Fennell, M.D.
Department of Pediatrics
School of Medicine
Oral Roberts University
7777 South Lewis Avenue
Tulsa, OK 74174
(918)495-7279

Ramon Torres-Pinedo, M.D.
Department of Pediatrics
University of Oklahoma Health
Science Center
PO Box 26901
Oklahoma City, OK 73190
(405)271-4000, ext 5884

PENNSYLVANIA

John T. Boyle, M.D.
Department of Pediatrics
Children's Hospital of Philadelphia
34th and Civic Center Boulevard
Philadelphia, PA 19104
(215)596-9534

Ramamurti Chandra, M.D.
Chief, Pediatric and Adolescent
Gastroenterology
Mercy Hospital
Pride and Locust Streets
Pittsburgh, PA 15219
(412)391-2216

Stanley E. Fisher, M.D.
Children's Hospital of Pittsburgh
125 DeSoto Street
Pittsburgh, PA 15213
(412)562-4642

Ian S.E. Gibbons, M.D.
Department of Pediatrics
Division of Gastroenterology
and Nutrition
Jefferson Medical College
1025 Walnut Street, Suite 1101
Philadelphia, PA 19107

Mary L. Rosenlund, M.D.
PO Box 264
Fairview Village, PA 19409

Steven M. Schwarz, M.D.
Children's Hospital of Philadelphia
One Children's Center
34th Street and Civic Center
Boulevard
Philadelphia, PA 19104
(215)596-9534

Maarten S. Sibinga, M.D.
St. Christopher's Hospital
for Children
2600 North Lawrence Street
Philadelphia, PA 19133
(215)427-5171

John B. Watkins, M.D.
Children's Hospital of Philadelphia
One Children's Center
34th Street and Civic Center
  Boulevard
Philadelphia, PA 19104
(215)596-9534

Steven Widzer, M.D.
St. Christopher's Hospital
  for Children
2600 North Lawrence Street
Philadelphia, PA 19133
(215)427-5181

Janis E. Zvargulis, M.D.
Department of Pediatrics,
Division of Gastroenterology
  and Nutrition
Jefferson Medical College
1025 Walnut Street, Suite 1101
Philadelphia, PA 19107
(215)329-0700

TENNESSEE

Fayez K. Ghishan, M.D.
Department of Pediatrics
Vanderbilt Medical School
Nashville, TN 37232

Harry L. Greene, M.D.
Department of Pediatrics
Vanderbilt Medical Center
Nashville, TN 37232
(615)646-3511

Randolph M. McCloy, M.D.
920 Madison Avenue, Suite 515 W
Memphis, TN 38103
(901)725-9123

Jose Roberto Moran, M.D.
Department of Pediatrics and
  Gastroenterology
Vanderbilt University Medical Center
D4200 Medical Center North
Nashville, TN 37232
(615)322-7449

Peter F. Whitington, M.D.
Assistant Professor of Pediatrics
University of Tennessee
951 Court Avenue, Room 545 D
Memphis, TN 38163

TEXAS

John M. Anderson, M.D.
University of Texas Health
  Science Center
5323 Harry Hines Boulevard
Dallas, TX 75235
(214)688-3437

Richard T. Calvin, M.D.
704 Longmire Road
Conroe, TX 77301

G. Kevin Donovan, M.D.
Kelsey Seybold Clinic
6624 Fannin Street
Houston, TX 77030
(713)797-1551

George D. Ferry, M.D.
Kelsey Seybold Clinic
6624 Fannin Street
Houston, TX 77030
(713)797-1551

Wallace A. Gleason, Jr., M.D.
Department of Pediatrics
University of Texas Health
  Science Center
7703 Floyd Curl Drive
San Antonio, TX 78284
(512)691-6263

J. Nevin Isenberg, M.D., Ph.D.
Department of Pediatrics
University of Texas Medical Branch
Galveston, TX 77550
(713)765-3773

Charles E. Mize, M.D.
Department of Pediatrics
University of Texas Health
  Science Center
5323 Harry Hines Boulevard
Dallas, TX 75235

Kathleen J. Motil, M.D.
Department of Pediatrics
Baylor College of Medicine
1200 Moursund
Houston, TX 77030
(713)790-6004

Buford L. Nichols, M.D.
Department of Pediatrics
Baylor College of Medicine
1200 Moursund
Houston, TX 77025
(713)521-3200

Geraldine K. Powell
Department of Pediatrics
University of Texas Medical Branch
Galveston, TX 77550
(713)765-1689

Alan D. Strickland, M.D., M.S.
Southwestern Medical School
Department of Pediatrics
University of Texas Health
  Science Center
5323 Harry Hines Boulevard
Dallas, TX 75235
(214)688-3111

UTAH

Linda S. Book, M.D.
Department of Pediatrics
University of Utah
50 North Medical Drive
Salt Lake City, UT 84132
(801)531-3464

John J. Herbst, M.D.
Department of Pediatrics
University of Utah Medical Center
Salt Lake City, UT 84132
(801)581-8227

VIRGINIA

Wallace F. Berman, M.D.
Medical College of Virginia
MCV Station, PO Box 743
Richmond, VA 23298
(804)786-9615

Martin F. Graham, M.D.
Medical College of Virginia
MCV Station, PO Box 529
Richmond, VA 23298
(804)786-9615

J. Rainer Poley, M.D.
Department of Pediatrics
Eastern Virginia Medical School
609 Colley Avenue
Norfolk, VA 23508
(804)489-5357

James L. Sutphen, M.D.
Department of Pediatrics
University of Virginia Medical Center
PO Box 386
Charlottesville, VA 22908
(804)924-2457

WASHINGTON

Dennis L. Christie, M.D.
Division of Gastroenterology
Children's Orthopedic Hospital and
  Medical Center
4800 Sandpoint Way, NE
Seattle, WA 98105

Charles H. Mitchell, IV, M.D.
2330 South 3rd
Ft. Lewis, WA 98433
(206)964-1437

WEST VIRGINIA

Ruth C. Harris-Adams, M.D.
26 Keeneland Drive
Huntington, WV 25705

WISCONSIN

Rajiv R. Varma, M.D.
8700 West Wisconsin Avenue
PO Box 105
Milwaukee, WI 53226
(414)257-6057

Steven L. Werlin, M.D.
Milwaukee Children's Hospital
1700 West Wisconsin Avenue
Milwaukee, WI 53226
(414)931-4090

CANADA

Joel W. Adelson, M.D.
Department of Gastroenterology
Montreal Children's Hospital
McGill University
2300 Tupper Street
Montreal, Quebec H3H 1P3 Canada
(514)937-8511

Ross C. deBelle, M.D.
Montreal Children's Hospital
2300 Tupper Street
Montreal, Quebec H3H 1P3 Canada
(514)937-8511, ext 437

Peter Roy Durie, M.D.
University of Toronto Hospital for
   Sick Children
555 University Avenue
Toronto, Ontario M5G 1X8 Canada

Charles T. Fried, M.D.
9737 112th Street
PH2
Edmonton, Alberta T5K 1L3 Canada

D. Grant Gall, M.D.
Faculty of Medicine, A.C.C.
University of Calgary
29th Street and 16th Avenue
Calgary, Alberta T2N 1N4 Canada

Kevin J. Gaskin, M.D.
University of Toronto Hospital for
   Sick Children
555 University Avenue
Toronto, Ontario M5G 1X8 Canada
(416)597-1500, ext 2215

John W. Gerrard, M.D.
Department of Pediatrics
University Hospital
Saskatoon, Saskatchewan S7N 0W8
   Canada

Leo Richard Haber, M.D.
Montreal Children's Hospital
2300 Tupper Street, Room A-801
Montreal, Quebec H3H 1P3 Canada
(514)937-8511, ext 437

J. Richard Hamilton, M.D.
University of Toronto Hospital for
   Sick Children
555 University Avenue
Toronto, Ontario M5G 1X8 Canada
(416)597-1500

Robert M. Issenman, M.D.
McMaster University Medical School
1433 Ontario Street
Burlington, Ontario L7S 1G5 Canada
(416)637-0352

Adrian B. Jones, M.D.
Department of Pediatrics
University of Alberta
4-117 Clinical Science Building
Edmonton, Alberta T6G 2G3 Canada
(403)432-6631

Seymour Mishkin, M.D.
Division of Gastroenterology
Royal Victoria Hospital
687 Pine Avenue, W
Montreal, Quebec H3A 1A1 Canada
(514)842-1231

Claude L. Morin, M.D.
Hospital Sainte-Justine
3175 Sainte-Catherine Road
Montreal, Quebec H3T 1C5 Canada
(514)731-4931, ext 247 or 248

Stanley P. Moroz, M.D.
Children's Centre, Health
   Sciences Centre
685 Bannatyne Avenue
Winnipeg, Manitoba R3E 0W1
   Canada

Claude E. Roy, M.D.
Hospital Sainte-Justine
3175 Sainte-Catherine Road
Montreal, Quebec H3T 1C5 Canada
(514)731-4931, ext 247

Andrew Sass-Kortsak, M.D.
University of Toronto Hospital for
   Sick Children
555 University Avenue
Toronto, Ontario M5G 1X8 Canada
(416)597-1500, ext 1753

Micheline T. Sainte-Marie, M.D.
University Hospital Center
2705 Laurier Boulevard
Sainte-Foy, Quebec G1V 4G2 Canada

Andree M. Weber, M.D.
Department of Pediatrics
Hospital Sainte-Justine
3175 Sainte-Catherine Road
Montreal, Quebec H3T 1C5 Canada
(514)731-4931, ext 247

NOVA SCOTIA

Philip C. Bagnell, M.D.
Department of Pediatrics
Izaak Walton Killam Hospital for
  Children
PO Box 3070
Halifax, Nova Scotia B3J 3G6
(902)424-6003

INDEX

Paradoxical reaction to sedatives, 29–30
Pederson, Dr. David R., 107
Pediatrician
  describing baby's symptoms to, 11–14
  dilemma of, 10–11
  finding trustworthy, 9–10
Pediatric gastroenterologists, 271–283
Pediatric urologists, 37–38
Pekkanen, John, *The Best Doctors in the U.S.*, 37–38
Penicillin, 74
Penis care, 38–39
Peristalsis, 50
Personality of baby
  with colic, 94–96
  coping with irritable, 96–99
  test for determining, 83–87
Phaire, Thomas, *Boke of Chyldren*, 113
Phenobarbital, 18
Phimosis, 39
Physician, *see* Pediatrician
Pickler, Dr. Emmi, 158–159
Pierpont, Dr. Mary Ella, 104
Pregestimil, 23
Pregnancy, and exposing fetus to music, 111–112
Pregnancy, and irritability of baby
  from birth complications, 17–18
  from drugs taken during, 18–21, 30
  from drugs taken during labor, 19, 20–21
  from high blood pressure during, 18
  from oxygen deprivation, 17, 21
Premature babies, 17–18, 92, 138
Preschoolers, 21
Projectile vomiting, 137–138
Prolactin, 71, 78
Prostaglandin, 74
Protein intolerance, 22, 26

Quiet sleep, 179–180, 181–182
Quinn, Susan, "The Competence of Babies," 128

Rebelsky, Freda, 155
Rectal problems, 58–59
Redness, 12
Referred pain, 34
Relaxation, for parents, 235, 247–250
  with massage, 247
  with music, 248–250
  steps toward, 248
Relaxing baby
  with body immobilization, 175
  by breastfeeding, 176–177
  with motion, 174–175
  with sound, 174
  with swaddling, 175–176
  by wedging, 177
Robertson, Dr. R. M., 189
Runny nose, 22

Salt, Patricia, 207
Schmitt, Dr. Barton D., *Pediatric Telephone Advice*, 137–138
Sedatives
  alcohol, 31
  paradoxical reaction to, 29–30
  Phenobarbital, 30
  treating colic with, 29–33
Self-rocking, 106
Self-soothing ability of baby, 87–89
Selye, Hans, 229
Semper, Laurel, 109
Senna, 75
Separation, and sleep, 189–192
Separation anxiety, 91
Shaw, Judith, 214–216
Shutdown system, 166, 174–177
Skinner, B. F., 164
Skin sensitive, 92
Sleep
  and body cycles, 183–184
  cycles, 181–182
  erratic, 186–188

facts about, 182
and food habits, 189
objections of parents to
   sleeping with baby, 193–194
parents shaping habits, 194–198
patterns and birth trauma, 188
patterns and length of mother's
   labor, 188
and separation, 189–192
through the night, 182, 185–186
Smoking, *see* Cigarette smoking
Snugli, 107–108
Sobel, Dava, 150
Soothing ability of baby, 87–89
Soothing baby
   by body immobilization, 176
   by breastfeeding, 174–175
   with motion, 175–176
   with sound, 175
   with swaddling, 176–177
   tips on, 218–220
   by wedging, 177
Sore nipples, 44–45
Sounds
   awareness of, 109–112
   relaxing to, 175
Soy milk, 23–24
Soy substitutes, 23–24
Spitting up, 14, 136–137
   treatment for, 27, 137–138
Spoiling baby, 160–162
Stenosis, 56
Stern, Dr. Daniel, 111, 128
Steroids, 70
Steward, Abigail, 207
Stomach relaxers, 72
Stools, 13
Stress, of parents
   converting negative feelings to
      positive, 229–233, 236–246
   coping with, 229, 235, 247–250
   physical symptoms of, 227–228,
      244–246
   and "red alert," 228
   serious problems caused by, 246
Sucking
   as pacifier, 174–175
   problems, 138–139

Sudden infant death syndrome
   (SIDS), 146
Support groups, 223, 255–270
Swaddling, 176–177
Swelling, 12

Talking to baby, 109–112
Taloin ointment, 47
Teas, herbal, 75
Temperature, taking, 15–16
Tension, in parents, 8, 235
Tests
   for characteristics of baby,
      81–83
   for personality profile of baby,
      83–87
Theobromine, 62
Thermometers, 15
Thirst cries, 168
Thoman, Dr. Evelyn B., 127, 161
Thomas, Dr. David B., 20
Thrush, 44
Thumb-sucking, 133–135, 176
Tips
   bathing, 220
   decorating, 224
   diapering, 220–221
   exercise, 225
   food management, 217–218
   housework, 216–217
   laundering, 216–217
   massage, 225
   on R and R (Rest and
      Relaxation), 221–222
   on soothing baby, 218–220
   on support, 223
   for working mothers, 214–216
Tiredness cries, 168
Tobacco, *see* Cigarette smoking
Tympanometry, 28

Urinary tract infections, 34–38
   diagnosing, 37–38
   and foreskin, 39
   symptoms of, 36
   treatment for, 37–38
Urination cries, 170

Vestibular system, 105–106, 175
Vitamins
  allergic reactions to, 33, 76
  baby, effects of, 33
  and breast milk, 76
Volvulus, 56
Vomiting, 14, 22
  as milk reaction, 22
  projectile, 137–138
  treatment for, 27, 137–138
Vorster, Dr. D. S., 158

Walker, Dr. Allan, 23, 24, 51
Watson, Lauren, 143
Watson, Ted, 143
Webb, Dr. Wilse, 190
Wedging, 177

Weight gain, 27
Weight loss, 27
Wheezing, 14, 22, 26
White, Gregory, 72
White, Mary, 72
Witter, Frank, 30
Working mothers
  breastfeeding, 125–126
  guilt of, 213
  maternity leave, 213–214
  tips for, 214–216

Yeast infection, 44–45, 46
Yogurt, 45
Youcha, Geraldine, "First Baby in
    the House," 154

Especially for You and Your Family

Keeping Parents Out of Trouble
Dr. Dan Kiley

The author of *Keeping Kids out of Trouble* explains that parental permissiveness does children more harm than good. Common sense, responsibility, and self-discipline are qualities nurtured through enlightened control of children's lives by their parents.

A pocket-size paperback   (J90-254, $3.50)

Dear Dr. Salk: Answers to Your Questions About Your Family
Dr. Lee Salk

The author answers parents' questions about contemporary problems confronting children. "He is refreshingly nonpontifical...his advice is eminently sensible." *(Publishers Weekly)*.

A pocket-size paperback   (J91-486, $2.50)

The Continuum Concept
Jean Liedloff

Based on the child-rearing techniques of the Yequana Indians of Venezuela, whose society boasts the absence of unhappiness in both children and adults, *The Continuum Concept* emphasizes a rediscovery in natural baby care that consists of warmth, security, and love from birth. The author offers practical advice on the topic, demonstrates what the deprivation of this experience can lead to, and proposes a program of crucial research in the field of baby care.

A pocket-size paperback   (J91-091, $2.50)

More Essential Books for Every Parent's Library

Couples with Children
Randy Meyers Wolfson and Virginia DeLuca

The inevitable changes that occur in a husband-wife relationship when there's a new baby in the house deal a great shock to a marriage. This book is the first to address these dramatic, stressful changes and offer support and advice for the first few months of parenthood. The authors include a detailed bibliography of books of interest to new parents as well as an excellent, extensive list of places to contact for support (clinics, counselors, etc.).

A pocket-size paperback   (J30-269, $3.50)

The Encyclopedia of Baby and Child Care
Lendon H. Smith, M.D.

An updated and revised edition of the all-inclusive reference guide to the health, treatment, and behavior of children from birth through adolescence. The book is separated into distinct, specialized encyclopedias on specific topics, such as "Emergencies and First Aid" and "Diet, Feeding and Nutrition"; each offers fully cross-referenced definitions, explanations, treatments, and even specialized medical terminology. An invaluable handbook for all parents and future parents.

Available in large-size quality paperback   (L37-502, $9.95, U.S.A.)
                                                    (L37-305, $11.50, Canada)

Dr. Turtle's Babies
William John Turtle, M.D.

All new parents find themselves plagued by questions on a variety of everyday situations—situations that can, without the proper answers, become real problems. Let a doctor answer your questions about:

- How to prepare for baby's homecoming
- When and how to feed an infant
- How to know when baby is sick
- When to call a doctor
- What to do about pacifiers and thumb-sucking
- How to discipline
- When to start toilet training
- How to create a safe, stimulating environment for baby
- How to schedule free time away from baby
- How to establish good and lasting emotional patterns.

A pocket-size paperback   (L31-065, $3.95, U.S.A.)
                                 (L31-066, $4.95, Canada)

Anyone Can Have a Happy Child
Jacob Azerrad, Ph.D.

The author, a clinical psychologist, bases his program for successful parenting on the premise that a happy child is one who has a positive outlook on life, self-esteem and the esteem of others, and the ability to express warmth and understanding.

A pocket-size paperback   (J90-795, $2.95)

Are You and Your Children Ready for School?

What Did You Learn in School Today?
Bruce Baron, Christine Baron, and Bonnie MacDonald

This is a revolutionary new title that can help parents guide their children through the American educational system, making sure that their children are learning what they should when they should. Three leading California educators, who are also parents, reveal exactly what parents can do to monitor and enhance their children's educational development from infancy through twelfth grade.

Available in large-size quality paperback

(J37-210, $7.95, U.S.A.)
(J37-285, $9.50, Canada)

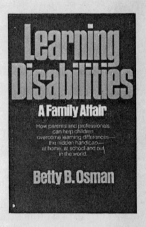

Learning Disabilities
Betty B. Osman

You're sure your child is at least of average intelligence. Then why does he or she have so much trouble learning a particular subject in school, where he is in space, how to get people to like him? Betty B. Osman, who diagnoses and treats children with learning disabilities, offers this book to help you understand and deal with the problems that face the child with this hidden handicap—and his family.

Available in large-size quality paperback   (L97-732, $5.95, U.S.A.)
(L97-777, $6.95, Canada)

Look for this—and other Warner bestsellers—in your bookstore. If you can't find them, you may order directly from us by sending your check or money order for the retail price of the book plus 75¢ per order and 50¢ per copy to cover postage and handling to: WARNER BOOKS, P.O. Box 690, New York, NY 10019. New York State and California residents must add applicable sales tax. Please allow 4 weeks for delivery of your books.